Teaching Research Methods in Psychology

ELGAR GUIDES TO TEACHING

The Elgar Guides to Teaching series provides a variety of resources for instructors looking for new ways to engage students. Each volume provides a unique set of materials and insights that will help both new and seasoned teachers expand their toolbox in order to teach more effectively. Titles include selections of methods, exercises, games and teaching philosophies suitable for the particular subject featured. Each volume is authored or edited by a seasoned professor. Edited volumes comprise contributions from both established instructors and newer faculty who offer fresh takes on their fields of study.

For a full list of Edward Elgar published titles, including the titles in this series, visit our website at www.e-elgar.com.

Teaching Research Methods in Psychology

Edited by

Regan A. R. Gurung
School of Psychological Science, Oregon State University, USA

Stephanie M. Byers
School of Psychological Science, Oregon State

ELGAR GUIDES TO TEACHING

Cheltenham, UK • Northampton, MA, USA

© The Editors and Contributing Authors Severally 2026

Every effort has been made to trace all the copyright holders but if any have been inadvertently overlooked please notify the publisher.

All rights reserved. No part of this publication may be reproduced, stored in a retrieval system or transmitted in any form or by any means, electronic, mechanical or photocopying, recording, or otherwise without the prior permission of the publisher.

Published by

Edward Elgar Publishing Limited
The Lypiatts
15 Lansdown Road
Cheltenham
Glos GL50 2JA
UK

Edward Elgar Publishing, Inc.
William Pratt House
9 Dewey Court
Northampton
Massachusetts 01060
USA

Authorised representative in the EU for GPSR queries only: Easy Access System Europe – Mustamäe tee 50, 10621 Tallinn, Estonia, gpsr.requests@easproject.com

A catalogue record for this book is available from the British Library

Library of Congress Control Number: 2025949680

This book is available electronically in the Elgaronline
Psychology subject collection
https://doi.org/10.4337/9781035359943

Printed on elemental chlorine free (ECF)
recycled paper containing 30% Post-Consumer Waste

ISBN 978 1 0353 5993 6 (cased)
ISBN 978 1 0353 5994 3 (eBook)
ISBN 978 1 0353 9059 5 (ePub)

Printed and bound in the USA

To Melina A. R. Gurung and all my research methods students who rose up to the challenge of learning the new language of research, pushed yourselves to complete an entire study from idea to paper in one ten-week term, and who now are champions for ensuring the validity and reliability of the scientific enterprise in all that you do and whereever your lives take you.
Regan A. R. Gurung

To my grandmother, Leonor Castañeda, who proudly exclaimed "vas a ser famosa" when I received my first research award in graduate school. I don't know about being famous, but I certainly hope that I have made you proud. Thank you for your love, patience, and support as I've learned how to be a scientist from the ground up. You made it possible.
Stephanie M. Byers

Contents

List of figures	ix
List of tables	x
List of contributors	xi
Preface	xiii
Supplementary material	xv

1 The case for teaching research methods in psychology: An introduction 1
   Regan A. R. Gurung and Stephanie M. Byers

PART I MODERNIZING AND REDESIGNING PSYCHOLOGICAL RESEARCH METHODS

2 From content to application: Reinventing research methods for today's psychology students 7
   David B. Strohmetz, Natalie J. Ciarocco and Gary W. Lewandowski, Jr.

3 Considerations for structuring (or restructuring) your research methods course 19
   Andrew N. Christopher, W. Robert Batsell, Jr., Autumn B. Hostetter and Eric Hill

4 Teaching psychological research methods at community colleges: Enhancing diversity in psychology through inclusive practices 36
   Todd Allen Joseph and Heather Schoenherr

PART II FOSTERING SCIENTIFIC THINKING IN PSYCHOLOGICAL RESEARCH METHODS

5 Teaching research methods in content courses 52
   Celeste Pilegard and Rian E. Drexler

6 'I've done my research': Teaching research methods to combat false information 65
   Holly Zell

7	Choose your words wisely: Recognizing and resolving lexical ambiguity when teaching research methods *Victoria L. Cross*	78
8	Learning how to read primary literature: A 'Focus Article' activity for research methods in psychology *Nicole Alea Albada and Vanessa E. Woods*	95
9	Engaging students in real and open science *Jordan R. Wagge*	111

PART III PROMOTING AND SUSTAINING CLASS ENGAGEMENT IN PSYCHOLOGICAL RESEARCH METHODS

10	Using alternative teaching methods to promote student engagement in research methods courses *Bryan K. Saville*	130
11	The 'Students as Partners' framework in teaching research methods *Sangeeta Gupta, Ethan Fireside and Alyssa Peters*	144
12	Redirecting the focus of an online research methods course: Engaging the disengaged *Jisook Park and Darin Challacombe*	158
13	Bridging the gap between research and civic engagement through a case study of a culturally responsive research methods course *Lauren Mathieu-Frasier and Reiko Habuto-Ileleji*	171

PART IV TEACHING ABOUT STATISTICS AND RESEARCH TOOLS IN PSYCHOLOGICAL RESEARCH METHODS

14	'It is impossible to run a full experiment in one term!' Using secondary datasets to create effective short-term research projects *Jacqueline A. Goldman*	186
15	Measure once: Covering measurement in a research methods course *Rosalyn Stoa*	199

| 16 | Talking about numbers: Essential statistics for research methods
Andrew Olstad, Jacqueline A. Goldman and Regan A. R. Gurung | 216 |
| 17 | Facilitating research: NVivo lab manual for undergraduate students
Marcie Coulter-Kern and Hannah Marie | 228 |

Index 247

List of figures

6.1	Using research methods skills to assess social media information	69
6.2	Assessing and critiquing sampling and generalizability	72
7.1	Model of intention and interpretation of the word 'manipulated'	91
15.1	Bullseye example	202
15.2	Trinitarian view of validity mapped onto new approaches	204
15.3	Teaching dimensionality	207
16.1	A p-value for a simple linear regression	219
16.2	Plotting miles per gallon by engine cylinder	222
17.1	NVivo interface: Ribbon View, Navigation View, List View, Detail View	232
17.2	Example of bad coding	237
17.3	Example of good coding	239
17.4	Project map with codes	241
17.5	Project map using participants and attribute values	242

List of tables

5.1	Strategies for integrating research methods into content courses	58
7.1	Synonyms	83
7.2	Homonyms with multiple scientific meanings	84
7.3	Homonyms with scientific and lay meanings	87
8.1	Summary of the Focus Article psychology subareas and full reference for articles	101
8.2a	Student responses to mid-quarter survey about the Focus Article activity. Survey question: Self-directed learning	104
8.2b	Student responses to mid-quarter survey about the Focus Article activity. Survey question: Learning to read literature	104
8.2c	Student responses to mid-quarter survey about the Focus Article activity. Survey question: Sense of community	105
8.2d	Student responses to mid-quarter survey about the Focus Article activity. Survey question: Relevance to real world	105
9.1	How research projects in psychology courses help meet APA undergraduate learning goals	113
9.2	Basic instructions and recommendations for completing CREP projects	121
12.1	Fort Hays State University (FHSU) online psychology graduate research methods objectives and corresponding key assignments	162
13.1	First semester student-led projects	180
13.2	Second semester student-led projects	182
15.1	Think-pair-share: Item improvement	210
17.1	Design framework example	231

List of contributors

Nicole Alea Albada, University of California, Santa Barbara, United States of America.

W. Robert Batsell, Jr., Kalamazoo College, United States of America.

Stephanie M. Byers, Oregon State University, United States of America.

Darin Challacombe, Fort Hays State University, United States of America.

Andrew N. Christopher, Albion College, United States of America.

Natalie J. Ciarocco, Monmouth University, United States of America.

Marcie Coulter-Kern, Manchester University, United States of America.

Victoria L. Cross, University of California, Davis, United States of America.

Rian E. Drexler, University of California, San Diego, United States of America.

Ethan Fireside, Hood College, United States of America.

Jacqueline A. Goldman, Oregon State University, United States of America.

Sangeeta Gupta, Hood College, United States of America.

Regan A. R. Gurung, Oregon State University, United States of America.

Reiko Habuto-Ileleji, Ball State University, United States of America.

Eric Hill, Albion College, United States of America.

Autumn B. Hostetter, Kalamazoo College, United States of America.

Todd Allen Joseph, Hillsborough Community College, United States of America.

Gary W. Lewandowski, Jr., Monmouth University, United States of America.

Hannah Marie, Bowling Green State University, United States of America.

Lauren Mathieu-Frasier, Ball State University, United States of America.

Andrew Olstad, Oregon State University, United States of America.

Jisook Park, Fort Hays State University, United States of America.

Alyssa Peters, Hood College, United States of America.

Celeste Pilegard, University of California, San Diego, United States of America.

Bryan K. Saville, James Madison University, United States of America.

Heather Schoenherr, College of Western Idaho, United States of America.

Rosalyn Stoa, Colorado State University, United States of America.

David B. Strohmetz, University of West Florida, United States of America.

Jordan R. Wagge, Avila University, United States of America.

Vanessa E. Woods, University of California, Santa Barbara, United States of America.

Holly Zell, Oregon State University, United States of America.

Preface

Scientific research is threatened. In the months that preceded the publication of this volume, a rash of federal actions in the United States of America changed the very nature of how research is done. Many research grants were canceled and faculty around the United States experienced significant challenges to continuing with their research agendas. In addition to these issues with conducting research, many of the usual checks and balances to how research is communicated also fell by the wayside. Major social media organizations scaled back on their fact-checking activities, making it very difficult for the untrained lay person to be able to successfully separate the wheat from the chaff. Cases of fabricated research citations being used in official reports due to AI use also increased.

Both the changes and threats to research funding and the rise of unchecked social media postings about research findings underscore the need for every student to have a good working knowledge of the research process. Those charged with conveying and cultivating this knowledge, the thousands of instructors worldwide, have a difficult task. All of us who teach research methods courses have to contend not only with student fears and misgivings about the class, for example, their fears of not understanding the topic, but we also have to teach in a higher education environment fraught with more stressors than ever before.

Research methods is an extremely important class that provides students with basic foundational tools to conduct research but more importantly to be savvy consumers of research. As we demonstrate in more detail in our introductory chapter, the research methods course is a critical requirement for the psychology major and for many other disciplines and majors as well. Students can get more out of an upper-level psychology class (or even reading news reports of research) from being cognizant of the basic elements of scientific research, especially research design, validity, and reliability. Often taken right after the introductory psychology class, sometimes concurrently or with a prerequisite statistics class, research methods is optimally taken before higher-level content courses. A student who successfully navigates the research methods course should get more out of higher level content courses due to having more insight into the research literature in those courses.

Our goal in editing this book was to provide a pragmatic resource for all instructors of the research methods course around the planet. We first wanted to make clear why the course is important and what the scope of the course is. We also wanted to provide many new ideas for course design and redesign. We understand how many constraints there are on instructor time and wanted to provide a variety of ways to help instructors be both effective and efficient. We capitalize on the expertise of over 20 different instructors of the course. Collectively, our authors have more than 300 years of experience teaching this course. Our ask to the authors was direct – write a chapter that showcases innovations in teaching research methods and leans on the lessons learned in teaching the course. The volume in front of you is a veritable treasure trove of insights, experiences, and practices. For pragmatic materials and assignments, see select chapter appendices on the book's Open Science Framework page: osf.io/pd7wb/.

We are thankful to many individuals for their help in getting this project off the ground:

Regan is thankful to Edward Elgar Publishing and Daniel Mather for the invitation to develop this project, and to all the authors who gave their time and expertise in writing their chapters. As someone who is constantly working to make his research method class as engaging and useful as possible, this opportunity to take a deep dive into the "hows and whys" of teaching the course was welcome. He is especially thankful for all his research methods students and his undergraduate mentors working on their honors and independent projects: they all made sure he was always thinking of the best way to teach research methods. He owes a special debt of gratitude to his wife Martha Ahrendt for all her help and support during this project. There are many house projects that he did not get down to doing while working on this book, and he was cut some slack. Finally, Regan would like to thank his co-editor Stephanie for all her hard work on this project. It was enjoyable sharing ideas and discussing a plan of action for the book with her.

Stephanie has greatly enjoyed the experience of being the book's co-editor, as it has allowed her to apply her skills as a journal editor as well as a creative writer. She has always had a penchant for writing and has aspired to publish a book, and now she can say that she has finally done it. In addition to thanking Edward Elgar Publishing and Daniel Mather for this great opportunity, she thanks every author for sharing their indispensable wisdom, and Regan for inviting her to work on this project. In particular, she thanks Regan for his great patience as she learned the ropes of book publishing. Much like the research process, learning how to prepare a book for publication was not a linear process. And yet, it was this nonlinearity that made for an exciting and rewarding learning experience.

Supplementary material

Supplementary materials for Chapters 2, 3, 8, 9, 10, 11, 12, 13, 16 and 17 of this book can be found online at: https://doi.org/10.4337/9781035359943.

1. The case for teaching research methods in psychology: An introduction

Regan A. R. Gurung and Stephanie M. Byers

'I wonder if what a student does before class will influence how much attention they pay in class, and how well they learn the material?' This question came up at one of our dinner tables. It was posed by Regan's daughter. It is a simple question but one many teachers have probably asked themselves. We have both looked out at our classes and seen thumbs scrolling reels, or fingers placing AirPods and selecting songs. The answer to this question can have significant practical implications for how we teach (Gurung & Gurung, 2025). The answers can be descriptive ('What do students do before class?'), associative ('Students who practiced mindfulness before class also had higher scores in class'), or even causal ('Practicing mindfulness before class led to higher attention in class'). Most importantly, to answer the question one needs to know about research methods.

Most disciplines, especially those in the social sciences, require students to gain research methods knowledge and be able to interpret data (Class, 2024; Jang & Sung, 2024; Kiryakova-Dineva & Yaneva, 2025). Unfortunately, many students perceive learning research skills in psychology as significantly less interesting than psychological content areas and lacking in relevance to their own future careers. In addition, they also find it especially difficult as it requires new skills (Lloyd-Lewis et al., 2024; Rajecki et al., 2005; Vittengl et al., 2004). Understanding research methods is one of the major student learning outcomes for both the psychology major (APA, 2023), as a key component of psychology programs (Dunn et al., 2010), and for the Introductory Psychology class as well (Gurung et al., 2016; Gurung & Neufeld, 2022). Most universities require the course for the major (Norcross et al., 2016; Stoloff et al., 2010) and many even offer upper-level capstone research courses (Strain and Moen, 2025).

Being knowledgeable about how research is conducted and having the ability to interpret data are components of being a skillful psychology student

(Naufel et al., 2025) and a psychologically literate student as well (McGovern et al., 2010). However, there has been limited discussion of how best to teach these skills. In one review of the research methods pedagogical research, Wagner et al. (2010) surveyed articles published over a ten-year period, 1997 to 2007, and identified 195 articles from 61 journals. The main categories discussed included teaching ethics, quantitative topics, qualitative topics, mixed methods, disciplinary specific methods, and special techniques for teaching research methods.

More recently, numerous psychologists have taken a close look at the research methods course. In a study of faculty perceptions of the research methods course, Ciarocco et al. (2017) found faculty recognized the importance of the course and identified course design issues (e.g., fitting in statistics, writing, and being engaging) as the biggest challenge. In another national study, Gurung and Stoa (2020) identified the most important concepts in the course from both a faculty and student perspective. For example, instructors considered ethics, extraneous/control/third variables, sources of information, confounding variables, and communicating research as some of the most important topics. Not surprisingly, student academic characteristics such as their GPA were strongly associated with their positive attitudes toward research methods. A similar study of over 200 students showed that validity is one of the hardest concepts for students to understand (Stoa et al., 2022). Most recently, Strohmetz et al. (2023) measured student perceptions of the course and identified key challenges (scientific writing and data analysis).

We divided this volume into four parts, each covering chapters with similar themes. After this introductory chapter, Part I opens with three chapters that detail ways to modernize and redesign the psychological research methods course. In Chapter 2, Strohmetz et al. contextualize the need to update pedagogical practices in psychological research methods for a new generation of students, identifying ways to modify and update pedagogical strategies while redesigning assignments and course structure. In Chapter 3, Christopher et al. identify ways in which research methods course delivery can differ, thus prompting instructors to consider making key changes to their course by taking into account the influence of factors like course goals, the scope of assignments, and the use of generative AI. In Chapter 4, Joseph and Schoenherr identify roadblocks that instructors face in teaching research methods at community colleges, and how these roadblocks can result in equity issues. After outlining these barriers and their ramifications, the authors discuss ways in which psychological research methods education can be improved to better serve community college students and the field of psychology at large.

Part II of the book focuses on fostering scientific thinking in psychological research methods. In Chapter 5, Pilegard and Drexler emphasize the importance of teaching research methods in content courses and discuss strategies that instructors can implement to support research methods thinking across the curriculum. This is complemented by Zell's discussion in Chapter 6 on the importance of prompting students to critically assess claims and the veracity of sources in an effort to combat media misinformation. Noting that variability in scientific lexicon can inhibit student learning in research methods courses, Cross identifies ways to recognize and resolve lexical ambiguity in an effort to better support their learning in Chapter 7. In Chapter 8, Alea Albada and Woods outline a 'Focus Article' activity that scaffolds scientific thinking and reading skills to promote students' understanding of primary literature. Closing Part II, Wagge's Chapter 9 discusses ways to engage students in open science practices by engaging them in replication studies, as well as by analyzing data using open-access secondary datasets.

In Part III, our authors introduce novel ways to promote and sustain class engagement in psychological research methods. In Chapter 10, Saville discusses alternatives to traditional teaching methods and how the efficacy of these alternative teaching methods has been empirically supported. This is followed by Gupta et al.'s Chapter 11, which details the learning value in collaborative practices in research methods courses that encourage students to become co-creators in the research process. Focusing on online courses, Park and Challacombe discuss the role of the researcher-consumer model in fostering student interest in Chapter 12. In Chapter 13, Mathieu-Frasier and Habuto-Ileleji present a case study of a culturally responsive advanced research methods course and discuss strategies for teaching research methods in a culturally responsive way.

Part IV of the book dives into teaching students about statistics and research tools in psychological research methods. It begins with Goldman's Chapter 14, which serves as a guide for research methods instructors who are interested in having students analyze secondary datasets in their course. On the topic of measurement, Stoa's Chapter 15 outlines ways that research methods instructors can teach students about scale development and psychometric tools. In Chapter 16, Olstad et al. introduce ways to teach students about statistical concepts in research methods courses, noting that there can be variations in student knowledge and recollection of statistics concepts. Lastly, in Chapter 17 Coulter-Kern and Marie provide a hands-on guide for undergraduate use of the qualitative research tool NVivo, created specifically to increase undergraduate students' access to qualitative research tools.

When reading this volume, it should be evident that our authors care deeply about research methods pedagogy and have written their chapters with the noble intent of providing you with the tools and knowledge necessary to embark on the journey of teaching this course. Many have also shared their own assignments, available at our book's Open Science Framework page: osf.io/pd7wb/. Through their various approaches, strategies, and examples, we have faith that our authors will guide you toward teaching your best research methods course yet.

REFERENCES

American Psychological Association. (2023). *APA Guidelines for the Undergraduate Psychology Major: Version 3.0.* https://www.apa.org/about/policy/undergraduate-psychology-major.pdf

Ciarocco, N. J., Strohmetz, D. B., & Lewandowski, G. W., Jr. (2017). What's the point? Faculty perceptions of research methods courses. *Scholarship of Teaching and Learning in Psychology, 3*(2), 116–131. https://psycnet.apa.org/record/2017-27109-001

Class, B. (2024). Teaching research methods in education: Using the TPACK framework to reflect on praxis. *International Journal of Research & Method in Education, 47*(3), 288–308.

Dunn, D. S., Brewer, C. L., Cautin, R. L., Gurung, R. A. R., Keith, K. D., McGregor, L. N., Nida, S. A., Puccio, P., & Voigt, M. J. (2010). The undergraduate psychology curriculum: Call for a core. In D. F. Halpern (Ed.), Undergraduate Education in Psychology: A Blueprint for the Future of the Discipline, 47–61. American Psychological Association. https://psycnet.apa.org/record/2009-13068-003

Gurung, M. A. R., & Gurung, R. A. R. (2025, May 20). *Primed for success: How what you do before class influences learning* [Poster presentation]. Spring Poster Symposium, Oregon State University, Corvallis, OR, United States.

Gurung, R. A. R., Hackathorn, J., Enns, C., Frantz, S., Cacioppo, J. T., Loop, T., & Freeman, J. E. (2016). Strengthening introductory psychology: A new model for teaching the introductory course. *American Psychologist, 71*(2), 112–124. https://doi.org/10.1037/a0040012

Gurung, R. A., & Neufeld, G. E. (2022). *Transforming Introductory Psychology: Expert Advice on Teacher Training, Course Design, and Student Success.* American Psychological Association.

Gurung, R. A. R., & Stoa, R. (2020). A national survey of teaching and learning research methods: Important concepts and faculty and student perspectives. *Teaching of Psychology, 47*(2), 111–120. https://doi.org/10.1177/0098628320901374

Jang, A., & Sung, M. (2024). Issues and challenges of qualitative research methods education in communication. *Asian Communication Research, 21*(2), 276–291.

Kiryakova-Dineva, T., & Yaneva, D. (2025). Top 6 literacies in marketing education: State-of-the-art approach. *Contemporary Educational Technology, 17*(1), ep544.

Lloyd-Lewis, B. L., Miller, D. J., & Krause, A. E. (2024). Against all odds: Students' interest in, and perceived value of, research and nonresearch psychology subjects. *Psychology Learning & Teaching, 23*(1), 65–89. https://doi.org/10.1177/14757257231222647

McGovern, T. V., Corey, L., Cranney, J., Dixon, W. E., Jr., Holmes, J. D., Kuebli, J. E., Ritchey, K. A., Smith, R. A., & Walker, S. J. (2010). Psychologically literate citizens. In D. F. Halpern (Ed.), Undergraduate Education in Psychology: A Blueprint for the Future of the Discipline, 9–27. American Psychological Association. https://doi.org/10.1037/12063-001

Naufel, K. Z., Spencer, S. M., & Richmond, A. S. (2025). Workforce readiness and guidelines 3.0: Is it time to update the skillful psychology student? *Scholarship of Teaching and Learning in Psychology*, *11*(1), 91–102. https://doi.org/10.1037/stl0000353

Norcross, J. C., Hailstorks, R., Aiken, L. S., Pfund, R. A., Stamm, K. E., & Christidis, P. (2016). Undergraduate study in psychology: Curriculum and assessment. *American Psychologist*, *71*(2), 89–101. https://doi.org/10.1037/a0040095

Rajecki, D., Appleby, D., Williams, C., Johnson, K., & Jeschke, M. (2005). Statistics can wait: Career plans, activity, and course preferences of American psychology undergraduates. *Psychology Learning & Teaching*, *4*, 83–89.

Stoa, R., Chu, T. L., & Gurung, R. A. R. (2022). Potential potholes: Predicting challenges and learning outcomes in research methods in psychology courses. *Teaching of Psychology*, *49*(1), 21–29. https://doi.org/10.1177/0098628320979881

Stoloff, M., McCarthy, M., Keller, L., Varfolomeeva, V., Lynch, J., Makara, K., Simmons, S., & Smiley, W. (2010). The undergraduate psychology major: An examination of structure and sequence. *Teaching of Psychology*, *37*(1), 4–15. https://doi.org/10.1080/00986280903426274

Strain, M. L., & Moen, K. C. (2025). Enhancing instructor and student experiences: A guide to successful capstone research courses. *Teaching of Psychology*, *52*(2), 236–241. https://doi.org/10.1177/00986283241257677

Strohmetz, D. B., Ciarocco, N. J., & Lewandowski, G. W., Jr. (2023). Why am I here? Student perceptions of the research methods course. *Scholarship of Teaching and Learning in Psychology*, 11(2), 273–283. https://doi.org/10.1037/stl0000353

Vittengl, J. R., Bosley, C. Y., Brescia, S. A., Eckardt, E. A., Neidig, J. M., Shelver, K. S., & Sapenoff, L. A. (2004). Why are some undergraduates more (and others less) interested in psychological research? *Teaching of Psychology*, *31*(2), 91–97. https://doi.org/10.1207/s15328023top3102_3

Wagner, C., Garner, M., & Kawulich, B. (2010). The state of the art of teaching research methods in the social sciences: Towards a pedagogical culture. *Studies in Higher Education*, *36*(1), 75–88. https://doi.org/10.1080/03075070903452594

PART I

Modernizing and redesigning psychological research methods

2. From content to application: Reinventing research methods for today's psychology students

David B. Strohmetz, Natalie J. Ciarocco and Gary W. Lewandowski, Jr.

Research methods in psychology is a paradoxical course. Along with the introductory psychology course, research methods is a ubiquitous part of the undergraduate psychology curriculum in the United States. Departments consider this course foundational to the major as it introduces students to the scientific underpinnings of psychology (Ciarocco et al., 2017; Gurung & Stoa, 2020; Stoa et al., 2022). Students utilize the skills they develop in this course as they pursue their educational and professional goals (Strohmetz et al., 2015). However, students are reluctant to take research methods courses (Rajecki et al., 2005) and instructors find these courses challenging to teach (Ciarocco et al., 2017; Gurung & Christopher, 2020). Moreover, the research methods course may result in students having more negative if not ambivalent attitudes toward research (Sizemore & Lewandowski, 2009).

One possible explanation for these negative attitudes toward the research methods course, despite its utility, is that what students primarily learn in the course is fundamentally different from other psychology courses. In more content-focused psychology courses, the emphasis is on knowledge acquisition where students learn key concepts and theories relevant to a specific area of psychology. However, the emphasis in the research methods course is on students learning how to think and reason like psychological scientists. Given these differing emphases, pedagogical strategies used in content-focused courses to increase student learning and engagement may not be as effective in a research methods course. While research methods students do learn key methodology concepts through more traditional instructional approaches such as lecturing, they still may not embrace or appreciate the value of scientific reasoning to their lives and potential careers (Holmes & Beins, 2009; Lloyd-Lewis et al., 2024; Sizemore & Lewandowski, 2009). Moreover, more traditional lecture-based approaches to teaching the research methods course can leave instructors feeling frustrated and overwhelmed (Ciarocco et al., 2017).

In this chapter we describe how we reinvented our research methods course using a scaffolded approach to strengthen student learning and perceptions of the utility of psychological science in their lives. This approach prioritizes continuously engaging students in the research process as they learn key concepts and develop important skills. Our goal is to make the research methods course an enriching learning experience for both instructors and students.

2.1   RATIONALE FOR REINVENTING RESEARCH METHODS

Now in their third iteration, the *APA Guidelines for the Undergraduate Psychology Major* (APA, 2023) continue to include scientific inquiry and critical thinking, communication through writing, and statistical reasoning among the desired learning outcomes for psychology students. The research methods course is well suited for addressing these learning outcomes (Ciarocco et al., 2017; Gurung & Neufeld, 2022; Naufel et al., 2018). In this course, students typically learn to identify and evaluate existing research on a question, propose testable hypotheses, design and conduct an appropriate study to test those hypotheses, employ statistics to draw conclusions based on the obtained data, and structure an APA-style research report to communicate the study findings. If research methods is a core course in the psychology major (Dunn et al., 2010), why do instructors find the course challenging to teach?

One reason is that instructors struggle with how to design a single course in which students can learn the entire research process, including how to write literature reviews, design research studies, draw appropriate conclusions based on collected data, and communicate the findings using APA style (Ciarocco et al., 2017). While research methods instructors value having students design and conduct research as a pedagogical strategy (Gurung & Stoa, 2020), time constraints may lead them to focus primarily on 'covering the material' (Ciarocco et al., 2017). For example, the time instructors spend helping students master the nuances of APA style may come at the expense of helping students become better writers in general (e.g., Ciarocco & Strohmetz, 2022). This emphasis on knowledge acquisition can limit students' opportunities to meaningfully engage in the research process and develop important skills.

In addition, instructors report that students are not equally prepared or motivated to be successful in a research methods course even if they completed the prerequisites for this course (Ciarocco et al., 2017). Students can be anxious about enrolling in the course as it requires them to engage in scientific thinking, statistical reasoning, and APA-style writing (Ciarocco et al., 2017;

Strohmetz et al., 2023). Students may also be hesitant to participate in active learning activities such as group research projects (Strohmetz et al., 2023), preferring more passive instructional approaches like lecture-based teaching (Deslauriers et al., 2019; Vittengl et al., 2004).

With over 65 combined years of experience teaching research methods, the authors of this chapter faced similar challenges teaching the undergraduate research methods course. We developed numerous learning activities and demonstrations to teach specific research concepts (Strohmetz et al., 2017). While our students did achieve the desired learning outcomes and went on to be successful in the major and beyond, we felt that something was missing. Students were learning about research, but they did not seem to embrace the value of becoming scientific thinkers themselves (refer also to Holmes & Beins, 2009). We were not adequately conveying the thrill we experience when engaging in the scientific process and its utility for everyday life (Naufel et al., 2018).

Were we missing an educational opportunity for our students? We decided that it was time to rethink and reinvent how we teach research methods, redesigning the course so that it not only strengthens student learning but also enhances students' attitudes toward the value of scientific thinking and cultivates skills they can use beyond the course (Ciarocco et al., 2013). We wanted our students to share the joy we experience when posing an interesting question, designing a way to test it, and finding out if we were right.

2.2 REINVENTION THROUGH SCAFFOLDING

We felt the best way to reinvent our approach to teaching research methods was through a version of scaffolding. Scaffolding helps provide students some structured support to help them solve a problem or carry out a task before they can do it on their own (Wood et al., 1976). Our overall approach to teaching specific research designs was for students to:

1) analyze how experts in the field use the design to answer their research question;
2) personally experience the design in action;
3) develop and execute the design to answer their own research question.

Following the 'gradual release of responsibility model' (Pearson & Gallagher, 1983), we show how research is done, do it together, and then give the students the chance to do it themselves. While this approach was originally developed for a four-credit, in-person research methods course that included a separate lab period, it has been successfully implemented in a three-credit, in-person course without an accompanying lab. One of the authors is currently experimenting with how to adapt this approach for a fully asynchronous online course. Refer to the Supplementary Material for an overall summary of our scaffolding approach.

2.2.1   Scaffolding Step One: Read Example of Design in Action

We spend the first few weeks of the course introducing students to the fundamental elements of any research design. Students learn basic concepts like hypothesis formulation, manipulation and measurement of variables, random sampling versus random assignment, and considerations of reliability and validity. Throughout the course we repeatedly address ethical considerations when conducting psychological research. Armed with this foundational knowledge, we introduce students to increasingly sophisticated research designs. Typically, we will begin with a simple experiment and then progress through multi-group, within-subjects, factorial, and mixed designs. The first author has also begun with observational research, then correlational research, before introducing these experimental designs.

We introduce each design by first having students read a short peer-reviewed research article employing that design to answer a research question. Short, engaging, and user-friendly research articles are ideal for this purpose. With the support of the Society for the Teaching of Psychology, we compiled a list of exemplar studies that one can use to introduce various research designs (Ciarocco et al., 2010). We also find the short report nature of the journal *Psychological Science* a great resource for this purpose, as are other journals that publish brief reports such as the *Journal of Experimental Psychology: General* and the *Journal of Applied Psychology*. As part of this design introduction, we ask students to identify the research goal, design elements of the study (e.g., sample, independent and dependent variables), basic findings, and their initial thoughts on the study's strengths and limitations.

There are a variety of ways to do this depending on your course goals and modality. Students could submit a written summary and initial critique of the study (refer to Supplementary Material for an example assignment and rubric), create an online discussion post, take a short comprehension quiz, or any combination of these ideas to ensure they have completed the reading. We use students' responses as the starting point for a dissection of the design the researchers employed to answer their question.

For example, when introducing within-subjects designs, we have had students read a study on how the scent of a loved one impacts sleep (Hofer & Chen, 2020). In that study, participants spent two nights with a loved one's scent and two nights with a control scent while researchers recorded sleep efficiency via a physiological measure, along with a self-report measure of sleep quality nightly. The physiological measure indicated better sleep efficiency when the participants physically slept with their loved one's scent. The self-report measure also indicated better perceived sleep quality when the participants *believed* they were sleeping with their loved one's scent.

Interestingly, participants did not always correctly identify whether they were sleeping with their loved one's scent or the control scent. This indicates that participants' beliefs about the scent predicted their self-reported sleep quality, but the physiological measure of sleep efficiency reacted to sleep with the actual scent of the loved one. In addition to the basic elements of within-subjects design, this study introduces students to design considerations such as the importance of including behavioral measures along with self-reports and how demand characteristics can influence findings.

2.2.2 Scaffolding Step Two: Experience Design in Action

After reviewing a published study employing the research design, we move to the next phase of scaffolding. We want students to personally experience the design in action through either an in-person or virtual demonstration. In these demonstrations, students serve as participants in that design and then use their study experiences to deconstruct the design elements. You can find example demonstrations for each key research design at https://teachpsychscience.org (for a discussion of the resources available on this site, refer to Strohmetz et al., 2017). The APA Online Psychology Laboratory (https://opl.apa.org) is another resource where students can personally experience a research design in action. These demonstrations are designed for easy implementation and are not necessarily based in theory or any prior topical readings.

To illustrate, we begin the 2 x 2 factorial design demonstration by asking students whether they are quicker at handwriting letters or numbers. Based on arbitrary assignment, such as the last digit of their mobile number, we then place students into one of four groups: 1) a group that will use their dominant hand to write a capital letter; 2) a group that will use their non-dominant hand to write a capital letter; 3) a group that will use their dominant hand to write a number; or 4) a group that will use their non-dominant hand to write a number. We then give students 10 seconds to complete this task according to their assigned group.

This demonstration becomes the framework for dissecting a factorial design. We begin by asking students to identify the independent variables, dependent variables, and conditions involved. We then extend the discussion to considerations of experimental control (e.g., What if someone didn't start and stop on time?) and individual differences (e.g., What if someone naturally writes larger than others?). We then compile their data.

Using this shared experience, we then provide a more traditional lecture on factorial designs, repeatedly using the demonstration as a shared frame of reference. This activity also provides an opportunity to discuss the role of hypothesis testing in experiments. For example, we have students propose potential main effect and interaction hypotheses for the demonstration experiment. Using the data generated through their study participation, we have the class engage in statistical reasoning to test those hypotheses. Generally, we have found that working through the exemplar article, demonstration, and content material takes the equivalent of one in-person class meeting (about 75 minutes). We do assign students the relevant textbook chapter to read before class to provide additional foundational understanding.

2.2.3 Scaffolding Step Three: Design Own Study

We now move to the last phase of our scaffolding. Students have read about the design in action, participated in a design demonstration as participants, and learned design-specific content through class lecture and discussion. They are ready to take the lead and develop their own research study using that same design. Students can do this in a variety of ways, such as individually, in pairs, or in small groups of three to five. When working in groups, we typically have students use web-based tools like Google Docs to provide them with an opportunity to strengthen their collaboration skills.

We begin the 'do it yourself' phase by providing students the same broad research topic, such as influences on attraction, first impressions, perception of products, or effects of brand exposure. We ask them to formulate a question based on this topic they can test using the targeted research design. As our goal is for students to develop a study by utilizing the research design concepts they are learning, we do not require students to do any initial background research on the topic or find underlying theory for their hypotheses. This is not to insinuate that developing research questions grounded in theory from an extensive review of the literature is unimportant. Rather, we address that learning outcome in a different part of the course with a traditional semester-long class research project resulting in a formal APA-style research report. We simply want students to focus on learning the mechanics of the targeted research design.

We use the equivalent of another class meeting (~ 60 minutes) to have students work through a guided activity that helps them plan their design. Students develop a research question, propose a testable hypothesis, and determine and operationally define their independent and dependent variables. This exercise alone provides students with the opportunity to apply class concepts, but for better mastery, we also have students develop the study materials and create a procedure for data collection. At this point, students formalize their study design by creating a method section of an APA-style research report including participants, materials, design, and procedure sections.

You can have students then execute their design and collect data using Google Forms, Qualtrics, or good old-fashioned paper and pencils. Students send links to their studies to friends and families or approach people on campus to complete their studies through their mobile devices or on paper. As this is a class demonstration and not research for dissemination, formal IRB approval is not required. However, students must have us review their proposal and obtain our approval prior to any data collection.

Once students have their data, they are then to use the appropriate statistics to test their hypotheses and write an APA-style results section. When actual data collection is not feasible, we provide students with a generated data set based on their design (refer also to Goldman, Chapter 14, this volume). ChatGPT and other AI data tools are useful for generating data sets.[1] Finally, we have students write an abridged version of an APA-style discussion section, starting with a summary of their findings in the context of their hypotheses and a brief possible explanation for their results, using what they have learned in their other psychology classes. More importantly for learning purposes, students also analyze the strengths and weaknesses of their design protocol. This is critical because as a quickly formulated student demonstration, the studies usually have many opportunities for improvement.

Through the scaffolded experiences of reading an exemplar study, participating in an actual study, and implementing the design themselves, students have multiple opportunities to learn different experimental methodologies. They can learn when and how researchers in the field use the design, what it is like to take part in the design, and how to implement it themselves. We do acknowledge that our scaffolding approach requires one to reduce actual lecture time spent 'covering the content.' However, we strongly believe that the best way to truly learn research, and the joy in the process, is through getting direct experience. The question is, what impact does our reinvented approach to teaching research methods have on students and their learning?

2.3 RESEARCH SUPPORTING THE EFFICACY OF REINVENTING RESEARCH METHODS

A 'Reinvented Research Methods' approach is only worth the effort if it helps student learning and engagement with the material. As researchers dedicated to fostering empirical inquiry among our students, we were curious about the new method's efficacy and conducted a systematic evaluation to identify pedagogical benefits. Specifically, we surveyed students enrolled in research methods courses to assess their attitudes toward research, statistics, and scientific writing before and after the implementation of the 'Reinventing Research Methods' curriculum (Ciarocco et al., 2013). The control group experienced the standard or traditional research methods course, which was primarily lecture-based and centered around a single comprehensive research project spanning the entire semester. In contrast, the experimental group engaged with the 'Reinventing Research Methods' framework, as outlined previously.

Our results indicated that students in the 'Reinventing Research Methods' course reported significantly greater confidence in their ability to use APA style, a stronger perception of the utility of research and statistics, and a greater affinity for statistical analysis (Ciarocco et al., 2013). Additionally, they exhibited increased confidence in their statistical competencies. Crucially, the more interactive and applied 'Reinventing Research Methods' model did not compromise conceptual learning. Exam scores were comparable and overall course grades remained consistent between groups. In other words, concept mastery did not change, but enthusiasm for the material increased. We were pleased with these findings given that boosting students' perception of research is traditionally difficult (e.g., Holmes & Beins, 2009; Lloyd-Lewis et al., 2024; Sizemore & Lewandowski, 2009). Moreover, a more favorable initial perception could have positive trickle-down effects as students take additional research and upper-level courses (Ciarocco et al., 2013).

Anecdotal evidence also suggests that this pedagogical shift has had lasting effects on students. The complexity and sophistication of our departmental undergraduate thesis projects have increased, with students demonstrating a higher level of preparedness. Former students frequently reach out to share that their extensive undergraduate research experience has provided them with a competitive edge in graduate studies, as they have repeatedly engaged in the full research process at the undergraduate level. Furthermore, from an instructional perspective, faculty members reported greater enjoyment in teaching the course in this manner. It is difficult to know if greater faculty enjoyment is due to the experience of revitalizing the course or from teaching students who are more positive and engaged. However, regardless of the reason, improving faculty's experience teaching a notoriously challenging course is a worthwhile benefit.

As William Butler Yeats eloquently stated, 'Education is not the filling of a pail, but the lighting of a fire.' The traditional lecture approach largely focuses on filling the pail, whereas the 'Reinventing Research Methods' model aims to ignite intellectual curiosity (Schumacher et al., 2025). By presenting research as an engaging and practical endeavor, we enable students to appreciate its significance and applicability to their everyday lives. The fact is most psychology graduates will not pursue careers as researchers (Lin et al., 2018). Therefore, our objective is to cultivate an appreciation for the research process, equip students with a foundational understanding of scientific inquiry, and foster a critical-thinking mindset that will extend to other areas of their lives. These skills will serve them well in making informed decisions, whether in personal matters such as evaluating medical treatments or in professional settings that demand evidence-based decision-making.

2.4 REINVENTING RESEARCH METHODS TO DEVELOP EMPLOYABLE SKILLS

A primary goal in our courses is to provide students with skills that extend beyond the classroom and enhance their career readiness (Ciarocco & Strohmetz, 2020). While the principal focus of a research methods course is to develop students' scientific competencies, the 'Reinventing Research Methods' framework also provides an opportunity for students to acquire and refine essential skills for professional success. The revised framework aligns with Goal 5 of the *APA Guidelines for the Undergraduate Psychology Major* (APA, 2023), which emphasizes professional development. Specifically, this objective encourages students to: 1) apply psychological knowledge and skills to their career aspirations, 2) develop self-efficacy and self-regulation, 3) refine project management skills, and 4) enhance teamwork capacity. Employers highly value these competencies, irrespective of academic discipline (Gray, 2021; Landrum & Harrold, 2003; Landrum et al, 2010). Students who can provide concrete examples of leadership, teamwork, problem-solving, and effective communication will have a competitive advantage when pursuing employment opportunities post-graduation (Halonen, 2019). Given that experiential learning is often the most effective means of skill development, the 'Reinventing Research Methods' approach serves as an ideal environment for students to cultivate these essential skills.

Throughout the course, students work collaboratively on research projects, yet each individual assumes a designated primary leadership role within their team. For example, one student serves as the project manager, overseeing and coordinating the group's efforts. Another student takes responsibility for organizing data collection, ensuring everyone knows the procedure and carries it out reliably. A third member serves as the primary data analyst, tasked with conducting statistical analyses and interpreting results accurately. While these roles provide structure, there is intentional flexibility, as all students are ultimately accountable for the project's success – an experience reflective of real-world professional environments. To further enhance skill acquisition, students rotate roles across different research projects, allowing them to develop proficiency in multiple domains.

These hands-on experiences enable students to articulate, with confidence, their competencies during job interviews. By participating in the 'Reinventing Research Methods' framework, students gain valuable insights into project management, problem-solving, collaboration, and communication – key attributes sought by employers. As a result, students are better prepared to navigate the demands of the professional world and contribute meaningfully to their chosen careers.

2.5 CONCLUSION

Our 'Reinventing Research Methods' approach transforms a traditionally challenging psychology course into an engaging journey of scientific discovery by guiding students from observing experts to conducting their own research. This scaffolded method not only preserves academic rigor but ignites students' passion for research while building critical professional skills. By creating opportunities for students to engage firsthand in the best parts of research, instructors can enhance student confidence, improve attitudes toward research, and better prepare graduates for future success. The bonus is that doing so can help instructors rediscover their own joy in teaching one of the discipline's most important courses.

NOTE

1. An example prompt for generating data for one condition using an OpenAI resource might be: 'Generate 25 whole numbers ranging from 1 to 7 where the mean is approximately 2.9 and the standard deviation is approximately 1.7.' You can also generate pairs of scores for correlational design demonstrations using prompts such as 'Generate 25 pairs of whole numbers ranging from 1 to 7 where their correlation is approximately 0.29'.

REFERENCES

American Psychological Association (2023). *APA Guidelines for the Undergraduate Major: Version 3.0*. https://www.apa.org/about/policy/undergraduate-psychology-major.pdf

Ciarocco, N. J., Lewandowski, G. W., Jr., & Van Volkom, M. (2013). The impact of a multifaceted approach to teaching research methods on students' attitudes. *Teaching of Psychology, 40*(1), 20–25. https://doi.org/10.1177/0098628312465859

Ciarocco, N. J., & Strohmetz, D. B. (2020). Psychology for the workforce: Using the classroom to help students develop and market their employable skills. In T. M. Ober, E. S. Che, J. E. Brodsky, C. Raffaele, & P. J. Brooks (Eds.), *How We Teach Now: The GSTA Guide to Transformative Teaching*, 286–297. http://teachpsych.org/ebooks/howweteachnow-transformative

Ciarocco, N. J., & Strohmetz, D. B. (2022). Teaching APA style: Missing the forest for the trees? *Scholarship of Teaching and Learning in Psychology, 8*(4), 399–403. https://doi.org/10.1037/stl0000304

Ciarocco, N., Strohmetz, D. B., & Lewandowski, G. W., Jr. (2010). *Exemplar Studies for Teaching Research Methodology*. Society for Teaching of Psychology. http://teachpsych.org/resources/Documents/otrp/resources/ciarocco10.pdf

Ciarocco, N. J., Strohmetz, D. B., & Lewandowski, G. W., Jr. (2017). What's the point? Faculty perceptions of research methods courses. *Scholarship of Teaching and Learning in Psychology*, *3*(2), 116–131. https://doi.org/10.1037/stl0000085

Deslauriers, L., McCarty, L. S., Miller, K., Callaghan, K., & Kestin, G. (2019). Measuring actual learning versus feeling of learning in response to being actively engaged in the classroom. *Proceedings of the National Academy of Sciences – PNAS*, *116*(39), 19251–19257. https://doi.org/10.1073/pnas.1821936116

Dunn, D. S., Brewer, C. L., Cautin, R. L., Gurung, R. A. R., Keith, K. D., McGregor, L. N., Nida, S. A., Puccio, P., & Voigt, M. J. (2010). The undergraduate psychology curriculum: Call for a core. In D. F. Halpern (Ed.), *Undergraduate Education in Psychology: A Blueprint for the Future of the Discipline*, 47–61. American Psychological Association. https://doi.org/10.1037/12063-003

Gray, K. (2021, December 3). *Competencies: Employers Weigh Importance Versus New Grad Proficiency*. National Association of Colleges and Employers. https://www.naceweb.org/career-readiness/competencies/competencies-employers-weigh-importance-versus-new-grad-proficiency

Gurung, R. A. R., & Christopher, A. (2020). Teaching the foundations of psychological science. In J. Zumbach, D. Bernstein, S. Narciss, & G. Marsico (Eds.) *International Handbook of Psychology Learning and Teaching*, 421–435. Springer International Publishing. https://doi.org/10.1007/978-3-030-28745-0_20

Gurung, R. A. R., & Neufeld, G. (2022). *Transforming Introductory Psychology: Expert Advice on Teacher Training, Course Design, and Student Success*. American Psychological Association.

Gurung, R. A. R., & Stoa, R. (2020). A national survey of teaching and learning research methods: Important concepts and faculty and student perspectives. *Teaching of Psychology*, *47*(2), 111–120. https://doi.org/10.1177/0098628320901374

Halonen, J. S. (2019, February). *Defending the Major: Exploiting the Workforce Advantage of the Psychology Degree*. Psychology Student Network. https://www.apa.org/ed/precollege/psn/2019/02/defending-major

Hofer, M. K., & Chen, F. S. (2020). The scent of a good night's sleep: Olfactory cues of a romantic partner improve sleep efficiency. *Psychological Science*, *31*(4), 449–459. https://doi.org/10.1177/0956797620905615

Holmes, J. D., & Beins, B. C. (2009). Psychology is a science: At least some students think so. *Teaching of Psychology*, *36*(1), 5–11. https://doi.org/10.1080/00986280802529350

Landrum, R. E., & Harrold, R. (2003). What employers want from psychology graduates. *Teaching of Psychology*, *30*(2), 131–133. https://doi.org/10.1207/S15328023TOP3002_11

Landrum, R. E., Hettich, P. I., & Wilner, A. (2010). Alumni perceptions of workforce readiness. *Teaching of Psychology*, *37*(2), 97–106. https://doi.org/10.1080/00986281003626912

Lin, L., Ghaness, A., Stamm, K., Christidis, P., &; Conroy, J. (2018, October 1). Do psychology degree holders work in psychology jobs? *Monitor on Psychology*, *49*(9). https://www.apa.org/monitor/2018/10/datapoint

Lloyd-Lewis, B. L., Miller, D. J., & Krause, A. E. (2024). Against all odds: Students' interest in, and perceived value of, research and nonresearch psychology subjects. *Psychology Learning and Teaching*, *23*(1), 65–89. https://doi.org/10.1177/14757257231222647

Naufel, K. Z., Appleby, D. C., Young, J., Van Kirk, J. F., Spencer, S. M., Rudmann, J., Carducci, B. J., Hettich, P., & Richmond, A. S. (2018). *The Skillful Psychology*

Student: Prepared for Success in the 21st Century Workplace. American Psychological Association. https://www.apa.org/careers/resources/guides/transferable-skills.pdf

Pearson, P. D., & Gallagher, M. (1983). The instruction of reading comprehension. *Contemporary Educational Psychology, 8*(3), 317–344. https://doi.org/10.1016/0361-476X(83)90019-X

Rajecki, D. W., Appleby, D., Williams, C. C., Johnson, K., & Jeschke, M. P. (2005). Statistics can wait: Career plans activity and course preferences of American psychology undergraduates. *Psychology Learning and Teaching, 4*(2), 83–89. https://doi.org/10.2304/plat.2004.4.2.83

Schumacher, A., Kammerer, Y., Scharinger, C., Gottschling, S., Hübner, N., Tibus, M., Kasneci, E., Appel, T., Gerjets, P., & Bardach, L. (2025). How do intellectually curious and interested people learn and attain knowledge? A focus on behavioral traces of information seeking. *European Journal of Personality, 0*(0). https://doi.org/10.1177/08902070241309124

Sizemore, O. J., & Lewandowski, G. W., Jr. (2009). Learning might not equal liking: Research methods course changes knowledge but not attitudes. *Teaching of Psychology, 36*(2), 90–95. https://doi.org/10.1080/00986280902739727

Stoa, R., Chu, T. L. Alan, & Gurung, R. A. R. (2022). Potential potholes: Predicting challenges and learning outcomes in research methods in psychology courses. *Teaching of Psychology, 49*(1), 21–29. https://doi.org/10.1177/0098628320979881

Strohmetz, D. B., Ciarocco, N. J., & Lewandowski, G. W., Jr. (2017). TeachPsychScience.org: Sharing to improve the teaching of research methods. In R. S. Jhangiani & R. Biswas-Diener (Eds.), *Open: The Philosophy and Practices that are Revolutionizing Psychological Science and Education*, 237–244. Ubiquity Press. https://doi.org/10.5334/bbc

Strohmetz, D. B., Ciarocco, N. J., & Lewandowski, G. W., Jr. (2023). Why am I here? Student perceptions of the research methods course. *Scholarship of Teaching and Learning in Psychology, 11*(2), 273–283. https://doi.org/10.1037/stl0000353

Strohmetz, D. B., Dolinsky, B., Jhangiani, R. S., Posey, D. C., Hardin, E., Shyu, V., & Klein, E. (2015). The skillful major: Psychology curricula in the 21st century. *Scholarship of Teaching and Learning in Psychology, 1*, 200–207. https://doi.org/10.1037/stl0000037

Vittengl, J. R., Bosley, C. Y., Brescia, S. A., Eckardt, E. A., Neidig, J. M., Shelver, K. S., & Sapenoff, L. A. (2004). Why are some undergraduates more (and others less) interested in psychological research? *Teaching of Psychology, 31*(2), 91–97. https://doi.org/10.1207/s15328023top3102_3

Wood, D., Bruner, J. S., & Ross, G. (1976). The role of tutoring in problem-solving. *Journal of Child Psychology and Psychiatry and Allied Disciplines, 17*(2), 89–100. https://doi.org/10.1111/j.1469-7610.1976.tb00381.x

3. Considerations for structuring (or restructuring) your research methods course

Andrew N. Christopher, W. Robert Batsell, Jr., Autumn B. Hostetter and Eric Hill

Before you begin reading this chapter, we need to issue a warning. If you are here looking for 'the correct way' to teach research methods or parts of such a course, you will be sorely disappointed. This chapter will probably raise more questions for you and your department than it will answer. It is important to note that the authors of this chapter are from two relatively similar, but still different, small, liberal, all-undergraduate arts colleges located about 45 miles apart in south central and southwest Michigan along Interstate 94. Our department faculty interact in person several times a year, both socially and professionally. When we do, even with the intent of watching a Detroit Lions football game or having a cookout, we always seem to find ourselves discussing how best to teach our students about research methods (and by association, statistics). And after more than 20 years of such interactions, we still don't have the answers. What we do have and will share in this chapter are the issues we've discussed and our – sometimes different – perspectives on them. By sharing these issues and our sometimes different perspectives on them, we hope you and your department will come up with new ideas for teaching this material to your own students.

This chapter is loosely organized around four major considerations for research methods and related classes (e.g., statistics): (1) the student audience, (2) the types of research projects, (3) the types of writing assignments, and (4) the potential role of artificial intelligence (AI).

3.1 THE STUDENT AUDIENCE FOR THIS CONTENT

All courses have certain challenges that teachers must overcome to maximize student learning. For instance, when teaching Introductory Psychology – especially in the fall semester when first-semester students will comprise the majority of students in class – teachers encounter a wide range of student interest in the course, ranging from none whatsoever to those who are there (they think) to solve their personal issues. In addition, in Introductory Psychology, the issue of what and how much content to cover has historically been an issue (see Gurung et al., 2016, and Gurung & Neufeld, 2022 for ideas).

Certainly, there is also no shortage of challenges in teaching research methods. Gurung and Christopher (2023) delineated three common challenges cited in the literature: the teacher-student enthusiasm gap is larger for these courses than for other psychology courses; students see the content as boring/irrelevant to them; and the material in these courses tends to be more difficult and abstract for students than in other courses they take. Here, in the first section of our chapter, we delve into these latter two challenges.

3.1.1 Students' Inherent Interest in Research Methods

At both of our colleges, we have noticed a distinct trend during the past 25 years, which has accelerated during the past decade. Specifically, whereas more than half of our psychology majors were aiming for some sort of graduate study in the early and mid 2000s, which often included a sizable number of students applying to PhD programs, that proportion is now much smaller, especially with respect to interest in research careers. There are still many students wanting to go into fields such as counseling, social work, and other person-to-person 'helping' settings. Indeed, according to the American Psychological Association's Center for Workforce Studies (Conroy et al., 2019), the majority of undergraduate psychology majors do not pursue an advanced degree. Of those who do pursue an advanced degree, about two-thirds of those students pursue an advanced degree outside of psychology (e.g., MSW). Although this trend likely affects much of the undergraduate curriculum, we focus in this section on if and how it should affect our teaching of methods and statistics.

Some of our majors freely report that they remained majors in spite of being required to take research methods and statistics courses. That tells us we need to do a better job of meeting them where their interests lie. Indeed, recent research (Strohmetz et al., 2023) on a sample of 168 research methods students at 21 different institutions suggests that they appreciate how these courses help them learn how to do research. However, this sample also indicated that such courses were viewed as simply preparation for graduate school rather than offering the chance to develop employable skills. Thus, we as teachers appear to have work to do to make these courses matter to all of our undergraduates, regardless of their aspirations for graduate study.

One way to increase the relevance of our courses is to create examples of what we know students *are* interested in (see also Strohmetz et al., (2023); Chapter 2, this volume). For example, many of our students are interested in going into marketing, human resource management, and other 'business-related' areas. There are ample examples we can pull from the 'business world.' For instance, Christopher et al. (2003) provide examples of methodologies and statistical techniques from research conducted on, broadly speaking, business topics. To take one example, to illustrate factorial designs, we use an experiment by Purohit and Srivastava (2001) that manipulated product manufacturing reputation (good or bad) and product warranty (better or worse than average). Although a complex methodological and statistical concept underlies this experiment, its specific focus is one to which students can readily relate. Similarly, we illustrate the statistical tests of one-sample t-test, independent samples t-test, one-way between-subjects ANOVA, and the 2 x 2 factorial ANOVA using taste tests involving Oreo cookies or diet soda. Indeed, Sizemore and Lewandowski (2011) found that students had a greater interest in methodological information after learning about those concepts applied to a setting in which they were inherently interested (see also Lawson et al., 2003).

In short, although it will require some effort on your part, finding examples in which students are interested will allow you to make the connection between their interests and this course material.

3.1.2 The Difficulty Level of the Material

Is there any better way to spend a Friday night than calculating a one-way repeated-measures ANOVA, pencil to paper? We think not! But as noted previously, our students apparently seem to think otherwise. We as teachers of this material no doubt 'geeked out' doing tasks such as these calculations. That's great for us, but we are not here for us – we are here for our students. And many of today's students say their biggest trepidation about methodological courses is data analysis (Strohmetz et al., 2023).

3.1.2.1 By hand or by computer?
During the past few decades, we have seen the development of sophisticated computer programs that can handle all of the statistics that are frequently included within a research methods class. Indeed, more recently, publicly available statistics programs like JASP (2024) and jamovi are now available for students to use at no cost. Despite the easy availability of these computer programs, one could certainly question whether they facilitate true mastery of the statistics or if students simply learn that the magic box determines statistical significance.

For some of us of a certain age, our first exposure to statistics involved calculations by hand, possibly with the help of a hand-held calculator or abacus. This approach requires the student to be familiar with the actual formula that underlies the statistic, along with each element of that formula. When one has to plug raw data into a formula, one starts to develop the ability to anticipate group differences when looking at the actual data, and not simply waiting until the statistics program delivers its final verdict. Moreover, when conducting statistics by hand, it may be easier to see how variance within a group can alter the error term, and ultimately, the statistic itself. Of course, some statistical calculations are quite unwieldy and would consume large chunks of class time. Indeed, recent research (e.g., Pirlott & Hines, 2025) suggests that at least with respect to one-way between- and within-subjects ANOVAs, students may better understand such material without having to do the associated hand calculations. Comparing one class that performed the hand calculations to another class that did not perform the calculations, these researchers found that the class without the calculations performed about 8% better on a quiz that assessed conceptual understanding of ANOVAs and about 6% better on ANOVA-related lab assignments.

So, what is the best approach? We believe that the balance falls on each instructor, but one approach is to provide more hands-on experience with an initial statistic (e.g., between-groups t-test; one-way ANOVA) in order for the students to understand how variations in some elements of the formula lead to alterations in the statistical output (e.g., t value, F score). Once this understanding has been established, other forms of that statistic (e.g., within-groups t-test, factorial ANOVA) can be introduced without walking the students through the by-hand calculations. Another approach that we have used is to demonstrate the statistic using a computer program, but with a small sample size so that the values in one group can be easily changed mid-session (e.g., to increase or decrease the variance of the group). The instructor can then demonstrate how that change in variance results in predictable differences in the output.

3.1.2.2 Statistical choice, assignments, and student knowledge

As mentioned earlier, many of the questions regarding the use of statistics in a research methods course are inextricably entwined. Of course, the best way to answer them is to start at the end: What are your learning goals related to statistics? Is it vital that every student memorizes the formula for each statistic? Or, is it sufficient that the student can interpret the statistic when they encounter it in another class or in the workplace? With seemingly fewer students choosing a career path through a psychology graduate program, the broader statistical understanding implied in the latter approach may be more appropriate (see Olstad et al., Chapter 16, this volume). From this perspective, we think two assessment approaches are most valuable.

The first is an end-of-term paper that requires students to apply their understanding of experimental design concepts, to calculate and to interpret statistics on data they collected, and to write up this final product according to technical writing guidelines. We still view this as the gold standard assessment of a research methods class as it prepares students for future work within the major, graduate school, and many postgraduate jobs. Yet, as valuable as this assignment can be, it is often not comprehensive in regard to statistics because student projects rarely include the range of statistics discussed during the term. Thus, it is necessary to include a second (or alternate) end-of-term assessment that presents statistics information in a range of different formats. Some of the approaches that we have used include: (1) a verbal description of the type of data collected in an experiment or project and the student identifies the correct statistic to use; (2) a picture of a line graph or a bar graph, and the student identifies the best statistic to use or interprets the data patterns; (3) a graphic of an output table from the statistics program in which the student identifies the different elements; and (4) a results section paragraph in which students need to identify the errors within the piece. With these approaches, we have been able to cover a wide range of statistics, using both a 'by hand' and 'by computer' approach.

3.2 OPTIONS FOR COURSE RESEARCH PROJECTS

Each of us as teachers easily recalls our first experience with psychological research. The rush of excitement from asking questions, collecting data, and drawing conclusions from one's own ideas is a powerful reinforcer. These opportunities were seminal in setting us on the path to our careers as experimental psychologists. It is likely all instructors of research methods want to re-create these exciting moments in their own students, and the student research project is the best means to do so. Some teachers believe that it may be professional malfeasance to teach a research methods class without a research project, but the nature of that project can have multiple consequences for both the student and the instructor. The most obvious factor that influences the number or type of projects is the duration of one's course. Some of us teach in a 15-week semester, whereas others are on a 10-week quarter, so this factor influences all subsequent decisions. Here are some key questions to consider when evaluating your research project.

3.2.1 Will Students Be Expected to Design Their Own Experiment?

The biggest benefit of having students design their own experiment is that it exposes the students to what are often the hardest parts of the research process for undergraduates: reading the literature, developing a unique question, and designing a valid study. However, each of these steps is very time intensive. Further, if a student is not very interested in a research-based career, they may choose to quit a stage (e.g., they do not read anything), and they are not likely to learn much about this process.

3.2.2 Will Each Student Have the Opportunity to Choose Their Research Question and Develop Their Own Study?

There are two primary benefits of this approach. First, students get to choose their own research topic, and students are generally most motivated when they feel they have ownership over the study.[1] Second, each student gets at least some rudimentary exposure to all foundational steps of the research process. This experience is especially valuable for the student who has little experience with research because this exposure might open an unexpected career path for them. Although this approach has the greatest potential benefit for the largest number of students, it can challenge the instructor. Depending on the class enrollment (and duration), instructors may be trying to give meaningful feedback on a large number of projects, particularly many in which they have minimal exposure to the literature.

3.2.3 Can Groups of Students Complete the Research Project?

A different approach is to have the entire class working on the same project. The instructor creates groups of 2–5 students, but here the instructor only needs to be responsible for a single area of the literature. If this area happens to fall within the instructor's area of expertise, the oversight will be even easier. Yet, many students may have little interest in their faculty member's area of expertise. Other concerns with this approach are that many of the groups may work on the same basic research question, which may promote oversharing of information and potential academic dishonesty.

3.2.4 Do Students Need to Collect Data?

We are strong advocates for students collecting data because so many lessons are learned when recruiting and interacting with human participants. Nonetheless, we acknowledge there are many situations in which data collection is not possible and perhaps not even necessary.[2] For example, at smaller institutions, it may not be possible to recruit a sufficient number of participants to conduct statistical tests. Also, it may be that the instructor's expertise is in an area of psychology in which the research topics do not lend themselves to undergraduates collecting potentially sensitive data. Another consideration is the oversight of ethical guidelines at one's institution. Although some Institutional Review Boards (IRB) may have provisions in which data collection for class purposes is exempt from review, others may require all projects to undergo a formal review. Obviously, this latter situation is likely to be much more involved (e.g., teaching the students about the IRB process, having them complete the IRB form, additional time for the review process to occur). It also leaves significantly less time for the design phase of the study, potentially pushing students into choosing variables and materials with little to no grasp of previous research in that area. This time pressure is exacerbated during a 10-week quarter, so the faculty member should expect to be more hands-on with the students during the IRB application process. If these conditions are present at one's institution, it may be best for the instructor to create a data set that can be used by all groups (or variations on the data sets to reduce academic dishonesty).

3.2.5 Are Public Data Available for the Research Project?

A newer possibility is the availability to the public of large databases. Here, the instructor introduces students to the database site and allows them to choose the questions and corresponding variables of greatest interest to them. This approach is particularly useful if time is limited because one forgoes the IRB review and participant recruitment. This approach is most beneficial for research methods classes that introduce correlational and multiple regression statistics, but opportunities for utilizing inferential statistics also exist. Some databases we have found useful include the General Social Survey (National Opinion Research Center, 2024) and the Google Dataset Search (Google, 2024). We caution that these sorts of data sets often need to be simplified in order to be made readily useful for most undergraduate students (see Goldman, Chapter 14, this volume for using secondary data as a research project; in addition, Wagge, Chapter 9, this volume, details the *Journal of Open Psychology Data*, which provides data sets that teachers can use in a similar way to how we use public databases).

3.2.6 What Approach Have We Found Works Best?

One approach that works for us is a modified replication project. Here, student groups are given a target article in the first week of class and instructed to build a project that replicates some portion of that report. Because the instructor has chosen the set of target articles, this reduces the time for students to find research articles and acquaint themselves with that literature. In addition to replicating part of the original study, students are instructed to add another variable (or at least another level to one of the variables from the original report). After reading the target article and related articles, students discuss which questions remain and what would be an effective way to test the most interesting remaining questions. We have observed students have an easier time building a valid experiment because they can rely on the method section of their target article. Given student interest and resource considerations, we have found it best to amass a set of target article possibilities from cognitive or social psychology papers, especially ones with minimal equipment needs, college-age participants, and experimental designs/statistics suitable for undergraduates. In addition, each group now has at least two hypotheses to test (the replication hypothesis and their novel hypothesis). Depending on their results, the opportunity to compare their results with those from their target article (the replication hypothesis) often leads to deeper thinking about the difficulties in repeating certain findings and information that is often omitted from published research reports. This can provide valuable teaching opportunities regarding the replication crisis in psychology and the need for better practices. Finally, this approach allows students to emulate professionally peer-reviewed methodologies instead of trying (or struggling) to develop their own, which we have found is not realistic in a semester, much less a quarter term (see Wagge, Chapter 9, this volume, for more on replication projects).

3.3 TYPES OF WRITING ASSIGNMENTS

The last step of the scientific method is to communicate one's findings to others, and the best vehicle remains the written word. So, it seems obvious, at least to us, that students in a research methods class should write something in some way, shape, or form. However, there are many variations in writing styles and paper types. Here are some choices we have wrestled with to improve student writing and learning in our own research methods classes.

3.3.1 APA Writing versus Technical Writing

As fewer students plan for graduate study in psychology, the need wanes for undergraduates to master APA style (see also Ciarocco & Strohmetz, 2022 for other considerations about the importance of APA style for our students). But do they need to learn any technical writing format? We argue that they do! Even though students think APA writing requirements are an archaic form of torture, we think it is important first to teach students that most disciplines have a prescribed system of communication (i.e., a technical writing format), and mastery of one often results in positive transfer to a new one. As a colleague, Eric Landrum, once said, although employers may not care if an employee knows APA style, they do care if an employee can follow directions (for ideas on teaching APA style, consult Boysen, 2019; Britto & Britto, 2022; and Fallon et al., 2018). These technical writing formats often include a template for the order of subsections, the presentation of data and figures, and the listing of sources. The purpose of this formatting is to aid the reader, because once the reader understands the formatting and style of a given system, they can quickly find specific information, even within a lengthy report. Therefore, we have found an effective approach is first to teach students how to *read* a report before they learn how to *write* a report. For example, we have had students work in small groups and make a presentation about the information (both general and specific to the research topic) contained in each of the various sections of an empirical article. In addition, we have devised 'reading assignments' in which we ask students to answer specific questions from each part of an empirical article, with specific focus on the method and results sections (see Christopher & Walter, 2006 and Kershaw et al., 2023 for more ideas for teaching students how to read empirical articles). From this perspective, then, students can learn that APA style is the approach that psychologists have used to communicate with one another and it would benefit them to know this style.

We have found, anecdotally, that APA style can be made more palatable to students through a combination of assignments and gamification. For example, students are often overwhelmed by the sheer number of rules and variations that apply to APA reference style. We often begin with an assignment in which students find and format five sources. Most students tend to make the same mistakes, so one can briefly teach them the basics of a journal article reference or book chapter reference. This message is reinforced in a subsequent class focused on correct citation of sources within the text of the paper. Here, pairs of students compete in a reference-in-text game in which they are shown a citation and asked how it should be referenced in text, which allows for variations in names, dates, number of authors, etc. Students are allowed to use their *APA Style Manual*, but they must also provide the page number that contains the rule for that citation type. Our students grow quite passionate during this game, and not just for the candy given to the winning team! This exercise emphasizes that APA's basic style applies to most journal article references, even though many variations exist within the *APA Style Manual*.

3.3.2 Variations in Writing Assignments

Requiring students to complete an APA-style paper at the end of the term is a common requirement in most research methods classes, but that does not mean there are no opportunities for variation! Here, we describe some different approaches to designing this capstone paper assignment. Of course, one can vary the number of papers that students are expected to write, or whether they need to complete all sections of an APA-style report, but decisions like these are highly contingent on the type of research project that was conducted, the length of one's term, the number of enrolled students, and the type of grading that you plan to employ.

In our collective experiences, undergraduates receive little instruction in technical writing, so writing these initial papers can be challenging and anxiety inducing (for students and teachers alike!). Indeed, we have observed the best approach is to provide multiple opportunities for students to write and revise to develop this important skill. A successful approach is to separate each of the subsections of the APA paper into different writing assignments. In this case, students are first given extensive instruction in the conventions of a specific APA section (e.g., method) before they submit their work for review. During the grading process, we have found it best to grade the work with the same scrutiny and standards that the final version will receive (one does not want to be 'moving the goalposts' for subsequent versions, and we believe consistency is important in how grading is done throughout the course). Once students receive detailed feedback, they should have a sufficient window of time to process and make corrections, otherwise many of them will only correct 'the low hanging fruit' (e.g., APA reference violations) and not tackle the larger structural problems. Yet, if too much time is allowed for corrections, we have found students may forget some of their earlier choices, and then they ask the faculty members to recall the particulars about writing suggestions they made weeks before. Much like some journals give authors deadlines for revising and resubmitting their manuscripts, we like to give our students a deadline, usually one to two weeks, to revise their work, depending on the number of students in the class and whether or not they have submitted newer work since their most recent feedback.

Instructors using this approach will need to decide how many times students can submit their work for review and how much to weigh the grades of earlier versus final efforts. Although some students avail themselves of every opportunity to re-submit their work, others simply take the first grade they were assigned. Because instructors cannot increase student conscientiousness, it is key for the instructor to protect their own time. In this approach, students should have one opportunity to re-submit the work to improve their grade. In some cases, we have allowed students to make up half of their missing points (e.g., if the original assignment received 60% of the points, a revision that was greatly improved could receive up to 80% of the points). This grading system favors students who put the most work into the original draft, and it also may favor those who entered the class with stronger writing skills. Thus, to encourage students to continue to build on and improve their writing skills, we have since shifted to a grading approach in which students can earn up to 100% of the original grade if their revised work meets the standards of the assignment (see Soysa et al., 2013 for a discussion and examples of writing assignments that can be used to enhance student writing skills throughout the curriculum). Also, we have found it very rare for students to try to 'game' the system by submitting clearly inferior work with the intention that the feedback will direct them to everything they will need to fix. Indeed, the instructor can ensure this does not happen by making sure that their feedback does not involve re-writing the student's work, but simply identifying where errors are occurring. Sometimes students may choose not to do earlier drafts at all if they know that only the final grade will count. We have found that a strict policy requiring a first draft (or else a zero is earned on the final draft) tends to discourage students from opting out of opportunities to receive feedback on earlier drafts.

3.3.3 Individual Writing versus Group Writing Assignments

The more writing feedback students receive, the more likely their writing will improve. Yet, this often means that the instructor is spending even more time grading these assignments, which quickly becomes impractical. One solution is to utilize group writing assignments (see Pham, 2023 for a discussion and empirical test of this technique), which reduce the time the instructor spends grading. Graded group assignments allow for students with varying skills to tutor and support other members within their group, but these assignments may result in some students engaging in social loafing or simply not engaging with the material. As neither approach is clearly superior, blending individual and group writing assignments can be an effective compromise. Now, each student submits their own version of the final written project, so all students must be responsible for learning all of the course material. Yet, earlier in the term, particularly on results writing assignments, group grading can be a benefit. For example, an assignment that requires use of a computer statistics program, data analysis and interpretation, and a written results section will demand a wide set of diverse skills for successful completion. As few students may have strong skills early in the term, allowing them to work with each other and to learn from their peers who are more advanced can be a good vehicle to raise the skill level across all members.

3.3.4 Does Your Class Have a Capstone Experience?

For many students, completion of a research methods class is a major achievement in their undergraduate journey. Arguably, the best means to capture the extent of student progress is the comprehensive written report that requires students to display their acquired skills in experimental design, statistical competence, and technical writing. Yet, simply submitting a final paper may seem underwhelming and solitary after a full term of hard work. Depending on the size and structure of your research methods class, it may be worth considering if there are other ways to recognize your students' accomplishments. For this reason, many research methods instructors have incorporated a final research conference in which students can present their work in either a talk or poster format. Over the years, we have evolved toward a model in which a group of students will design and conduct their study as a team, but then each member is expected to conduct the statistics and write their own version of the final paper. In the last week of the term, the group members reconvene to create a poster version of their project. We have found that group talks are too stressful and time-consuming when students need to be focused on writing their final paper. Further, quietly listening to one presenter at a time quickly dampens student enthusiasm. Instead, during a poster conference, students are free to visit other posters, chat with others, and demonstrate their knowledge of their project. We further enhance the 'celebratory' nature of their accomplishment by purchasing food for this event, offering a minimal extra-credit prize for the best poster and the best project, and inviting guest judges (i.e., other faculty) who interact with the student presenters. This event helps the students end their project (and the class) on an upbeat note, and the instructors have a final opportunity to highlight the students' progress while developing another important research skill – effective oral communication of one's project.

3.4 USES FOR GENERATIVE AI

Admittedly, we were hesitant about the onset of Generative AI (GenAI) in the academic arena (and if you feel the same way, we strongly recommend Bowen & Watson's (2024) excellent primer on using AI as a teacher). However, it was also immediately clear to us that AI was not going to be a passing fad and that we needed to learn about and incorporate it into our teaching. This belief was borne out, albeit anecdotally, when one of our students – in the spring of 2023, less than four months after the release of ChatGPT 3.5 – reported that in a job interview, they were asked about how they had used AI in their classes. In our minds, this train had already left the station. As a colleague put it, 'There is no getting ahead of AI. Either grab onto the life preserver or drown.' Fortunately, Slade et al. (2024) provide ten different potential academic student uses of AI. Here, we focus on how it can be used specifically in teaching research methods.

We see two general ways that GenAI could be used in research methods classes. The first involves having students use GenAI themselves. The second involves teachers' use of GenAI as a 'teaching assistant' for the course. We will provide thoughts to ponder for each of these two possibilities.

3.5 STUDENT USE OF GENAI

We believe one of the most valuable things we can help students develop is how to create prompts that generate useful information. Within methods courses, particularly for ones that require students to have a research idea of any sort, as Slade et al. (2024) suggested, GenAI can help generate ideas based on student interests. As noted previously, many students want to pursue 'non-research' careers (e.g., counseling). We are not trained in these areas, and even if we were, sampling such populations in a 10- or 14-week term is practically impossible. However, we have helped a few of our students interested in such work generate ideas for their class research projects, and the output we received served as a starting point for their own projects. Naturally, it is *critical* to input the constraints on the project (e.g., undergraduate student researcher, time constraint, equipment/technology availability, needing to use a sample of college students) or else it will spit out a great idea – for a doctoral dissertation. That said, it will give students a starting point, from which they can, with your help, formulate a doable project.

Once a student has a general idea for a project, with an independent/predictor variable and dependent/criterion variable in mind, GenAI can also help with constructing operational definitions for those variables (we would suggest using GenAI in addition to consulting prior research here). For instance, many students want to study the construct of anxiety. Of course, there are literally dozens of ways to measure this construct. With prompts that consider constraints on the project, GenAI can offer some ideas to help students jump-start their work in terms of measuring their variables. Indeed, last fall, one student used an AI platform to manipulate the gender (male or female) and pitch (high or low) of a voice that read information aloud to a participant. It was a convenient 2 x 2 experiment that likely would have been much more difficult to operationalize if not for this platform (which, we caution, the student did pay for – a point to which we will return later).

We caution that some students will use GenAI as a 'plug-and-chug' tool, without critically examining the output. We find AI to be helpful in part because we understand the information in these courses – our students do not, and even when they do understand something, they are hesitant to feel as though they understand something. Thus, undergraduates struggle to critically examine AI output related to methodological and statistical concepts, and teachers need to help them think through what they have received. Last spring, we ran some questions from a homework assignment through ChatGPT during a class meeting. It provided some very impressive answers, far more detailed than what we covered in class or what was covered in course readings. In fact, one student – a very perceptive one – said that if he submitted the AI output, he knew his instructors would know he had not written the response himself!

Indeed, we must caution that some students will likely use GenAI to do their homework, especially if they are feeling very pressed for time or otherwise overwhelmed by the assignment. Frankly, as students get better at prompt generation, it is quite possible that GenAI can generate answers that would be more than sufficient to earn a passing grade on some assignments. Indeed, we have found GenAI to be quite good at our multiple-choice items, but as we just mentioned, it is less adept at answering more open-ended questions – at least without relatively sophisticated prompts. We suggest providing time in class for students to get some work done on traditionally out-of-class assignments so that teachers can monitor who does and does not seem to be understanding the information before a final summative assessment of the assignment occurs.

To date, we have only used free ChatGPT platforms. From student self-report data, some have accessed paid GenAI platforms. We have encouraged use of the free platforms, but have not advocated for or demonstrated using any platform that costs money. Our reasoning is not to save ourselves that money but because for a not inconsequential number of our students, it is an expense they cannot easily absorb. We do not want to exacerbate economic inequities that already exist among our students.

3.5.1 Instructor Use of GenAI

Regarding GenAI as a 'teaching assistant,' we have used the technology in several ways in research methods courses. One helpful use of GenAI is for updating homework and other smaller assignments, to avoid using the same scenarios year after year. Simple GenAI prompts to, for example, 'produce an assignment that assesses this same information, but with a different scenario and with different numbers to be used in the calculations' can provide quite useful output! Likewise, if you give tests in your classes, not only can GenAI help you produce at least decent free-response items, it can also rewrite existing multiple-choice questions that assess the same material.

In addition to helping with assessments, AI can be helpful when looking for new ideas for class demonstrations. Admittedly, we have never actually used AI for this purpose, as we have historically relied on journals such as *Teaching of Psychology* and the *Scholarship of Teaching and Learning*, as well as interactions with colleagues at conferences such as the Annual Conference on Teaching and the National Institute on the Teaching of Psychology. That said, we have used AI to jump-start other classes with new demonstrations and in-class activities. We strongly advise not waiting until the morning of your class meeting to use AI in this regard, and some of the suggestions it provides will require finetuning and gathering of materials that may not be readily available in your office.

We do offer three cautions here. First, as implied previously, what we have received from ChatGPT is rarely perfect – we need to spend time, and sometimes a lot of time, editing and finetuning its products. Second, although we are not sure if this is actually the case or not, it is possible that feeding our work into GenAI makes it available for future AI use. If that is so, then what you put in will, to some degree, now be 'out there' for future AI prompts to tap into. As such, we have been extraordinarily careful not to put proprietary information (e.g., data sets, student writing, copyrighted material) into GenAI platforms. Third, there are ethical concerns around using AI. For instance, it is energy-intensive and thus detrimental to the environment. There is also a question of when one should and should not cite AI as a source of information. It is our opinion that any finished product (such as a class activity or assessment tool) in which AI played a role, even if only at the outset of its creation, should credit this.

If you are interested in learning other ways to use GenAI, consult Carter (2025) for simple but highly helpful suggestions. In addition, Afful and Christopher (in press) detailed ways that mid- and late-career faculty are using AI in different aspects of their academic responsibilities.

3.6 CONCLUSION

Considering that the basic elements of a research methods class (experimental design, statistics, and technical writing) have changed little over the past 30 years, it may be surprising to see how much this course can change from term to term. But, much like the idea that an experiment can always be improved, our research methods classes can as well. We hope this chapter captures the conversations and changes that we have attempted over the past two decades, and that it provides some actionable (both big and small) strategies to help you and your department colleagues think about four major challenges in teaching research methods and related courses.

NOTES

1. There are certainly advantages to using 'prefabbed' alternatives to having students choose their research question and develop their own study. For instance, teachers can target a class research project on a topic of their own expertise. We have found that this approach allows the teacher to better serve the students in terms of applying course material to the project because the teacher does not need to stretch into different content areas (e.g., cognitive, social, personality, etc.) and topics within those content areas.
2. In situations where data collection is not possible, students could generate their own hypotheses without empirically testing them. Similarly, they could write sample IRBs, discussing how they would collect data. They could also record themselves doing a sample data collection session. None of these activities necessarily need to be done within the context of a full-scale research project!

REFERENCES

Afful, S. E, & Christopher, A. N. (in press). Maintaining balance and preventing burnout: Advice for mid- and later-career faculty. In D. Dunn & A. S. Richmond (Eds.), *The Oxford Handbook of Undergraduate Psychology Education*. Oxford University Press.

Bowen, J. A., & Watson, C. E. (2024). *Teaching with AI: A Practice Guide to a New Era of Human Learning*. Johns Hopkins University Press.

Boysen, G. A. (2019). An evaluation of production versus error-recognition techniques for teaching APA-style citations and references. *Teaching of Psychology, 46*(4), 328–333. https://doi.org/10.1177/0098628319872609

Britto, M. & Britto, S. (2022). A successful approach to assist students in gaining familiarity and knowledge of APA style and format. *Ticker: The Academic Business Librarianship Review, 7*(1), 3. https://doi.org/10.3998/ticker.2932

Carter, K. (2025, January 3–6). *AI for You: 20 Practical Tips for Psychology Teachers* [Conference presentation]. National Institute on the Teaching of Psychology, Clearwater Beach, FL.

Christopher, A. N., Marek, P., & Benigno, J. (2003). Economic psychology: Its connections with research-oriented courses. *Teaching of Psychology, 30*(3), 209–215. https://doi.org/10.1207/S15328023TOP3003_02

Christopher, A. N., & Walter, M. I. (2006). An assignment to help students learn to navigate primary sources of information. *Teaching of Psychology, 33,* 42–45.

Ciarocco, N. J., & Strohmetz, D. B. (2022). Teaching APA style: Missing the forest for the trees? *Scholarship of Teaching and Learning in Psychology, 8*(4), 399–403. https://doi.org/10.1037/stl0000304

Conroy, J., Christidis, P., Fleishmann, M., & Lin, L. (2019, September). Datapoint: How many psychology majors go on to graduate school? News on psychologists' education and employment from APA's Center for Workforce Studies. American Psychological Association. https://www.apa.org/monitor/2019/09/datapoint-grad-school

Fallon, M., Mahon, M. A., & Coyle, M. (2018). Watching screencasts help students learn APA format better than reading the manual. *Teaching of Psychology, 45*(4), 324–332. https://doi.org/10.1177/0098628318796415

Google (2024). Google dataset search. https://datasetsearch.research.google.com/

Gurung, R. A. R., & Christopher, A. N. (2023). Teaching the foundations of psychological science. In J. Zumbach, D. A. Bernstein, S. Narciss, & G. Marsico (Eds.), *International Handbook of Psychology Learning and Teaching.* Springer International Handbooks of Education. Springer. https://doi.org/10.1007/978-3-030-28745-0_20

Gurung, R. A. R., Hackathorn, J., Enns, C., Frantz, S., Cacioppo, J. T., Loop, T., & Freeman, J. E. (2016). Strengthening introductory psychology: A new model for teaching the introductory course. *American Psychologist, 71*(2), 112–124. https://doi.org/10.1037/a0040012

Gurung, R. A. R., & Neufeld, G. (Eds.). (2022). Introduction: The introductory psychology initiative. In R. A. R. Gurung & G. Neufeld (Eds.), *Transforming Introductory Psychology: Expert Advice on Teacher Training, Course Design, and Student Success,* 3–6. American Psychological Association. https://doi.org/10.1037/0000260-001

JASP Team (2024). JASP (Version 0.19.3) [Computer software]. https://jasp-stats.org/

Kershaw, T. C., Fugate, J. M. B., & O'Hare, A. J. (2023). Teaching undergraduates to understand published research through structured practice in identifying key research concepts. *Scholarship of Teaching and Learning in Psychology, 9*(2), 216–233. https://doi.org/10.1037/stl0000239

Lawson, T. J., Schwiers, M., Doellmann, M., Grady, G., & Keinhofer, R. (2003). Enhancing students' ability to use statistical reasoning with everyday problems. *Teaching of Psychology, 30*(2), 107–110. https://doi.org/10.1207/S15328023TOP3002_04

National Opinion Research Center (2024). The General Social Survey. https://gss.norc.org/

Pham, V. P. H. (2023). The impacts of collaborative writing on individual writing skills. *Journal of Psycholinguistic Research, 52*, 1221–1236. https://doi.org/10.1007/s10936-023-09939-2

Pirlott, A. G., & Hines, J. C. (2025). Eliminating ANOVA hand calculations predicts improved mastery in an undergraduate statistics course. *Teaching of Psychology, 52*(2), 127–132. https://doi.org/10.1177/00986283231183959

Purohit, D., & Srivastava, J. (2001). Effect of manufacturer reputation, retailer reputation, and product warranty on consumer judgments of product quality: A cue diagnosticity framework. *Journal of Consumer Psychology, 10*(3), 123–134. https://doi.org/10.1207/s15327663jcp1003_1

Sizemore, O. J., & Lewandowski, G. W. (2011). Lesson learned: Using clinical examples for teaching research methods. *Psychology Learning & Teaching, 10*(1), 25–31. https://doi.org/10.2304/plat.2011.10.1.25

Slade, J. J., Byers, S. M., Becker-Blease, K. A., & Gurung, R. A. R. (2024). Navigating the new frontier: Recommendations to address the crisis and potential of AI in the classroom. *Teaching of Psychology, 52*(3). https://doi.org/10.1177/00986283241276098

Soysa, C. K., Dunn, D. S., Dottolo, A. L., Burns-Glover, A. L., & Gurung, R. A. R. (2013). Orchestrating authorship: Teaching writing across the psychology curriculum. *Teaching of Psychology, 40*(2), 88–97. https://doi.org/10.1177/0098628312475027

Strohmetz, D. B., Ciarocco, N. J., & Lewandowski, G. W., Jr. (2023, January 12). Why am I here? Student perceptions of the research methods course. *Scholarship of Teaching and Learning in Psychology, 11*(2), 273–283. https://dx.doi.org/10.1037/stl0000353

4. Teaching psychological research methods at community colleges: Enhancing diversity in psychology through inclusive practices

Todd Allen Joseph and Heather Schoenherr

One of the major concerns about the future of psychological science is the lack of diversity in our discipline (Evans, 2021; Huff, 2021). We believe community colleges represent a powerful yet underutilized pipeline for diversifying the field of psychology at both educational and professional levels. Enrolling nearly half of all undergraduates in the United States, these institutions serve students from historically marginalized and underserved backgrounds, including first-generation, low-income, and non-traditional students (Fink et al., 2023). Positioned to address structural inequalities in higher education, particularly those related to access, affordability, and academic preparedness, community colleges play a critical role in democratizing educational opportunities. However, their potential to diversify psychology can only be realized if students are provided with early, meaningful opportunities to develop research skills. Such preparation is essential to ensure students are academically competitive upon transfer and well-positioned for graduate training and career advancement (Hughes et al., 2019; Kotter-Grühn & Grühn, 2024).

Psychology, as a scientific discipline, has profoundly influenced contemporary understandings of human behavior, mental health, social interaction, and cognitive processes (Landrum et al., 2022). Despite these contributions, psychology instruction faces ongoing challenges in adequately reflecting the diversity inherent within the broader population. The American Psychological Association (APA) has repeatedly emphasized the critical need to diversify psychology's workforce, not only to ensure that the discipline is inclusive but also to enhance the cultural relevance and effectiveness of psychological research, practice, and education (Evans, 2021; Huff, 2021).

The importance of diversity within psychology extends beyond representation; it fundamentally affects the quality and applicability of psychological knowledge and services. Culturally competent psychological research and practice are essential for addressing the unique mental health needs and behavioral concerns of increasingly diverse populations (Chu et al., 2022). In the United States, demographic shifts toward greater racial, ethnic, socioeconomic, and cultural diversity demand that psychology, as both a science and a profession, proactively adapts and expands its scope to remain relevant and effective in the services it provides.

However, current data show that the psychology workforce remains disproportionately White and does not reflect the diversity of the broader US population. As of 2023, 78.66% of psychologists identified as White, while only 7.78% were Hispanic, 5.49% Black/African American, 4.37% Asian, 1.12% American Indian/Alaska Native, and 0.03% Native Hawaiian/Pacific Islander (APA, 2022a). With such limited representation of minoritized groups, the discipline risks becoming increasingly disconnected from the diverse communities it aims to understand and serve (Huff, 2021). This disparity is particularly problematic because the effectiveness of psychological services and interventions often hinges on providers' ability to relate culturally and contextually to their clients (Chu et al., 2022). Similarly, the absence of diverse perspectives within psychological research limits the generalizability and applicability of research findings, reinforcing existing biases and inequalities (Thalmayer et al., 2021). Without intentional efforts to diversify the educational pipeline, the field will continue to reinforce existing biases and fall short of producing research and services that apply to all communities.

Teaching psychological research methods at community colleges is therefore not just an academic imperative; it is a strategic intervention with far-reaching implications. APA's Introductory Psychology Initiative (APA, 2022b; Gurung et al., 2016) emphasizes research methods as the foundational core upon which all other components of introductory psychology education should be structured, reinforcing the centrality of research skills in psychology curricula as highlighted by the *APA Guidelines for the Undergraduate Psychology Major 3.0* (APA, 2023) and adhering to *The Principles of Quality Undergraduate Education* (BEA, 2023). To achieve this vision, stronger transfer partnerships, support from organizations, and program and course level investments can ensure community college students are equipped with foundational research skills and integrated into the broader research community.

Whether teaching at a community college or a university, it is essential for educators to understand the consequences of delayed research training and work collaboratively to bridge the gap. Community college transfer students often bring diverse, non-traditional experiences that enrich research learning and the career readiness of all students they interact with. By introducing research methods early at community colleges and fostering cross-institutional partnerships, transfer barriers can be reduced and more diverse talent retained within the field of psychology. Successful partnerships between community colleges and universities not only help to diversify the psychology pipeline, but they also help to fill seats at four-year colleges and universities that are facing a looming demographic cliff. This chapter invites educators to recognize the value of early research training and to commit to coordinated efforts that ensure community college students are not left behind in the psychology pipeline.

4.1 HISTORICAL OVERVIEW OF COMMUNITY COLLEGES

The establishment and evolution of community colleges represent a significant chapter in the broader narrative of American higher education. Originating in the early twentieth century, community colleges were initially conceptualized as junior colleges, intended primarily to provide the first two years of higher education and prepare students to transfer to four-year institutions. The first junior college, Joliet Junior College, was founded in Illinois in 1901, marking the beginning of a nationwide trend toward creating accessible and affordable pathways to higher education (Cohen & Bisker, 2010).

Throughout the first half of the twentieth century, the junior college movement expanded significantly, driven by the growing public demand for educational accessibility, changing labor market demands, and progressive educational philosophies advocating for democratization of education. The post-World War II era witnessed a substantial surge in community college growth because of the influx of veterans seeking educational opportunities through the GI Bill. This period saw not only an expansion in the number of institutions, but also significant diversification in their educational missions and program offerings, including vocational and technical training, adult education, and community service (Drury, 2003). In the mid 1900s, psychology courses were regularly offered at community colleges to support education, nursing, and business programs.

By the 1960s and 1970s, community colleges had firmly established themselves as multifaceted institutions serving diverse educational, economic, and community needs. This era was marked by the rapid expansion of community colleges, driven by a combination of demographic growth, evolving labor market requirements, and the increasing need for accessible higher education opportunities for historically underserved populations, including racial and ethnic minorities, women, and economically disadvantaged individuals.

Despite their significant role in higher education, community colleges have historically struggled with persistent underfunding and undervaluation relative to four-year institutions (Kisker et al., 2023). These financial and reputational challenges have often resulted in limited resources for curriculum development, faculty support, research opportunities, and student services, particularly impacting courses and programs that require intensive resources, such as psychological research methods.

Today, community colleges remain critical entry points to higher education, providing essential pathways for diverse populations to access education, workforce development, and upward social mobility. Their ongoing evolution continues to reflect broader societal changes, economic trends, and educational innovations, making them essential partners in addressing contemporary challenges, such as diversifying the psychological sciences through inclusive research education.

Research methods courses remain underrepresented in community college psychology curricula. Norcross et al. (2016) noted an increase in the proportion of community colleges offering research methods (from 13% to 41% from 1997 to 2014), but this remains lower than four-year universities where nearly all offer research methods and 98% require it for degree completion. One contributing factor may be that research methods is often classified as an upper-division course, which complicates its inclusion in associate degree programs designed for lower-division credit transfer. However, as Ciarocco et al. (2017) highlighted, research methods courses serve a vital role in building foundational skills, such as critical thinking and scientific literacy, which are essential skills for all courses in the major and for workforce readiness. Consequently, transfer students, many of whom come from underrepresented or disadvantaged backgrounds, may arrive at transfer institutions underprepared or be required to retake courses, delaying their progress and increasing financial burdens (Joseph, 2023). Understanding who these students are and what they need is key to closing these gaps and supporting their success in psychology.

4.2　CHARACTERISTICS OF COMMUNITY COLLEGE STUDENTS

Community colleges serve a remarkably diverse student population, reflecting the broader societal shifts toward increased educational accessibility and equity. According to the American Association of Community Colleges (2022), community colleges enroll approximately 41% of all undergraduate students in the United States. Among these students, approximately 55% are students of color and 29% are first-generation college students. Furthermore, 65% of community college students attend part-time, and the average age is 28, indicating a significant presence of non-traditional students.

Many community college students juggle multiple responsibilities, including employment and caregiving (American Association of Community Colleges, 2022). Approximately 62% of full-time community college students are employed, with many working over 20 hours per week. Additionally, 15% are single parents balancing education with child-rearing responsibilities. Financial challenges are also prevalent, with about 42% of community college students receiving Pell Grants because of their low-income status (American Association of Community Colleges, 2022).

Despite these obstacles, extensive research by the Jack Kent Cooke Foundation (JKCF;2019) showed community college students who transfer to selective four-year institutions often perform equally well or even surpass the achievements of students who enter these institutions directly from high school or transfer from other four-year colleges. JKCF's findings reveal that community college transfer students typically graduate at higher rates, achieve higher GPAs, and pursue graduate education at rates comparable to their peers who started at four-year institutions.

Diego Dulanto's story provides an illustrative example of the community college student experience. Born in Peru and brought to the United States as a child, Diego grew up navigating the complexities of being undocumented. As a Deferred Action for Childhood Arrivals recipient, Diego faced financial and institutional barriers that restricted his educational choices. Community college became his accessible entry point into higher education, chosen primarily for its affordability and proximity to his home.

At community college, Diego quickly distinguished himself academically, excelling in his courses and demonstrating exceptional intellectual curiosity and becoming a leader in his college's chapter of Psi Beta. However, despite his academic success, Diego encountered substantial obstacles. His institution lacked significant research opportunities, particularly in psychology, limiting his exposure to the essential experiences needed for successful transfer and future educational pursuits. Having participated in Psi Beta's National Research Project, Diego had a better introduction to psychological research than many other transfer students, but his path was still quite difficult.

Limited availability of courses at his community college (research methods, in particular) and transfer barriers challenged Diego's aspirations to continue in psychology at a four-year institution. Despite these challenges, Diego persisted, navigating complex bureaucratic pathways to ensure credit transfer and advocating for himself through institutional channels. His story exemplifies the resilience and determination characteristic of many community college students who, despite systemic and structural barriers, remain committed to advancing their educational and professional goals.

As more community college students like Diego transfer to four-year institutions, it is essential that university faculty understand the unique characteristics, strengths, and challenges these students bring with them. When faculty recognize and support the varied backgrounds of transfer students, they contribute to a richer, more dynamic academic community in which all students deepen their understanding of diversity and benefit from a broader range of perspectives and experiences.

4.3 INCREASING DIVERSITY THROUGH COMMUNITY COLLEGE RESEARCH METHODS EDUCATION

Effectively teaching psychological research methods at community colleges offers a transformative opportunity to diversify the field of psychology. Community colleges provide a critical pathway for students from historically marginalized, underserved, and disadvantaged backgrounds, offering an accessible entry point to higher education that is crucial for diversifying psychology's workforce.

APA underscores that cultural competence is essential in psychological practice and research, highlighting the importance of training psychologists who can effectively work with diverse populations (DeAngelis, 2015). Community colleges, with their diverse student populations, offer fertile ground for cultivating culturally competent future psychologists. By providing research methods training, community colleges can equip students with the foundational skills required to critically examine psychological phenomena through a culturally informed lens.

Gay (2002) highlights the importance of culturally responsive teaching practices, which create learning environments for all students to thrive. Such practices include incorporating students' cultural characteristics into instruction, highlighting the work of scholars from diverse backgrounds, and promoting culturally relevant curriculum content. Building on this, Rogelberg et al. (2020) argue that embedding culturally responsive pedagogy into psychology courses enhances empathy, understanding, and a sense of belonging, making students from underrepresented backgrounds feel more welcome.

When applied to research methods education, culturally responsive teaching can take many forms: integrating diverse research examples and case studies, examining the cultural contexts of psychological theories, and using collaborative learning to encourage peer-to-peer engagement across differences. Community-based research projects (see Harvey et al., 2023) also offer powerful applied learning opportunities that use lived experiences to ground psychological inquiry. These strategies not only strengthen students' methodological skills but also nurture the cultural awareness and empathy essential for conducting inclusive, ethical research. These approaches have the potential to help students develop empathy and skills to develop into culturally competent psychology professionals.

4.4 BARRIERS TO RESEARCH METHODS EDUCATION

Teaching psychological research methods at community colleges presents a range of significant challenges that can affect students' academic and professional development. One of the most persistent obstacles is the research methods transfer problem, a well-documented issue in psychology education (Stringer, 2022). Although research methods is a foundational course in the psychology curriculum, many community colleges cannot offer it because of its classification as an upper-division course by state and institutional policies. This designation restricts access to essential research training, placing community college students at a disadvantage when transferring to four-year institutions. While transfer students may complete research methods after transitioning, they often do so later in their academic careers than their non-transfer peers who are often encouraged to take the course before their junior year. As a result, transfer students miss out on early involvement in research labs and other experiential learning opportunities that require prior completion of research methods. However, in regions where community colleges can offer this course, students who complete it before transfer often perform as well as or better than their university peers in upper-division coursework, giving them a competitive advantage in research-focused environments (Rudmann, 2022; Stringer, 2022).

Even when research methods courses are available at community colleges, transferability frequently becomes a significant obstacle (Robinson et al., 2025). Four-year institutions often do not accept these credits as equivalents to their courses, leading students to retake research methods courses upon transfer. This redundancy can cause increased tuition costs, prolonged time to graduation, and higher student debt (The Center for Higher Education Policy and Practice, 2024). Because of these barriers, students may also experience psychological impact, such as frustration, decreased motivation, and self-doubt (Fann, 2013). It can be particularly frustrating when a four-year institution will not award credit for a research methods course taught at a community college by a faculty member who also teaches the same course as an adjunct at that same transfer-receiving institution.

Institutional policies at four-year universities further exacerbate this problem. Many universities maintain rigid curricula that do not adequately recognize or accommodate coursework completed at community colleges (Taylor & Jain, 2017). Misalignment between community college offerings and four-year curricula can mean community college students are viewed as underprepared, despite successfully completing rigorous coursework. This perceived deficiency can hinder students' acceptance into competitive programs and research opportunities at the four-year level, limiting their career trajectories and future academic prospects.

Another substantial barrier is the lack of institutional resources at community colleges (Hewlett, 2018). Chronic underfunding often means limited access to faculty who have training in psychological research methods, inadequate laboratory and technology infrastructure, and insufficient library resources. These constraints significantly limit the scope and quality of research education that some community colleges can offer.

The consequences of these barriers are far-reaching. Students lacking early and comprehensive training in research methods are at a distinct disadvantage when applying for advanced study opportunities, internships, and employment within psychology. Falling behind their university peers in opportunities, transfer students may struggle to develop the confidence and academic identity needed to succeed, challenges that are often intensified by the stigma associated with starting at a community college (Shaw et al., 2018). This dynamic not only reinforces existing inequities within higher education and the psychology workforce but perpetuates broader social and economic inequalities, as students from marginalized backgrounds remain systematically excluded from key educational experiences that facilitate upward mobility and professional success. Targeted policy interventions, enhanced institutional collaboration, and increased resource allocation must address the significant hurdles created by institutional and systemic barriers.

4.5 SOLUTIONS AND OPPORTUNITIES

Key initiatives and educational models have proven effective in overcoming these barriers, significantly enhancing the academic success and professional preparedness of community college students. By strategically addressing these areas, community colleges can significantly enhance the diversity, equity, and cultural competence of psychology as a discipline, preparing a diverse cohort of culturally competent psychologists equipped to meet the needs of an increasingly diverse population. The following section describes these strategies at various systematic levels.

4.5.1 Institutional Partnerships and Transfer Receptive Cultures

Creating institutional partnerships and developing transfer-receptive cultures between community colleges and four-year institutions are critical strategies for improving student outcomes (Jain et al., 2011). Successful model partnerships involve comprehensive articulation agreements, aligned curricula, and structured pathways designed to facilitate seamless student transfers. Examples of successful institutional partnerships include collaborations between community colleges and local universities to establish clear, articulated pathways, specifically in psychology majors. These agreements often include shared faculty development programs, aligned learning objectives, and joint advising structures that comprehensively support students through every stage of their academic journey.

Transfer-receptive cultures are intentionally designed environments at four-year institutions that prioritize and actively support transfer student success (Fink & Jenkins, 2017). Such environments include dedicated transfer advising offices, orientation programs tailored for transfer students, and academic and social integration support systems. Institutions recognized by the JKCF as exemplary in transfer student support often provide scholarships, research opportunities, and robust mentoring programs specifically targeting community college transfer students.

These strategies play a vital role in enhancing transfer students' academic preparation, particularly in areas such as psychological research methods where early exposure and support are crucial. Faculty and administrators should investigate whether such partnerships currently exist between their institutions and local community colleges. Additionally, conducting surveys of transfer students can help identify gaps in support and areas where transfer culture or articulation agreements may be improved to ensure equitable outcomes for all students.

4.5.2 Program and Course-Level Research Experiences

While faculty may have limited influence over institutional partnerships and course designations, they have direct control over curriculum and pedagogy, thus making integration of research experiences across the psychology curriculum a powerful way to foster research skill development at community colleges, which can be done with limited resources. For example, course-based undergraduate research experiences (CUREs) offer a scalable and highly effective solution for integrating research training into community college psychology curricula (Bangera & Brownell, 2014). Unlike traditional research experiences that often require significant extracurricular time commitments, CUREs embed authentic research projects within regular coursework. This approach significantly broadens access to research opportunities, particularly benefiting community college students balancing demanding personal and professional obligations.

Successful examples of CURE implementation include projects where students conduct community surveys on mental health awareness or experimental research on cognitive processes, such as memory and attention. At several community colleges, psychology instructors have successfully incorporated longitudinal observational studies into developmental psychology courses, allowing students to engage in real-world research experiences directly aligned with course learning objectives.

Research findings from CUREs have been presented at local, regional, and national conferences, providing students with professional exposure and networking opportunities. Students consistently report that CURE participation enhanced their understanding of research methodologies, strengthened their analytical skills, and increased their overall engagement and interest in psychological science.

In addition to CUREs, APA offers accessible resources that faculty can use to integrate research experiences into content courses at the community college level. For example, the Online Psychology Laboratory provides experiment ideas, resources, and data to allow for structured research experiences that require limited resources from the faculty or the institution, making this an accessible way to integrate research learning opportunities in various classes. Another is the APA Project Assessment (PASS), a searchable database of instructor-created assessments aligned with the *APA Guidelines for the Undergraduate Psychology Major 3.0* (APA, 2023). PASS allows educators to filter assessments by learning goal or topic, such as 'Goal 2: Scientific Inquiry and Critical Thinking,' making it easier to embed research-based assessments in existing courses.

Finally, faculty should encourage students to seek undergraduate research opportunities and internships outside of their institutions. These experiences not only provide access to research training that may not be available locally but also promote collaboration with individuals from diverse backgrounds. Many of these programs offer stipends to help offset living expenses, making the opportunities more accessible to students with financial needs. Engaging in such programs is invaluable for developing a broad range of research experiences, which are essential for competitive graduate school applications and successful entry into the psychology workforce.

4.5.3 Leveraging Organizational Resources to Support Research Skill Development

Because institutional partnerships and course designation decisions often fall outside the direct control of faculty, leveraging external resources from professional organizations presents a practical solution for supporting research skills development at community colleges. One notable organization leading these efforts is Psi Beta, the national honor society for psychology students at community colleges. Psi Beta plays a vital role in expanding access to psychological research experience for students who might not otherwise have the opportunity.

A cornerstone of Psi Beta's work is its annual National Research Project (Psi Beta, 2025). Each year, Psi Beta selects a timely psychological research topic, providing community college students across the nation with the opportunity to engage collaboratively in empirical research. Past projects have explored relevant psychological themes such as resilience, stress management, academic persistence, and social media impacts on mental health. Participation in the NRP offers students practical, hands-on experiences, from designing methodologies to collecting and analyzing data. These experiences empower students by encouraging the development of critical thinking, statistical analysis, and collaborative skills. For instance, students who participated in a recent NRP investigating social isolation reported significant gains in their ability to design surveys, analyze data using statistical software, and interpret findings in real-world contexts. Outcomes from these projects are frequently presented at regional and national conferences, enhancing students' professional profiles and providing valuable networking opportunities.

Psi Beta also supports research development through its Undergraduate Research Toolkit, a publicly accessible resource that provides faculty and students with tools to understand ethical research practice, data analysis, and strategies for effective dissemination (Psi Beta, n.d.b). Complementing these efforts, the *Psi Beta Journal of Student Research* offers a peer-reviewed publication outlet exclusively for community college student researchers, helping students build a professional research portfolio and gain recognition within the psychological community (Psi Beta, n.d.a).

Another significant resource offered by Psi Beta is the National Psychology Summit. This virtual conference is strategically designed to be accessible and affordable, eliminating significant barriers such as travel costs and scheduling conflicts, enabling broader student participation. Open to the public, the conference has featured diverse programming, including keynote speeches from renowned psychologists; interactive workshops; and structured poster sessions showcasing community college and university student research. An impactful component is the 'Café Conversations' series, where students interact directly with psychology professionals from various sub-disciplines, such as clinical, cognitive, developmental, forensic, and industrial-organizational psychology. Student feedback from these sessions has consistently highlighted the benefits of gaining direct insights into career pathways and the practical application of psychological research. The asynchronous poster sessions at the summit allow students to present their empirical research findings to a national audience. Psychology professionals rigorously judge these sessions, providing valuable constructive feedback to students. Several past participants have reported that the experience significantly enhanced their confidence in research communication skills, leading to successful transfers and admissions to competitive psychology programs at four-year institutions.

To further acknowledge student research development, Psi Beta created the Jerry Rudmann Research Award. This award recognizes members who demonstrate emerging competencies in research skills, communication, ethics, and service. This award offers another way for students to gain recognition for research skills outside of formal coursework.

Collectively, these solutions offer comprehensive pathways for overcoming barriers, promoting equity, and enhancing diversity within the psychology workforce. Professional organizations, like APA and Psi Beta, should continue advocating for community college students and facilitating comprehensive resource sharing and professional development opportunities. Expanded collaboration between community colleges, four-year institutions, and professional organizations can significantly enhance educational equity and inclusivity within psychology education. For example, Psi Chi (the honor society for psychology students at four-year institutions) updated policies to be more community college friendly by basing membership eligibility on community college GPA, rather than waiting for transfer students to establish a four-year college GPA.

4.6 CONCLUSION: PATHWAY TO EQUITY AND CULTURAL COMPETENCE

Community colleges have a unique and critical role in advancing equity, diversity, and cultural competence within psychology. Serving nearly half of all undergraduates in the United States, many from historically marginalized and underserved backgrounds, these institutions are well-positioned to expand access to foundational psychological education, including research methods training. As this chapter has illustrated, community college students face distinct barriers: limited access to essential courses; inconsistent transfer policies; and constraints related to time, work, and financial resources. These challenges contribute to disparities in academic preparedness and limit opportunities for engagement in research, a key component of undergraduate psychology education (APA, 2023). Furthermore, the absence of research methods courses in community college curricula places students at a disadvantage, particularly when transfer institutions do not recognize equivalent coursework. However, initiatives such as Psi Beta's (2025) National Research Project, Psi Beta's National Psychology Summit, and APA's classroom resources offer scalable solutions. Integrating CUREs, strengthening transfer pathways, and building mentoring networks can further bridge opportunity gaps and support student success.

Ultimately, increasing access to psychological research methods and extracurricular research opportunities at community colleges is not just an equity issue; it is a strategic investment in the future of psychology. Collaboration across organizations and institutions, sustained institutional support, and flexibility in recognizing research preparedness are essential to realizing this potential. By working collectively, educators, institutions, and professional organizations can ensure community college students are prepared to lead, innovate, and diversify the future of psychological science.

REFERENCES

American Association of Community Colleges. (2022). *Fast Facts 2022*. https://www.aacc.nche.edu/2022/02/28/42888/

American Psychological Association (APA). (2022a). *Demographics of U.S. Psychology Workforce* [Interactive data tool]. https://www.apa.org/workforce/data-tools/demographics

American Psychological Association (APA). (2022b). *The APA Introductory Psychology Initiative (IPI)*. https://www.apa.org/ed/precollege/undergrad/introductory-psychology-initiative

American Psychological Association (APA). (2023). *APA Guidelines for the Undergraduate Psychology Major: Version 3.0*. https://www.apa.org/about/policy/undergraduate-psychology-major.pdf

Bangera, G., & Brownell, S. E. (2014). Course-based undergraduate research experiences can make scientific research more inclusive. *CBE Life Sciences Education, 13*(4), 602–606. https://doi.org/10.1187/cbe.14-06-0099

Board of Educational Affairs. (2023, March 1). *Principles for Quality Undergraduate Education in Psychology*. American Psychological Association. https://www.apa.org/education-career/undergrad/principles

Chu, W., Wippold, G., & Becker, K. D. (2022). A systematic review of cultural competence trainings for mental health providers. *Professional Psychology, Research and Practice, 53*(4), 362–371. https://doi.org/10.1037/pro0000469

Ciarocco, N. J., Strohmetz, D. B., & Lewandowski Jr, G. W. (2017). What's the point? Faculty perceptions of research methods courses. *Scholarship of Teaching and Learning in Psychology, 3*(2), 116–131. https://doi.org/10.1037/stl0000085

Cohen, A. M., & Bisker, C. B. (2010). *The Shaping of American Higher Education: Emergence and Growth of the Contemporary System* (2nd Ed.). Jossey-Bass.

DeAngelis, T. (2015). In search of cultural competence. *Monitor on Psychology, 46*(3). https://www.apa.org/monitor/2015/03/cultural-competence

Drury, R. L. (2003). Community colleges in America: A historical perspective. *Inquiry, 8*(1), 1–6. https://files.eric.ed.gov/fulltext/EJ876835.pdf

Evans, A. C. (2021). Diversifying the psychology pipeline. *Monitor on Psychology, 52*(7). https://www.apa.org/monitor/2021/10/ceo

Fann, A. (2013). Campus administrator and student perspectives for improving transfer policy and practice. *New Directions for Higher Education, 2013*(162), 27–38. https://doi.org/10.1002/he.20054

Fink, J., & Jenkins, D. (2017). Takes two to tango: Essential practices of highly effective transfer partnerships. *Community College Review, 45*(4), 294–310. https://doi.org/10.1177/0091552117724512

Fink, J., Tulloch, A. G., Steiger, J., & Reddy, V. (2023). *Advancing Equity with Effective Community College Transfer Pathways*. Campaign for College Opportunity.

https://collegecampaign.org/wp-content/uploads/2023/11/2023_AEEIEA_Briefs_TransferBrief_AdvancingEquity.small_.pdf

Gay, G. (2002). Preparing for culturally responsive teaching. *Journal of Teacher Education, 53*(2), 106–116.

Gurung, R. A. R., Hackathorn, J., Enns, C., Frantz, S., Cacioppo, J. T., Loop, T., & Freeman, J. E. (2016). Strengthening introductory psychology: A new model for teaching the introductory course. *American Psychologist, 71*(2), 112–124. https://doi.org/10.1037/a0040012

Harvey, H., Pierce, J., & Hirshberg, D. (2023). Using participatory research to develop a culturally responsive early childhood assessment tool. *Journal of Participatory Research Methods, 4*(2). https://doi.org/10.35844/001c.77624

Hewlett, J. A. (2018). Broadening participation in undergraduate research experiences (UREs): The expanding role of the community college. *CBE Life Sciences Education, 17*(3), Article es9. https://doi.org/10.1187/cbe.17-11-0238

Huff, C. (2021). Psychology's diversity problem. *Monitor on Psychology, 52*(7). https://www.apa.org/monitor/2021/10/feature-diversity-problem

Hughes, J. L., Li, M., McDonnell, E. R., Engsberg, E. V., & Goss, C. S. (2019). Professors' research expectations for admission to psychology graduate programs. *Psi Chi Journal of Psychological Research, 24*(1). https://doi.org/10.24839/2325-7342.JN24.1.2

Jack Kent Cooke Foundation. (2019). *Persistence: The Success of Students Who Transfer from Community Colleges to Selective Four-Year Institutions.* https://www.jkcf.org/research/persistence/

Jain, D., Herrera, A., Bernal, S., & Solorzano, D. (2011). Critical race theory and the transfer function: Introducing a transfer receptive culture. *Community College Journal of Research and Practice, 35*(3), 252–266. https://doi.org/10.1080/10668926.2011.526525

Joseph, T. A. (2023, February 17). *Eliminating Community College Transfer Barriers to Promote Fairness and Diversity* [Keynote]. Southeastern Teaching of Psychology Conference, Atlanta, GA.

Kisker, C. B., Cohen, A. M., & Brawer, F. B. (2023). *The American Community College.* John Wiley & Sons.

Kotter-Grühn, D., & Grühn, D. (2024). Availability and perceived importance of high-impact practices for psychology graduate program admission. *Teaching of Psychology, 52*(2), 210–218. https://doi.org/10.1177/00986283241235667

Landrum, R. E., Gurung, R. A., Nolan, S. A., McCarthy, M. A., & Dunn, D. S. (2022). *Everyday Applications of Psychological Science: Hacks to Happiness and Health.* Routledge.

Norcross, J. C., Hailstorks, R., Aiken, L. S., Pfund, R. A., Stamm, K. E., & Christidis, P. (2016). Undergraduate study in psychology: Curriculum and assessment. *American Psychologist, 71*(2), 89–101. https://doi.org/10.1037/a0040095

Psi Beta. (2025). *Annual National Research Project 2025–2026.* https://psibeta.org/psi-betas-annual-national-research-project-2024-2025/

Psi Beta. (n.d.a). *Psi Beta Journal of Student Research.* https://psibetajournal.org/

Psi Beta. (n.d.b). *Undergraduate Research Resources.* https://psibeta.org/ur_resources/

Robinson, D., Lee, S., Lazzara, J., Schoenherr, H., Waggoner Denton, A., Taylor, V. C., Bui, N., Boenau, M. E., & Orsillo, S. M. (2025). Fostering equity in two-year college psychology education: Using the APA *Guidelines 3.0* as a path for student success. *Scholarship of Teaching and Learning in Psychology, 11*(1), 49–64. https://doi.org/10.1037/stl0000413

Rogelberg, S. L., Summerville, K., & Ruggs, E. N. (2020). I-O psychology for everyone: Use of culturally responsive teaching to increase diversity and inclusion in undergraduate classrooms. *Industrial and Organizational Psychology, 13*, 509–514. https://doi.org/10.1017/iop.2020.78

Rudmann, J. (April, 2022). *Community College Research Methods White Paper Status Report*. Psi Beta National Council Meeting [Virtual].

Shaw, S. T., Spink, K., & Chin-Newman, C. (2018). "Do I really belong here?": The stigma of being a community college transfer student at a four-year university. *Community College Journal of Research and Practice, 43*(9), 657–660. https://doi.org/10.1080/10668926.2018.1528907

Stringer, H. (2022). Reducing barriers for community college students majoring in psychology. *Monitor on Psychology, 53*(6). https://www.apa.org/monitor/2022/09/barriers-community-college-psychology

Taylor, J. L., & Jain, D. (2017). The multiple dimensions of transfer: Examining the transfer function in American higher education. *Community College Review, 45*(4), 273–293. https://doi.org/10.1177/0091552117725177

Thalmayer, A. G., Toscanelli, C., & Arnett, J. J. (2021). The neglected 95% revisited: Is American psychology becoming less American? *American Psychologist, 76*(1), 116–129. https://doi.org/10.1037/amp0000622

The Center for Higher Education Policy and Practice. (2024). *The Cost of Today's College Credit Transfer System*. https://www.chepp.org/news/from-chepp/improving-credit-transfer-can-help-more-students-graduate-from-college/

PART II

Fostering scientific thinking in psychological research methods

5. Teaching research methods in content courses

Celeste Pilegard and Rian E. Drexler

Research methods is a required course in the curriculum of almost every undergraduate psychology program in the United States (Norcross et al., 2016). Why is it so important for psychology majors to understand scientific reasoning, inference, and evidence? Beyond being what distinguishes psychology from mere speculation about human behavior, such understanding helps psychology students within the discipline, both as producers or consumers of research (Morling, 2021), and is a critical component of the skills psychology students can bring into the larger workforce (Naufel et al., 2018). Skills around interpreting scientific information are central to the American Psychological Association's (APA) *Guidelines for the Undergraduate Psychology Major*, with research methods themes woven throughout the core competencies (APA, 2023). In this chapter, we argue that the teaching of research methods must not end in a dedicated research methods course. Instead, every course in the psychology curriculum should be infused with explicit epistemological concepts that emphasize where knowledge comes from in psychology. We discuss why this integrated approach is essential for developing scientific thinking and offer strategies that instructors can implement in their content courses to strengthen students' methodological reasoning.

5.1 WHAT SHOULD PSYCHOLOGY STUDENTS KNOW ABOUT RESEARCH IN PSYCHOLOGY?

The psychology curriculum should help students develop two complementary forms of scientific understanding. First, students need methodological competence, which includes understanding how to conduct and interpret psychological research through proper design, valid measurement, and appropriate inferences based on data (see *APA Guidelines for the Undergraduate Major*, Outcome 3.2: Interpret, design, and evaluate psychological research; APA, 2023). Second, they need meta-scientific understanding: knowing how psychological science itself functions as a knowledge-building enterprise, including its cumulative nature, social processes, and reliance on evidence (see *APA Guidelines for the Undergraduate Major*, Outcome 3.1: Exercise scientific reasoning to investigate psychological phenomena; APA, 2023).

5.1.1 Methodological Competence

The most obvious role of research methods in the psychology major is that it prepares students with the basic concepts and vocabulary they need for the rest of the psychology major; hence, a research methods class is often among the early requirements in the psychology curriculum. The components of this knowledge will be familiar to anyone who has read a research methods textbook, with key topics including measurement validity, reliability, random assignment, statistical inference, confounds, correlation versus causation, replication, and meta-analysis, among others. Mastering these concepts helps students understand how psychologists measure phenomena, gather evidence, and interpret findings to develop and verify knowledge. When students understand these concepts, they not only spot claims that don't match the evidence, but they can also explain what's wrong with them, such as when someone assumes causation without proper evidence.

These concepts are challenging for psychology majors (Gurung & Landrum, 2013; Gurung & Stoa, 2020); many key concepts in methodology involve mentally representing complex relationships between variables and probabilistic thinking, which takes practice to develop. For example, determining what makes a measurement valid involves a complex decision tree. Given this complexity, methodological concepts should be reinforced throughout the psychology curriculum so that students get the diverse examples and consistent practice they need to adequately learn the concepts and apply them to everyday situations.

5.1.2 Meta-Scientific Understanding

In addition to methodological competence, psychology students need to understand how psychological science functions as a knowledge-building enterprise. Scholars call the understanding of the beliefs and values inherent to the scientific process *nature of science* knowledge (Lederman, 2013) or epistemic beliefs (Bromme et al., 2010). Research has shown that epistemic beliefs correlate with achievement in a psychology course (Drexler & Pilegard, 2025) and that enhancing nature of science understanding supports critical thinking about science content (Greene & Yu, 2016). Whereas methodological competence helps students understand how to design studies and make inferences, meta-scientific understanding helps students grasp why these methods are valued for creating knowledge, why knowledge changes in psychology, and that not all claims about human behavior have the same knowledge-value.

5.1.3 Nature of Science in Psychology

The *APA Guidelines for the Undergraduate Major* identifies recognizing flaws in pseudoscience and favoring scientific reasoning as a key goal for our students (Outcome 2.1B; APA, 2023) – but what are the components of scientific reasoning that the psychology major should foster? In terms of the nature of science, the *Next Generation Science Standards* for K-12 education offer a useful starting point: science is a way of knowing about the natural world, it is based on empirical evidence, it is subject to change, and it is a human endeavor (National Research Council et al., 2013).

At a basic level, students must understand that psychological knowledge is empirically based: scientific claims in psychology must be grounded in systematic observations and data. Psychology graduates should understand when claims about human behavior require evidence, and that the quality of the evidence matters for the validity of claims. Building on this foundation is the recognition that knowledge in psychology is subject to change. Students must understand that even well-established theories in psychology represent our current best understanding of the available data rather than absolute, unchangeable facts. Changes to scientific knowledge reflect the cumulative nature of scientific knowledge; only as we gather new evidence do we strengthen, refine, discard, or change our theories.

A more complex component of the nature of science is that science is a human endeavor, influenced by social, cultural, and historical contexts. Students should understand that because scientists are human, research can include biases, errors, and even malpractice. Equally important, however, is that science achieves objectivity precisely through social processes: discussion, debate, critique, collaboration, consensus, and peer review help identify and correct for individual biases and assumptions (Longino, 1990; Oreskes, 2019). This balance between human subjectivity and objectivity in science is a particularly important concept for psychology graduates to understand. Students should neither naively accept scientific claims at face value nor become cynical about science based on individual examples of human error.

5.1.4 Developing Evaluativist Thinking

A goal for psychology graduates should be to develop an *evaluativist* thinking style. This concept comes from a developmental model of epistemic thinking styles that includes three major styles: absolutism, multiplism, and evaluativism (Kuhn et al., 2000). In an absolutist style, students believe that there is only one way of understanding the world, and that knowledge is objective and certain. A student using an absolutist thinking style might believe a single study proves a theory, or that anything their textbook or professor says must be true. In a multiplist style, students understand that there is more than one way to understand the world and believe that knowledge is entirely subjective and uncertain. A student using a multiplist style might have an attitude that knowledge is a matter of opinion, and therefore no method of evaluating claims is more useful than another. Evaluativism, by contrast, refers to an understanding that, even though knowledge is subjective and uncertain, claims can be evaluated based on evidence. This thinking style helps students accept uncertainty in science, while still motivating them to use reliable methods to find the best explanations. Evaluativism is considered the most sophisticated epistemic thinking style and has been connected to better reasoning abilities and educational performance (Weisberg et al., 2021).

This thinking style connects to what McIntyre (2019) describes as the *scientific attitude*: '(1) We care about empirical evidence; (2) We are willing to change theories in light of new evidence' (p. 48). Such an attitude will help psychology graduates beyond the classroom as they encounter new claims and evidence not covered in our classes. Psychology graduates should be motivated to integrate new evidence with their existing knowledge and update their knowledge when appropriate. To achieve this, we must design our courses to give students the tools (i.e., methodological competence and meta-scientific knowledge) to engage in evaluativism-style thinking. Strategies to help students develop those tools will be presented later in this chapter (see section 'How to Teach Research Methods Across the Curriculum').

5.2   WHY TEACH RESEARCH METHODS IN CONTENT COURSES?

Developing sophisticated scientific thinking skills is not trivial; that even educated adults struggle with scientific reasoning has been a persistent puzzle of developmental psychology (Shtulman & Walker, 2020). However, we are not advocating redesigning the psychology curriculum by replacing content courses with additional research methods classes. Such an approach would be misguided. It is productive toward our current goals for the psychology curriculum to focus mostly on content courses: students can't learn to reason about science if they don't have knowledge to reason with. Rather than choosing between content and methodology, psychology instructors should view their content courses as having two explicit and mutually reinforcing goals: developing content knowledge and developing scientific thinking.

5.2.1 Scientific Thinking Needs Scientific Knowledge

When we sequester research methods concepts into a single course, we risk falling for a repeatedly discredited idea: that transferable critical thinking skills can be taught independently of content knowledge (Mayer, 2008; Perkins & Salomon, 1989). When a course is designed to teach general thinking skills, such as critical thinking, problem-solving, or general intelligence, the benefits tend to be modest or nonexistent, with little or no transfer to new tasks (Ritchhart & Perkins, 2005). The reason this approach fails is likely because it reflects an incomplete view of how critical thinking develops. There is little evidence for critical thinking as a general skill; rather, critical thinking is largely domain-specific, and interventions to improve critical thinking will be more successful when they are grounded in disciplinary knowledge (Bensley & Spero, 2014; Greene & Yu, 2016; Willingham, 2019). What is recognized as 'critical thinking' is often the application of a variety of disciplinary skills and structures that require repeated, applied practice to acquire.

The discipline-specific nature of thinking skills has implications throughout higher education. A common structure for many undergraduate majors is to require a series of prerequisite formal skills courses before starting the content-based major courses that apply those skills. As Nathan (2012) argues, this approach misunderstands how abstract knowledge develops. Concrete applications provide the foundation that helps students develop meaningful understanding of abstract concepts. This aligns with Agarwal's (2019) findings that challenge traditional hierarchical assumptions about knowledge acquisition. In psychology, this means that students develop their understanding of concepts like confounding variables not by memorizing abstract definitions, but through seeing how specific confounds, such as socioeconomic status or selection bias, operate across different studies.

5.2.2 Research Methods Themes Should Be Made Explicit

Psychology is a science, and so all content courses should, at least *implicitly*, convey research methods themes. However, evidence suggests that explicit instruction about the nature of science is far more effective than implicit or discovery-based approaches (Abd-El-Khalick & Lederman, 2023). Lederman and Lederman (2019) make the argument that students cannot read their teachers' minds, and thus need adequate scaffolding to arrive at appropriate conclusions about how the science content relates to the nature of science.

Even when students have the appropriate research methods knowledge, they need cues to know when to activate it and apply it to the novel lesson (Gick & Holyoak, 1980; Meylani, 2024). Research method concepts are abstract, and often the same underlying concept can manifest in an unlimited variety of surface features. While experts in an area easily see the structural features of new information in their domain of expertise, novices tend to focus on the surface (Chi et al., 1981). Students are less likely to internally cue themselves to connect their previous research methods knowledge to new content information, and thus benefit from explicit guidance from instructors to make necessary connections. With practice, students will be more prepared to make those connections spontaneously, as they must in the world outside the classroom.

5.3 HOW TO TEACH RESEARCH METHODS ACROSS THE CURRICULUM

Given the challenges in developing thinking skills, the limitations of isolated research methods courses, and the domain-specific nature of critical thinking, we should consider the entire psychology curriculum as an opportunity to develop scientific thinking. Integrating research methods into content courses requires starting from a simple perspective: our courses must teach the process of science, not just its products. By making the epistemological foundations of psychological knowledge explicit, instructors help students understand not just what we know, but how we know it and why we trust this knowledge. The following strategies offer practical approaches for psychology instructors to incorporate research methods throughout the curriculum (see Table 5.1 for a summary).

5.3.1 Remind Your Students What They Already Know

We are not suggesting that every psychology class should dedicate weeks to re-teaching research methods. However, as psychologists, we understand that transferring knowledge between contexts is challenging, and that it's easy to fail to activate the necessary prior knowledge to understand something new.

Depending on the context and target concept, one of the following strategies may be appropriate: reminders, re-teaching, or supplemental materials. A reminder is just a brief refresher. For example, when you first mention 'control' and 'experimental' groups in discussing a study, take a moment to help students recall what these terms mean (and remember that there are many similar-sounding terms that can easily blend together in students' minds: consider 'control,' 'confound,' 'construct,' 'condition,' 'confederate,' 'convenience,' and 'constant'; see Cross, Chapter 7, this volume). More complex concepts may require re-teaching. Consider how many years of psychology education you needed before confidently distinguishing between mediation and moderation; even if these topics were covered in a research methods course, students might not have fully grasped them the first time. For important topics, you may also supply supplemental materials for students to review independently,

Table 5.1 Strategies for integrating research methods into content courses

Strategy	Description	Implementation example
Remind your students what they already know	Activate prior research methods knowledge	• Brief refreshers of key terms • Re-teaching complex research methods concepts • Providing supplemental materials for review
Present claims as inferences based on evidence	Frame scientific knowledge as conclusions drawn from evidence rather than established facts	• Teaching individual studies with method, results, and conclusions • Emphasizing science as cumulative enterprise • Pairing classic studies with recent meta-analyses
Emphasize within-group variation	Balance discussion of group differences with attention to within-group variation	• Showing visualizations of distributions rather than just means • Discussion of degree of overlap between groups
Support students' causal reasoning	Provide explicit frameworks for evaluating causal claims	• Diagramming alternative explanations for causal relationships • Discussing alternative explanations for relationships, identifying necessary evidence to rule out alternatives
Don't avoid the 'warts' of science	Acknowledge uncertainties, limitations, and ongoing debates	• Discussing the replication crisis • Addressing historical biases in psychological research • Showing how science changes over time
Assess methodological reasoning	Include methodological reasoning in course assessments	• Exam questions on evidence for claims • Causal diagram exercises

or implement low-stakes assignments to check for foundational knowledge and assign or suggest additional materials based on students' performance. Even if you are confident that a topic was thoroughly covered in a prerequisite course, remember for some students that prerequisite course may be several years removed, and some students might have transfer credit from courses with different coverage.

5.3.2 Present Claims as Inferences Based on Evidence

Perhaps the most critical principle for teaching research methods across the curriculum is consistently presenting scientific claims as inferences based on evidence rather than as established facts. Students should not view science as an oracle they can consult to know the truth of the universe, but rather as a method of knowing the world that involves testing theories through observation. When introducing a psychological concept or theory, explicitly discuss the evidence behind it. Rather than stating 'people encode memories differently based on how deeply they process information,' try teaching Craik and Tulving (1975), including the method, results, and conclusions. This approach models scientific thinking for students and reinforces the connection between claims and evidence: students should develop the mental habit of expecting a scientific claim to be followed by its supporting evidence.

Additionally, instructors should help students understand science as a cumulative enterprise. Individual studies should not be presented as definitive; emphasize how knowledge builds through multiple studies, replications, and meta-analyses. Many classic studies are useful to teach because they established important research paradigms and generated extensive subsequent research, even though the original studies often had methodological limitations such as very small sample sizes. If you teach a classic study with methodological flaws, complement that with a recent meta-analysis showing whether the original effect holds up.

5.3.3 Emphasize Within-Group Variation Alongside Between-Group Differences

Psychology often focuses on group differences, but failing to discuss within-group variation can lead students to develop an oversimplified understanding of psychological phenomena. Instructors may be surprised at how easily students can misinterpret group differences. For example, students may assume little or no overlap between groups when they see a bar graph showing two different means (Wilmer & Kerns, 2022). In reality, even large effect sizes involve substantial overlap between groups (e.g., an effect size of $d = 0.8$ involves a 68.9% overlap between two normal distributions; Grice & Barrett, 2014). When discussing many group differences, such as many gender differences, within-group variation may be much greater than between-group differences.

Emphasizing within-group variation helps combat essentialist thinking and reinforces important statistical concepts like distributions, central tendency, and variability that students learn in statistics and research methods courses. Error bars can help suggest variation, but they are often misunderstood compared to visualizations such as violin plots (Correll & Gleicher, 2014; see

Cumming & Finch, 2005 for guidance on interpreting error bars). Don't assume students understand the nature of group differences and explicitly discuss the degree of overlap between groups when presenting research findings on group differences.

5.3.4 Support Students' Causal Reasoning

The ability to repeat the maxim that 'correlation does not imply causation' is not the same as recognizing when causal claims are appropriate from given evidence. Inappropriate causal inferences are not uncommon among college students (Norris et al., 2003; Rodriguez et al., 2016). How can we help psychology students learn to avoid such errors?

One approach is to help students visualize relationships through simple diagrams (sometimes called directed acyclic graphs or DAGs in fields like causal inference; Pearl, 2009). Draw variables as nodes and causal relationships as arrows pointed from causes to effects. For example, in a basic diagram examining the relationship between stress and depression, a potential third variable like socioeconomic status (SES) would be drawn with arrows pointing from SES to both stress and depression, visually illustrating why we can't conclude that stress causes depression without accounting for SES. Seifert et al. (2022) showed that teaching students to diagram alternative explanations for causal claims (e.g., reverse causation, third variable problem) reduced causal theory error after the intervention. When discussing research findings, take time to explicitly work through causal claims. What alternative explanations might account for the observed relationship? What evidence would we need to rule out these alternatives? This kind of guided practice can help students develop more sophisticated causal reasoning skills.

5.3.5 Don't Avoid the 'Warts' of Science

Don't present an artificially sanitized version of psychology. Acknowledge the uncertainties, limitations, and ongoing debates in the field. Doing so doesn't undermine the authority of science; rather, it helps students understand how science works as a self-correcting process. If a claim you make is based on a single promising study that needs further replication, say so. Discuss issues like the replication crisis openly with students, explaining how psychologists are working to improve research practices. Share examples of how scientific knowledge has changed over time as new evidence has emerged. Don't conceal the problematic roots or ongoing biases that might be present in your field (e.g., Kennedy-Shaffer, 2024; Thomas et al., 2023) – instead, discuss how addressing such bias, and incorporating more diverse perspectives, can improve science's ability to describe the world objectively (Longino, 1990; Oreskes, 2019).

By addressing these 'warts' honestly, you help students develop a more accurate understanding of how science works and protect them from disillusionment when they encounter critiques of psychological science. This approach also models evaluativist thinking, showing students how scientists can acknowledge uncertainty while still valuing evidence-based approaches to knowledge.

5.3.6   Assess Methodological Reasoning

Include methodological reasoning as an explicit learning goal in your class, support students toward that goal, and assess it on exams and assignments. Inform students that exam questions will focus on the evidence for claims and ask questions that require students to make connections between claims and evidence. Ask students to draw causal diagrams depicting the relationships between variables. Assign popular press articles reporting on psychological research and ask students to evaluate the accuracy of the reporting. Mueller et al. (2020) provide more concrete examples of assessments designed specifically to measure students' scientific thinking skills in alignment with APA outcomes. While students shouldn't be expected to demonstrate perfect methodological reasoning – even professors make errors after many years of graduate school – including appropriate formative and summative assessments reinforces that understanding psychological phenomena and evaluating the evidence for them are inseparable aspects of psychology education.

5.4   CONCLUSION

When psychology instructors integrate research methods into content courses, they not only deepen students' understanding of course material but also equip them with thinking skills that extend beyond the classroom. The approaches outlined in this chapter help develop two important competencies. First, they build methodological literacy: the ability to understand research designs and accurately interpret findings. Second, and perhaps more importantly, they cultivate meta-scientific understanding, including an appreciation for how knowledge in psychology evolves and principles for evaluating scientific claims. Importantly, the approaches presented here don't require small or high-touch courses and align with approaches to implement APA guidelines in large-scale contexts (Cross et al., 2025).

We recognize that implementing these approaches presents challenges. Instructors may be concerned that covering the process of science adds to their already-packed syllabi, or that discussing the limitations and uncertainties of science may cause students to distrust the enterprise. However, teaching in this manner will help students practice thinking about scientific claims the way they will need to in the real world: by evaluating the available evidence and connecting that evidence to the claim.

To evaluate your own teaching practices, consider the following standards for teaching scientific thinking in psychology. These criteria can serve as benchmarks for assessing whether your courses effectively integrate methodological reasoning with content knowledge:

1. Present scientific claims as inferences based on evidence, not as proven facts.
2. Provide the evidence for scientific claims.
3. Describe within-group as well as between-group variation when characterizing group differences.
4. Discuss limitations to studies, including limits to internal, external, and measurement validity.
5. Provide context about the weight of scientific evidence, such as emphasizing that a claim is based on a single study and needs to be replicated, noting that an effect is robust and replicates widely, or addressing widespread replication failures.

By implementing these approaches across the psychology curriculum, we can help students develop the sophisticated scientific thinking skills they need to be informed consumers of psychological research, prepared for success in a world where evaluating evidence is more important than ever.

REFERENCES

Abd-El-Khalick, F., & Lederman, N. G. (2023). Research on teaching, learning, and assessment of nature of science. In N. G. Lederman, D. L. Zeidler, & J. S. Lederman (Eds.), *Handbook of Research on Science Education*, Vol. III, 850–898. Routledge.

Agarwal, P. K. (2019). Retrieval practice & Bloom's taxonomy: Do students need fact knowledge before higher order learning? *Journal of Educational Psychology*, *111*(2), 189–209.

American Psychological Association (APA). (2023). *APA Guidelines for the Undergraduate Psychology Major: Version 3.0.* https://www.apa.org/about/policy/undergraduate-psychology-major.pdf

Bensley, D. A., & Spero, R. A. (2014). Improving critical thinking skills and metacognitive monitoring through direct infusion. *Thinking Skills and Creativity*, *12*, 55–68.

Bromme, R., Pieschl, S., & Stahl, E. (2010). Epistemological beliefs are standards for adaptive learning: A functional theory about epistemological beliefs and metacognition. *Metacognition and Learning*, *5*, 7–26.

Chi, M. T., Feltovich, P. J., & Glaser, R. (1981). Categorization and representation of physics problems by experts and novices. *Cognitive Science*, *5*(2), 121–152.

Correll, M., & Gleicher, M. (2014). Error bars considered harmful: Exploring alternate encodings for mean and error. *IEEE Transactions on Visualization and Computer Graphics*, *20*(12), 2142–2151.

Craik, F. I., & Tulving, E. (1975). Depth of processing and the retention of words in episodic memory. *Journal of Experimental Psychology: General*, *104*(3), 268–294.

Cross, V. L., Albada, N. A., Ditta, A. S., Geller, E. H., Hendley, H. S., Paquette-Smith, M., Pilegard, C., & Woods, V. E. (2025). Scaling up APA Guidelines 3.0 for large-enrollment classes. *Scholarship of Teaching and Learning in Psychology*, *11*(1), 113–121.

Cumming, G., & Finch, S. (2005). Inference by eye: Confidence intervals and how to read pictures of data. *American Psychologist*, *60*(2), 170.

Drexler, R. E., & Pilegard, C. (2025). Does connecting the processes and products of science facilitate learning? A schema-based approach. In D. Barner, N.R. Bramley, A. Ruggeri and C.M. Walker (Eds.), *Proceedings of the 47th Annual Meeting of the Cognitive Science Society*, *47*, 6074–6080.

Gick, M. L., & Holyoak, K. J. (1980). Analogical problem solving. *Cognitive Psychology*, *12*(3), 306–355.

Greene, J. A., & Yu, S. B. (2016). Educating critical thinkers: The role of epistemic cognition. *Policy Insights from the Behavioral and Brain Sciences*, *3*(1), 45–53.

Grice, J. W., & Barrett, P. T. (2014). A note on Cohen's overlapping proportions of normal distributions. *Psychological Reports*, *115*(3), 741–747.

Gurung, R. A., & Landrum, R. E. (2013). Bottleneck concepts in psychology: Exploratory first steps. *Psychology Learning & Teaching*, *12*(3), 236–245.

Gurung, R. A., & Stoa, R. (2020). A national survey of teaching and learning research methods: Important concepts and faculty and student perspectives. *Teaching of Psychology*, *47*(2), 111–120.

Kennedy-Shaffer, L. (2024). Teaching the difficult past of statistics to improve the future. *Journal of Statistics and Data Science Education*, *32*(1), 108–119.

Kuhn, D., Cheney, R., & Weinstock, M. (2000). The development of epistemological understanding. *Cognitive Development*, *15*(3), 309–328.

Lederman, N. G. (2013). Nature of science: Past, present, and future. In S. K Abell & N. G. Lederman (Eds.), *Handbook of Research on Science Education*, 831–879. Lawrence Erlbaum.

Lederman, N. G., & Lederman, J. S. (2019). Teaching and learning nature of scientific knowledge: Is it déjà vu all over again? *Disciplinary and Interdisciplinary Science Education Research*, *1*, 1–9.

Longino, H. E. (1990). *Science as Social Knowledge: Values and Objectivity in Scientific Inquiry*. Princeton University Press.

Mayer, R. E. (2008). *Learning and Instruction*. Merrill Prentice Hall.

McIntyre, L. (2019). *The Scientific Attitude: Defending Science from Denial, Fraud, and Pseudoscience*. The MIT Press.

Meylani, R. (2024). Innovations with schema theory: Modern implications for learning, memory, and academic achievement. *International Journal for Multidisciplinary Research*, *6*(1), 2582–2160.

Morling, B. (2021). *Research Methods in Psychology: Evaluating a World of Information*. W. W. Norton & Company.

Mueller, J. F., Taylor, H. K., Brakke, K., Drysdale, M., Kelly, K., Levine, G. M., & Ronquillo-Adachi, J. (2020). Assessment of scientific inquiry and critical thinking: Measuring APA Goal 2 student learning outcomes. *Teaching of Psychology*, *47*(4), 274–284.

Nathan, M. J. (2012). Rethinking formalisms in formal education. *Educational Psychologist*, *47*(2), 125–148.

National Research Council, et al. (2013). Appendix H – Understanding the scientific enterprise: The nature of science in the next generation science standards. *Next Generation Science Standards: For States, by States*, 2.

Naufel, K. Z., Appleby, D. C., Young, J., Van Kirk, J. F., Spencer, S. M., Rudmann, J., & Richmond, A. S. (2018). *The Skillful Psychology Student: Prepared for Success in the 21st Century Workplace*. https://www.apa.org/careers/resources/guides/transferable-skills.pdf

Norcross, J. C., Hailstorks, R., Aiken, L. S., Pfund, R. A., Stamm, K. E., & Christidis, P. (2016). Undergraduate study in psychology: Curriculum and assessment. *American Psychologist*, *71*(2), 89–101.

Norris, S. P., Phillips, L. M., & Korpan, C. A. (2003). University students' interpretation of media reports of science and its relationship to background knowledge, interest, and reading difficulty. *Public Understanding of Science*, *12*(2), 123–145.

Oreskes, N. (2019). *Why Trust Science?* Princeton University Press.

Pearl, J. (2009). *Causality* (2nd Ed.). Cambridge University Press.

Perkins, D., & Salomon, G. (1989). Are cognitive skills context-bound? *Educational Researcher*, *18*(1), 16–25.

Ritchhart, R., & Perkins, D. N. (2005). Learning to think: The challenges of teaching thinking. In K. J. Holyoak & R. G. Morrison (Eds.), *The Cambridge Handbook of Thinking and Reasoning*, 775–802. Cambridge University Press.

Rodriguez, F., Ng, A., & Shah, P. (2016). Do college students notice errors in evidence when critically evaluating research findings? *Journal on Excellence in College Teaching*, *27*(3).

Seifert, C. M., Harrington, M., Michal, A. L., & Shah, P. (2022). Causal theory error in college students' understanding of science studies. *Cognitive Research: Principles and Implications*, *7*(1), 4.

Shtulman, A., & Walker, C. (2020). Developing an understanding of science. *Annual Review of Developmental Psychology*, *2*(1), 111–132.

Thomas, A. K., McKinney de Royston, M., & Powell, S. (2023). Color-evasive cognition: The unavoidable impact of scientific racism in the founding of a field. *Current Directions in Psychological Science*, *32*(2), 137–144.

Weisberg, D. S., Landrum, A. R., Hamilton, J., & Weisberg, M. (2021). Knowledge about the nature of science increases public acceptance of science regardless of identity factors. *Public Understanding of Science*, *30*(2), 120–138.

Willingham, D. T. (2019). How to teach critical thinking. *Education: Future Frontiers*, *1*, 1–17.

Wilmer, J. B., & Kerns, S. H. (2022). What's really wrong with bar graphs of mean values: Variable and inaccurate communication of evidence on three key dimensions. *OSF Preprints*. https://osf.io/preprints/osf/av5ey_v1

6. 'I've done my research': Teaching research methods to combat false information

Holly Zell

6.1 WHY SHOULD I TAKE RESEARCH METHODS IF I DON'T WANT TO BE A RESEARCHER?

Many research methods teachers have likely heard this phrase or some variation of the phrase before. There are a variety of ways to answer this question including mentioning of transferable skills, an improved ability to read research papers, and the expansion of critical thinking (Naufel et al., 2018). While some students may find these to be valuable additions to their knowledge, others may continue to view the course as necessary but not useful (Gurung & Stoa, 2020).

In 2017, the American Psychological Association (APA) reported that of 3.5 million people in the United States with a psychology undergraduate degree, only about 4% of those went on to obtain a doctorate degree in psychology (APA, 2019). This number does not distinguish PhD degrees from PsyD degrees, which involve less research practice. This would seem to suggest that the vast majority of psychology undergrads do not wind up in research careers. With this knowledge, how can teachers balance the needs of those who do wish to pursue professional research careers with those who do not? How do we make these skills broadly accessible enough so that any student, regardless of career aspirations, can connect to the content and use it in their lives?

A highly salient topic in the age of social media and intensely divided politics surrounds false information and its often devastating consequences. The phrase 'I've done my research' (Small, 2021) shows up frequently in social media posts when false information is shared, and without empirical research skills it can be very challenging for individuals to know which information to accept or reject (Bergstrom & West, 2020). Importantly, as psychology teachers we must also consistently consider inclusivity in teaching. Learning about false information in the media within the classroom opens the opportunity to have discussions around how false information interacts with systemic oppression, and how strategies for dealing with false information can also act as tools for increasing justice and safety within our communities.

6.2   WHAT IS FALSE INFORMATION IN THE MEDIA?

False information in the media spans many areas of day-to-day life. It is very common to find difficulty in determining truth versus lack thereof in a wide variety of situations and topics. Often, misrepresentations and false information are presented as factual, leaving individuals to do their own work to determine the veracity of a source or a piece of information. A challenge therein is that not everyone knows how to do that work, or even that the work is necessary.

While some false information is spread intentionally, false information is also frequently unintentionally created and spread (Oregon Health News Blog, 2021). This may happen after someone misinterprets facts or research results and shares their misinterpretation as factual. This could also potentially happen in relation to biases people hold, especially in regard to information that confirms a person's pre-existing beliefs (Trethewey, 2019). For example, a person on social media who reads an article that references the side effects of a vaccine may retain this negative information and discard other information, such as the efficacy of the vaccine. They may then spread this information as the results of their *research*, truly believing that the information they are sharing is accurate and complete.

Regardless of the intention behind the message, false information can have severe consequences. A particularly ubiquitous example of this is false information spread during the COVID-19 global pandemic. A wide variety of rumors spread rapidly regarding the origins and spread of the disease (Bolsen et al., 2020), possible treatments (Levin et al., 2023), information around vaccines (Di Domenico et al., 2022), wearing face masks, and more (Taylor & Asmundson, 2021). These rumors fueled racist attacks against Asian individuals (Han et al., 2022; Park et al., 2024), promoted the idea that getting vaccinated against COVID-19 was dangerous (Di Domenico et al., 2022), and spread false information about treatments that could allegedly heal COVID-19 (Levin et al., 2023). During the height of the pandemic, the US president himself stated that the use of bleach could be a potential treatment, with no basis in actual science (McGraw & Stein, 2021).

Not only does this false information create confusion and stress in trying to determine what advice should be followed and what should be discarded, it has genuine life-or-death outcomes. Despite the fact that research demonstrated that those who were vaccinated were significantly less likely to die of complications of COVID-19 (de Gier et al., 2023), large swaths of Americans believed that the vaccine was more harmful than the disease, and many of those who opted to not become vaccinated died (Jia et al., 2023). Certainly, skills in research methods cannot fully eradicate these noted problems, but they can provide tools needed to prevent these outcomes for many. Especially in the context of the COVID-19 pandemic, social media was a particular source of false information perpetuation and must be considered specifically. When considering increasing the relevance of research methods courses for students, topics related to social media could prove both relatable and practical.

6.3 SPECIAL CONTEXT: SOCIAL MEDIA

In the age of widespread social media use, many are looking to social networking sites to receive their news and public information, and this can present many challenges. More than 70% of college students use social media daily, and many of those are on social media for a significant time each day (Baldwin-White & and Gower, 2023). While strictly speaking, news networks are supposed to verify information before reporting it (APA, 2024b), social media posts are held to no such standard. In 2025, Meta CEO Mark Zuckerberg announced that he would be removing fact checking from all Meta platforms (including Facebook, Instagram, and Threads) in the name of 'free speech' (McMahon et al., 2025). Fact checking involved employees of Meta reviewing posts and removing or labeling them if they contained factually incorrect information (Meta, 2025). While this system was imperfect in terms of combating false information, it at least created an opportunity for people to question the media they were consuming. Without this, social media users must use their own judgment to decide what to believe and what to discard.

Social media sites use algorithms to determine which types of content a person will see on their feed (Institute for Internet and the Just Society, 2021). This algorithm is built through an individual's engagement on the site including which accounts they follow, their searches, and which types of posts they interact with (Institute for Internet and the Just Society, 2021). This results in people frequently winding up in a sort of online echo chamber (Institute for Internet and the Just Society, 2021) and this can build quickly. As a social media user interacts with content on the site, the algorithm will subsequently feed them more and more related content. As their viewing of the content increases, they will also likely see their views shift as people tend to experience an increase in positive reactions to things they view more frequently (Zajonc, 1968). Also, because of their engagement with this content, they are less likely to come across any contradicting information to challenge their beliefs (Brady et al., 2023).

Without a critical eye in social media consumption, it is easy to not only consume false information but spread it as well. When a social media user views a post that they agree with or like, it usually takes just one click to share the post with their own followers, which increases engagement with the post. When that information is accepted at face value without investigating the veracity of the information therein, false information on social media spreads like a literal virus from one user to the next. We can use lessons and assignments within research methods courses to help students learn research skills and apply them to their social media use, such as the example assignment in the section below.

6.3.1 Connecting Social Media to Research Methods

A first topic in many research methods courses is examining what types of knowledge and evidence exist and how to distinguish research evidence from anecdotal or opinion-based information. For many undergraduate students, the distinctions between an article about research and a peer-reviewed research article are not clear. It is important to dedicate intentional class time to ensuring students know how to search for, identify, and select research articles in order to be successful in their courses (Lacum et al., 2014). It is also critical to teach students how to search for literature on a topic. Many lower-level courses provide papers for students to use, and while this can be effective in terms of ensuring students are using a desired source, it does not actually teach students about how to find their own literature.

An assignment I completed myself as an undergraduate and have also assigned as an instructor involves finding a news article about scientific research and then finding the original research article to compare and contrast the reporting of the research with the actual research results. This allows students to witness how sometimes research results reported by the media are not fully accurate or complete. This can be a valuable exercise, and it can also be pushed a step further.

In Figure 6.1 I outline an assignment to help students learn to identify, research, and assess information that they see on social media. Submittable assignments could include formal papers or more creative applications such as infographics or media presentations.

Figure 6.1 depicts a potential outline for an assignment where students find a topic of interest from social media and then follow a number of steps to assess that information and reassess their initial reactions. Holmes et al. (2015) note that repeated practice of critical thinking skills encourages future spontaneous use of said skills. This assignment has the potential for meaningful practice of critical thinking skills through encouraging skepticism of presented information. This assignment also has potential regarding helping students to learn about the creation of research questions (George Mason University, 2018). Regardless of the outcome that students find, there are opportunities

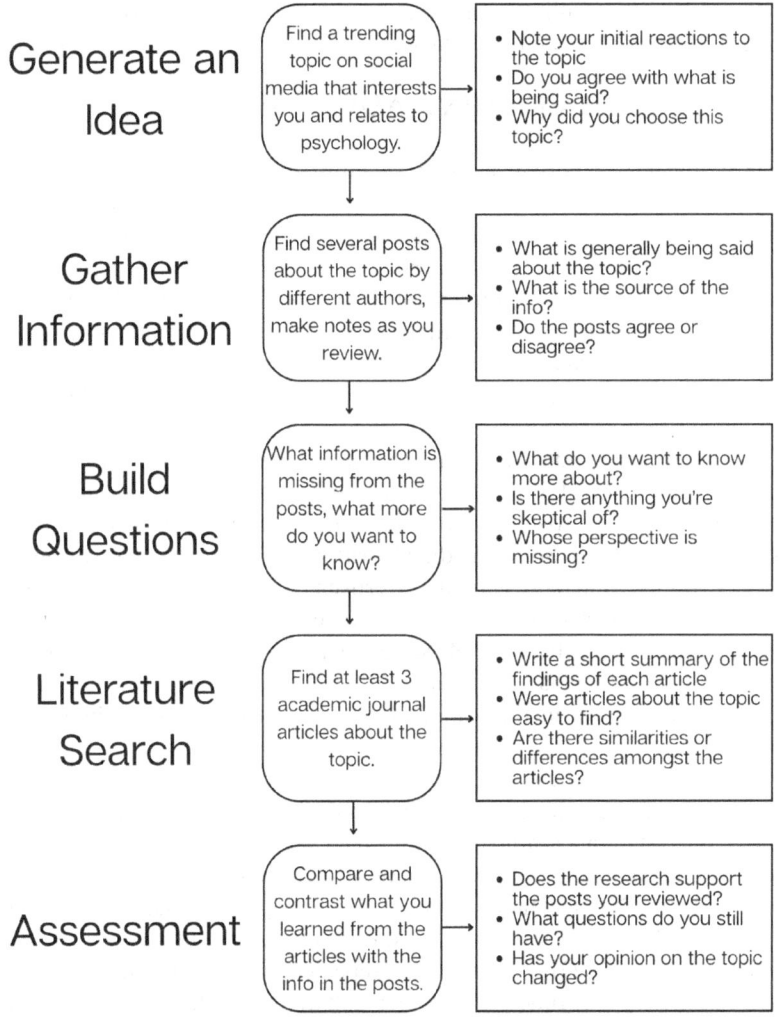

Source: Author's own work.

Figure 6.1   Using research methods skills to assess social media information

for learning. For example, if a student finds *no* literature on a topic, or only tangential topics, this can be a place to discuss identifying gaps. If the student finds articles with conflicting information, this can be a place to discuss examining study quality as well as replication.

6.4 SPECIAL CONTEXT: ADVERTISING

Even if students do not engage with social media at all, it is impossible that they do not interact with any false information in the media. While much of this chapter focuses on false information regarding current events and scientific research, it would be a mistake not to also consider how research methods skills can help students become better critics of advertising. Advertisements infiltrate nearly every area of life in the twenty-first century, both online and in person. While advertisements are generally prohibited from making outright false claims (Federal Trade Commission, 2013), they can still be incredibly and intentionally misleading.

It is important to note that social media and advertising have a very tight-knit relationship. Most, if not all, social media sites receive a majority of their revenue through advertising to platform users, including users who are minors (Raffoul et al., 2023). Social media algorithms will increase advertising of a product if a user interacts with an advertisement. Targeted advertising algorithms make it such that if a person searches for a particular product on a search engine, they will also likely see an increase in advertising for that product on their social media apps (Dutta, 2020). This means that oftentimes false information on social media platforms can interact specifically with targeted advertising.

For example, a user comes across a video that suggests that taking a certain supplement will help them lose weight rapidly with no scientific evidence presented. Interested in learning more, they then seek out information on the supplement to see how it works or what it costs. Even if the user decides they do not wish to buy the supplement at that time, it is highly likely that advertisements for that supplement, as well as other similar products, will increase dramatically (Froehlich, 2022). Increased and repeated exposure to the product can build familiarity over time, which may result in the user feeling more inclined to believe in the product or purchase it (Bornstein, 1989; Zajonc, 1968).

It can be a useful classroom activity to practice brainstorming using critical thinking skills (Doğan & Batdı, 2021), and this can be applied to assessing advertisements. For example, the instructor can display an advertisement for the class to look at, such as the fabricated one available in the book's Supplementary Materials.

The instructor can then ask the class to share what messages they perceive from the image, and what they think the advertisers want them to perceive. Students may say something like 'Supplement X is healthy,' 'Supplement X has vegetables in it,' or 'Supplement X is good for your heart.' This can then be discussed by contrasting what is actually *known* about Supplement X (nothing!). Students can then come up with a list of questions they have about the product to help them decide what they think about it.

This brainstorming using a critical lens can help to reinforce skepticism in terms of consuming advertising but also has the potential to help students adopt a critical lens while assessing research as well – a crucial skill for any research methods course.

6.5 HOW DO WE CRITICALLY EVALUATE A SOURCE? HOW DO WE CRITICALLY EVALUATE RESEARCH?

Research methods courses generally teach students how to read and evaluate research papers. These sources can be challenging to read for students, and intentional instruction regarding how to read them gives students a leg up on being able to evaluate their sources (Lacum et al., 2014). This can include teaching about the different types of research articles that exist, such as the various types of studies that can be conducted (qualitative, quantitative, longitudinal, cross-sectional), and different types of papers, including review types such as systematic reviews versus literature reviews. It is also useful to teach students about the different sections that are common within research papers and how to engage with them. Students occasionally find themselves hung up on complex statistics that they may not yet understand, and help navigating this in advance can reduce the likelihood of frustration when working on assignments.

An extremely important facet of critiquing research in terms of combating false information in the media is considering *generalizability* (Mitchell & Shivde, 2023). For example, a media report may use a sensationalist headline regarding a new study on the efficacy of a particular positive mental health habit. However, when the original research is reviewed, the actual study only tested introductory psychology students, or the study had a very small sample size. Researchers are aware that these issues should limit who the study is purported to apply to, but this is not always widely known information.

Beyond learning to critically evaluate media claims, it is also important that students in research methods courses learn to critically evaluate research evidence as well. While it may be beyond the scope of some courses to make in-depth critiques of complex statistical procedures, students can evaluate studies in terms of the representativeness of their sampling and sampling methods. Figure 6.2 outlines another variation on the previously discussed social media assignment, where students compare and contrast a media article with the original research article. In this proposed assignment, students place a special

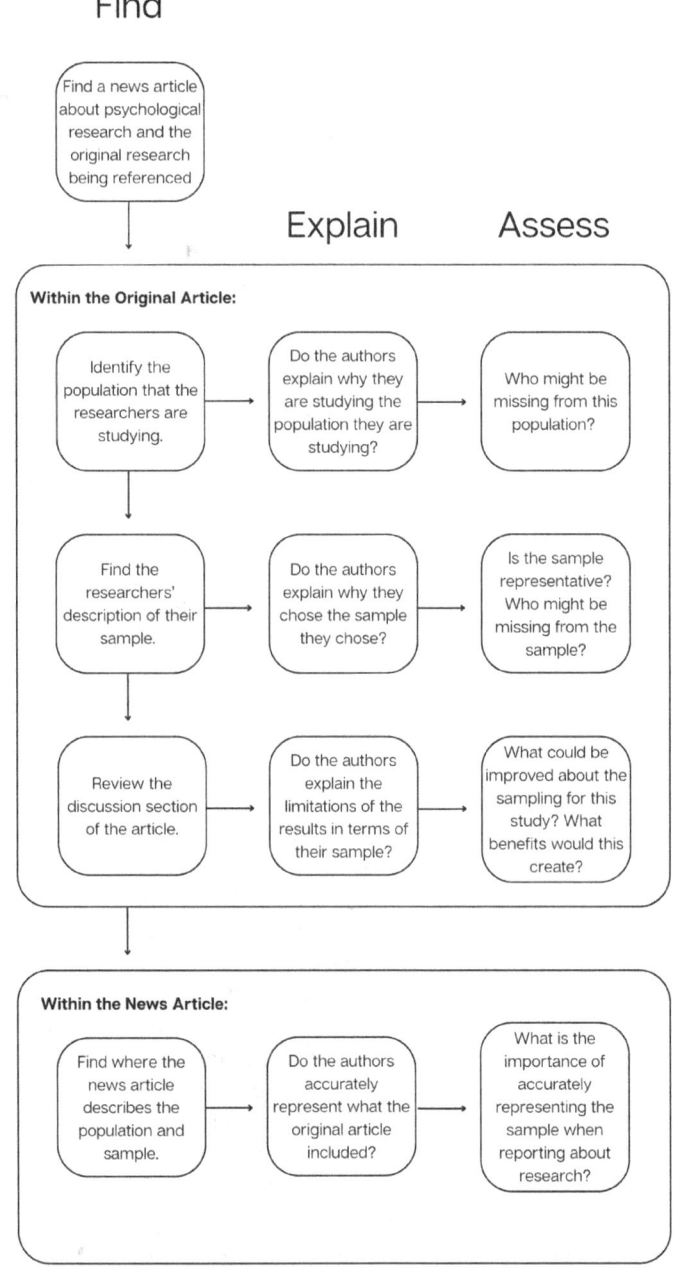

Figure 6.2   Assessing and critiquing sampling and generalizability

focus on sampling representativeness within the research and the accuracy of the generalizability of results within the media article.

Figure 6.2 describes a potential assignment wherein students assess both a research article and a media article before reporting the research results. By focusing in on population, sampling, and reporting, students can learn about the differences between a research population and a research sample, as well as apply their critical thinking skills to sampling methods and accurate reporting. These topics and this assignment can also potentially be places to include course content around psychology's history with poor representativeness in sampling or norming of tests (APA, 2024a; Apicella et al., 2020).

6.6 FALSE INFORMATION AND SYSTEMIC OPPRESSION

False information has the potential to harm anyone, and it is also known that it creates disproportionate burdens for minoritized communities (Lee et al., 2023). For example, the following was published in a 2025 executive order by the White House: 'Across the country today, medical professionals are maiming and sterilizing a growing number of impressionable children under the radical and false claim that adults can change a child's sex through a series of irreversible medical interventions' (The White House, 2025).

Taken at face value, these words are shocking. However, if one takes the time to do further reading, they will find that, firstly, medical professionals are not maiming children or sterilizing them. Surgical transition care is exceptionally rare for those under 18 years of age (Dai et al., 2024), and the types of treatments that are approved for youth under 18 are endorsed by the American Medical Association (American Medical Association, 2024) as well as the American Academy of Pediatrics (Wyckoff, 2023). The language itself in the statement, 'that adults can change a child's sex through a series of irreversible medical interventions' (The White House, 2025) also misleads. Medical professionals and trans people alike are aware that one cannot change their sex, but rather gender identity and expression. Despite the fact that this statement has multiple demonstrable falsehoods, it is being stated as fact on an official government website, written into executive order.

Psychology itself has a history of perpetuating harm through false information, and much of this history has real and current impacts on systemic oppression and false information today (Auguste et al., 2023). In 2021, the American Psychological Association issued an apology to people of color, acknowledging a decades-long history of false information and harm done to communities of color (APA, 2021). Many regard this apology as too little, much too late, and there is significant reason for this perspective (Auguste et al., 2021). One of the many reasons relates to the harm already done and the long-term rippling impacts of false information spread through scientific entities themselves. A project conducted by the APA into psychology's history of harms against people of color highlights a number of issues, including the creation and perpetuation of race hierarchies, promoting race as a biological construct, creating testing measures that discriminated against people of color, the promotion of segregation, and more (APA, 2024a).

It is not uncommon to hold the sentiment that we should *keep politics out of the classroom* and to some degree, we can acknowledge there are sometimes reasons for believing in this notion as an *inclusive practice*. However, it is critical to interrogate who specifically is being included when we ignore the impacts of political situations on our students, as well as the intersections of science and politics. If we seek to use research methods courses as a platform to help students navigate their everyday lives, we cannot ignore that some students are more impacted by false information than others. One of the topics we may teach in a research methods course is distinguishing personal opinion from scientifically supported information. Discussing political information in the context of scientific findings and consensus versus personal opinion can help our students learn something important about the scientific process while also creating space for discussion of important and currently relevant topics.

6.7   CONCLUSION AND TAKE-AWAYS

False information in the media is a serious problem facing our society and has the potential to have severe impacts on students' lives. While combating false information in the media may not be the primary focus of a research methods course, the transferable skills taught within these courses can be broadly applied to help teach students how to engage with, interrogate, and evaluate the media they are exposed to. These skills can be especially important in terms of combating false information that feeds into systemic oppression and false information about communities facing discrimination. Intentionally teaching these skills to apply broadly can also potentially increase the perceived usefulness of research methods courses for students who do not intend to pursue research careers.

REFERENCES

American Medical Association. (2024, May 21). *Advocating for the LGBTQ Community.* https://www.ama-assn.org/delivering-care/population-care/advocating-lgbtq-community

American Psychological Association. (2019). *Datapoint: How Many Psychology Majors go on to Graduate School?* https://www.apa.org/monitor/2019/09/datapoint-grad-school

American Psychological Association. (2021). *Apology to People of Color for Apa's Role in Promoting, Perpetuating, and Failing to Challenge Racism, Racial Discrimination, and Human Hierarchy in U.s.* https://www.apa.org/about/policy/racism-apology

American Psychological Association. (2024a). *Historical Chronology.* https://www.apa.org/about/apa/addressing-racism/historical-chronology

American Psychological Association. (2024b). *How and Why Does Misinformation Spread?* https://www.apa.org/topics/journalism-facts/how-why-misinformation-spreads

Apicella, C., Norenzayan, A., & Henrich, J. (2020). Beyond WEIRD: A review of the last decade and a look ahead to the global laboratory of the future. *Evolution and Human Behavior, 41*(5), 319–329. https://doi.org/10.1016/j.evolhumbehav.2020.07.015

Auguste, E., Bowdring, M., Kasparek, S. W., McPhee, J., Tabachnick, A. R., Tung, I., & Scholars for Elevating Equity and Diversity (SEED). (2023). Psychology's contributions to anti-Blackness in the United States within psychological research, criminal justice, and mental health. *Perspectives on Psychological Science, 18*(6).

Auguste, E., Nobles, W., & Rowe, D. (2021, November 21). Opinion | American Psychological Association's white supremacy apology falls short. *NBC News.* https://www.nbcnews.com/think/opinion/why-apa-s-apology-promoting-white-supremacy-falls-short-ncna1284229

Baldwin-White, A., & and Gower, K. (2023). Influence of social media on how college students perceive healthy relationships and consent. *Journal of American College Health, 71*(4), 1301–1309. https://doi.org/10.1080/07448481.2021.1927049

Bergstrom, C. T., & West, J. D. (2020). *Calling Bullshit: The Art of Skepticism in a Data-Driven World* (Illustrated edition). Random House.

Bolsen, T., Palm, R., & Kingsland, J. T. (2020). Framing the origins of COVID-19. *Science Communication, 42*(5), 562–585. https://doi.org/10.1177/1075547020953603

Bornstein, R. F. (1989). Exposure and affect: Overview and meta-analysis of research, 1968–1987. *Psychological Bulletin, 106*(2), 265–289. https://psycnet.apa.org/record/1990-00422-001

Brady, W. J., Jackson, J. C., Lindström, B., & Crockett, M. J. (2023). Algorithm-mediated social learning in online social networks. *Trends in Cognitive Sciences, 27*(10), 947–960. https://doi.org/10.1016/j.tics.2023.06.008

Dai, D., Charlton, B. M., Boskey, E. R., Hughes, L. D., Hughto, J. M. W., Orav, E. J., & Figueroa, J. F. (2024). Prevalence of gender-affirming surgical procedures among minors and adults in the US. *JAMA Network Open, 7*(6), e2418814. https://doi.org/10.1001/jamanetworkopen.2024.18814

de Gier, B., van Asten, L., Boere, T. M., van Roon, A., van Roekel, C., Pijpers, J., van Werkhoven, C. H. H., van den Ende, C., Hahné, S. J. M., de Melker, H. E., Knol, M. J., & van den Hof, S. (2023). Effect of COVID-19 vaccination on mortality by COVID-19 and on mortality by other causes, the Netherlands, January 2021–January 2022. *Vaccine, 41*(31), 4488–4496. https://doi.org/10.1016/j.vaccine.2023.06.005

Di Domenico, G., Nunan, D., & Pitardi, V. (2022). Marketplaces of misinformation: A study of how vaccine misinformation is legitimized on social media. *Journal of Public Policy and Marketing, 41*(4), 1–17. https://doi.org/10.1177/07439156221103860

Doğan, Y., & Batdı, V. (2021). Revisiting brainstorming within an educational context: A meta-thematic analysis. *Journal of Learning for Development, 8*(3), 541–556. https://doi.org/10.56059/jl4d.v8i3.495

Dutta, S. (2020, May 22). How does Instagram show me posts regarding what I have searched on Google. *The Startup.* https://medium.com/swlh/how-does-instagram-show-me-posts-regarding-what-i-have-searched-on-google-20744326a4a9

Federal Trade Commission. (2013). *Truth in Advertising.* https://www.ftc.gov/news-events/topics/truth-advertising

Froehlich, N. (2022). The truth in user privacy and targeted ads. *Forbes.* https://www.forbes.com/councils/forbestechcouncil/2022/02/24/the-truth-in-user-privacy-and-targeted-ads/

George Mason University. (2018). *How to Write a Research Question.* The Writing Center – George Mason University. https://writingcenter.gmu.edu/writing-resources/research-based-writing/how-to-write-a-research-question

Gurung, R. A. R., & Stoa, R. (2020). A national survey of teaching and learning research methods: Important concepts and faculty and student perspectives. *Teaching of Psychology, 47*(2), 111–120. https://doi.org/10.1177/0098628320901374

Han, S., Riddell, J. R., & Piquero, A. R. (2022). Anti-Asian American hate crimes spike during the early stages of the COVID-19 pandemic. *Journal of Interpersonal Violence, 38*(3–4), 3513–3533. https://doi.org/10.1177/08862605221107056

Holmes, N. G., Wieman, C. E., & Bonn, D. A. (2015). Teaching critical thinking. *Proceedings of the National Academy of Sciences, 112*(36), 11199–11204. https://doi.org/10.1073/pnas.1505329112

Institute for Internet and the Just Society. (2021, April 24). *Algorithms in Social Media Platforms.* https://www.internetjustsociety.org/algorithms-in-social-media-platforms

Jia, K. M., Hanage, W. P., Lipsitch, M., Johnson, A. G., Amin, A. B., Ali, A. R., Scobie, H. M., & Swerdlow, D. L. (2023). Estimated preventable COVID-19-associated deaths due to non-vaccination in the United States. *European Journal of Epidemiology, 38*(11), 1125–1128. https://doi.org/10.1007/s10654-023-01006-3

Lacum, E. B. V., Ossevoort, M. A., & Goedhart, M. J. (2014). A teaching strategy with a focus on argumentation to improve undergraduate students' ability to read research articles. *CBE—Life Sciences Education, 13*(2), 253–264. https://doi.org/10.1187/cbe.13-06-0110

Lee, A. Y., Moore, R. C., & Hancock, J. T. (2023, February 7). Designing misinformation interventions for all: Perspectives from AAPI, Black, Latino, and Native American community leaders on misinformation educational efforts. *Harvard Kennedy School Misinformation Review.* https://doi.org/10.37016/mr-2020-111

Levin, J. M., Bukowski, L. A., Minson, J. A., & Kahn, J. M. (2023). The political polarization of COVID-19 treatments among physicians and laypeople in the United States. *Proceedings of the National Academy of Sciences, 120*(7), e2216179120. https://doi.org/10.1073/pnas.2216179120

McGraw, M., & Stein, S. (2021). It's been exactly one year since Trump suggested injecting bleach. We've never been the same. *POLITICO.* https://www.politico.com/news/2021/04/23/trump-bleach-one-year-484399

McMahon, L., Kleinman, Z., & Subramanian, C. (2025, January 7). Meta to replace "biased" fact-checkers with moderation by users. *BBC.* https://www.bbc.com/news/articles/cly74mpy8klo

Meta. (2025). *How Fact-Checking Works.* Transparency Center, Meta. https://transparency.meta.com/features/how-fact-checking-works

Mitchell, K. J., & Shivde, G. (2023). Generalizability in psychology research: Beware the grinch. *Journal of Applied Research in Memory and Cognition, 12*(2), 180–184. https://doi.org/10.1037/mac0000118

Naufel, K. Z., Appleby, D. C., Young, J., Van Kirk, J. F., Spencer, S. M., Rudman, J., Carducci, B. J., Hettich, P., & Richmond, A. S. (2018). *The Skillfull Psychology Student: Prepared for Success in the 21St Century Workplace*. American Psychological Association. https://www.apa.org/education-career/guide/transferable-skills.pdf

Oregon Health News Blog. (2021). What misinformation looks like and tools to combat it. *Oregon.gov*. https://covidblog.oregon.gov/what-misinformation-looks-like-and-tools-to-combat-it/

Park, J. J., Lee, A.-H. A., Park, L. S.-C., Jaung, R., & Song, C. (2024). Korean residents' experiences of racism in Germany during the COVID-19 pandemic: Association with life satisfaction and sense of belonging. *Journal of International Migration and Integration*, 25(4), 2299–2320. https://doi.org/10.1007/s12134-024-01169-2

Raffoul, A., Ward, Z. J., Santoso, M., Kavanaugh, J. R., & Austin, S. B. (2023). Social media platforms generate billions of dollars in revenue from U.S. youth: Findings from a simulated revenue model. *PLOS ONE*, 18(12), e0295337. https://doi.org/10.1371/journal.pone.0295337

Small, M. F. (2021, February 13). "I've done my research." But have you? *Medium*. https://ms32-23594.medium.com/ive-done-my-research-but-have-you-447508b1343

Taylor, S., & Asmundson, G. J. G. (2021). Negative attitudes about facemasks during the COVID-19 pandemic: The dual importance of perceived ineffectiveness and psychological reactance. *PLOS ONE*, 16(2), e0246317. https://doi.org/10.1371/journal.pone.0246317

The White House. (2025, January 28). *Protecting Children from Chemical and Surgical Mutilation*. https://www.whitehouse.gov/presidential-actions/2025/01/protecting-children-from-chemical-and-surgical-mutilation/

Trethewey, S. P. (2019). Medical misinformation on social media: Cognitive bias, pseudo-peer review, and the good intentions hypothesis. *Circulation*, 140(14), 1131–1133. https://doi.org/10.1161/CIRCULATIONAHA.119.041719

Wyckoff, A. S. (2023). *AAP Reaffirms Gender-affirming Care Policy, Authorizes Systematic Review of Evidence to Guide Update*. American Academy of Pediatrics. https://publications.aap.org/aapnews/news/25340/AAP-reaffirms-gender-affirming-care-policy

Zajonc, R. B. (1968). Attitudinal effects of mere exposure. *Journal of Personality and Social Psychology*, 9(2, Pt. 2), 1–27. https://doi.org/10.1037/h0025848

7. Choose your words wisely: Recognizing and resolving lexical ambiguity when teaching research methods

Victoria L. Cross

As a scientist and an educator, you are an experienced thinker and speaker in science. You have learned the vocabulary and connotations of this language and are likely so fluent that you may not remember the struggles you experienced while developing that fluency. You may be aware of ongoing debates around the definitions of fundamental scientific concepts such as internal and external validity (e.g., see Reichardt, 2011; Shadish et al., 2002) or whether qualitative is synonymous with categorical (e.g., see Vogt & Johnson, 2016). These sophisticated discussions reflect a level of fluency that obscures the foundational challenges students face in simply acquiring basic terminology.

As we train the next generation of scientists, we must be sensitive to the struggle required to develop a basic scientific vocabulary, let alone join such nuanced debates. Developing a new lexicon is a long and effortful endeavor that will be fraught with mistakes. One of my students recently wrote about 'eternal validity,' another referred to the use of 'deferential statistics,' and a third suggested that 'ransom assignment' was used to create equivalent groups of participants. As much as I love the idea of validity that lasts forever and respectful statistics and am a little afraid of being kidnapped in my next study, I assure you that none of these phrases had been included in the lecture or textbook. However, the propensity to mishear and misunderstand complex new vocabulary is unsurprising and a natural part of learning a new language. To add to the challenge, the terminology used in science also includes many ambiguous words, potentially creating a chasm between your intention and your students' interpretation. This chapter describes the challenges of lexical ambiguity and highlights examples of ambiguous terms used in research methods to illustrate pedagogical principles that can help novices join the conversation. While validity may not last forever, we can take some concrete steps to assist our students in learning to speak and think in science.

7.1 SCIENCE IS A LANGUAGE

The core competencies in any research methods course rely on learning to speak the language of science (e.g., APA, 2023; Stoa et al., 2022). While there is much agreement between instructors about the essential core concepts of the research methods curriculum (Gurung & Stoa, 2020), to enhance their scientific literacy and communication, students must first learn the appropriate vocabulary and grammar. Science language acquisition should be included as an integral part of the curriculum; students will need to expend their efforts to learn this language and cannot be expected to absorb the terminology passively (Rector et al., 2013). Instructors must be thoughtful about the vocabulary they introduce and the context they include to scaffold the specific and nuanced meanings of new terms.

7.2 LEXICAL AMBIGUITY

Lexical ambiguity occurs when words have multiple potential meanings that can create confusion or misunderstanding. This phenomenon exists in all languages (e.g., Beekhuizen et al., 2021; Kaplan et al., 2009) but presents particular challenges in scientific discourse, where precision is essential. Within the vocabulary of research methods, lexical ambiguity takes several distinct forms that students must learn to recognize and that instructors could directly address. Synonyms – different words with similar meanings – can overwhelm students with unnecessary vocabulary. For example, it is unnecessary to introduce five different ways of labeling a between-groups design until students have a solid grasp on the concept. Homonyms – words that sound the same but have different meanings – create more insidious problems. Some homonyms exist entirely within scientific discourse, where the same term has multiple scientific definitions depending on context. Even more challenging are homonyms that bridge scientific and everyday language, where familiar words take on specialized meanings unrelated to students' prior understanding. The words 'positive' and 'negative' provide excellent examples of homonyms as they are used in multiple ways both within and outside of psychology and always require additional context to disambiguate whether we are discussing attitudes, connotations, electrical charges, medical diagnoses, feedback loops, reinforcement, a correlation coefficient, or an error (to indicate a few of their meanings). By explicitly examining their own vocabulary, instructors can develop targeted strategies to help students navigate these potential misunderstandings.

7.2.1 Ambiguity Can Create Barriers to Comprehension

Lexical ambiguity creates significant learning challenges. Technical vocabulary can make the material appear overwhelmingly complex and unapproachable (Kaplan et al., 2009). When presented with ambiguous words, students must navigate between everyday and scientific registers (Liu et al., 2022), and cognitive labor is required to determine a word's intended meaning (Gwilliams et al., 2024; Lemke, 1990).

Increased demand on cognitive labor can be detected in processing ambiguous words from initial perception to integration, disambiguation, and, perhaps, comprehension. Perceiving ambiguous words takes longer, whether presented in text and measured in eye fixation (Parker et al., 2024) or in audio and measured in duration to recognition (Sanker, 2019). Decoding ambiguous words requires more cognitive control than decoding unambiguous words (Liang et al., 2024; Rodd et al., 2002). To comprehend ambiguous words, their multiple meanings are activated (Sanker, 2019), incoherence must be recognized, and incorrect interpretations must be suppressed (Mason & Just, 2007; Rodd et al., 2004). When students encounter ambiguous words, they require additional processing time and resources.

Homonyms that have both a common lay meaning and a specific scientific meaning present an additional level of cognitive work. Evidence shows that the most frequent meaning of the word will be activated as a quick first guess (Witzel & Forster, 2014). As this heuristic (the dominance effect) will predictably activate the incorrect definition in novices, additional processing will be required to generate the appropriate definition and suppress the other meanings (Mason & Just, 2007; Sanker, 2019). For example, when an instructor uses the term 'manipulation' to indicate a step in an experimental procedure, they should anticipate that students will first activate the more frequent meanings, such as 'deceived,' and will need time and focus to disambiguate that term. This process relies on working memory capacity. Working memory capacity (as estimated by reading span) is positively related to effectively suppressing incorrect definitions (Mason & Just, 2007). If a student's working memory is already taxed, as one would expect when listening to a lecture or reading a textbook, they may not have sufficient working memory resources to fully disambiguate the vocabulary.

Misconceptions will occur when a novice fails to disambiguate the vocabulary and attempts to understand the material with the more familiar lay meaning of an ambiguous scientific term (Kaplan et al., 2012; Sanker, 2019). Even worse, lexical ambiguity can create hidden misconceptions: as a definition for the term is successfully identified by the student, these misconceptions may be compounded with a paralyzing lack of awareness. For example, a student may identify the meaning of 'positive' as 'good' and create the false belief that positive correlations describe good relationships. Research has established that misconceptions can be resistant to correction (e.g., Chi, 2005; Konold, 1995). Learning is not simply overwriting existing knowledge (Konold, 1995) but requires active construction (including deconstruction) as new information is integrated into existing knowledge. Identifying and resolving misconceptions will take time and effort from both the novice and the expert.

7.2.2 Ambiguity Can Be an Opportunity for Learning

As fluent speakers of science, we must resist the curse of knowledge and deliberately remind ourselves that the precise vocabulary of science is far from universally understood by students. Once we have more accurately estimated the distance between our knowledge and our students' knowledge, research has shown that we can create learning opportunities by explicitly pointing out ambiguous vocabulary (Anderson-Cook, 2010; Barwell, 2005; Liu et al., 2022) and providing adequate context for disambiguation (Hyland & Tse, 2007). An explicit approach has also been demonstrated to help students understand metaphors used in science (Brookes & Etkina, 2007), and acknowledging ambiguity can serve as a tool to prompt deeper exploration and develop a more robust understanding (Barwell, 2005; Kaplan et al., 2009).

Repeated exposure and explicit elaboration of all meanings of ambiguous words are needed to support students as they acquire this new vocabulary and learn to speak science. A single exposure to the new meaning was insufficient to eliminate the processing costs of encountering ambiguous words (Parker et al., 2024). One group of researchers has systematically investigated instructional methods to address lexical ambiguity in statistics education and found that clear and consistent exposure (Kaplan et al., 2009), drawing attention using a mnemonic device (Kaplan et al., 2014), and repeated assessment (Kaplan & Rogness, 2018) are effective ways to exploit the existence of lexical ambiguities as opportunities to reinforce student learning.

7.2.3 Ambiguity Can Be a Challenge for Assessment

Assessment of our students' developing vocabulary and comprehension of science needs to account for the challenges of lexical ambiguity. Self-assessment by a novice scientist is unlikely to be accurate for ambiguous terms. Zukswert et al. (2019) found that prior exposure to lay meanings of words newly introduced with biological meanings is negatively associated with accuracy in self-assessment of novice scientists' knowledge, leading to overconfidence. When the students in this study assessed their understanding of biology vocabulary and demonstrated that knowledge, they were least accurate at self-assessing their knowledge of ambiguous terms that had lay homonyms. This mismatch between confidence and accuracy may create issues for students if they rely on self-assessment to plan their study time, faculty if they assess student learning through any form of self-assessment, and researchers attempting to identify particularly difficult concepts through self-assessment (e.g., Gurung & Landrum, 2013; Stoa et al., 2022). When lexical ambiguities exist, demonstrated competence should be emphasized over self-assessment.

The development of a lexicon does not progress linearly. Students may be able to identify definitions but still misuse terms in context (Kaplan et al., 2009), making it difficult to identify clear milestones between novice and expert understanding (Talanquer, 2009). Assessment should be used to consistently reinforce scientific definitions, explicitly contrast them with lay definitions, and challenge students to use terms appropriately in context.

7.3 SPECIFIC EXAMPLES OF LEXICAL AMBIGUITY FROM RESEARCH METHODS IN PSYCHOLOGY

Lexical ambiguity compounds the cognitive challenges students face as they learn a new language. As fluent speakers of this language, we may no longer hear the ambiguity. To improve our teaching of research methods and invite our students into this language, we must recognize and acknowledge the ambiguous words we use in every class. The following section will highlight some common ambiguous terms, many of which are essential concepts (e.g., Gurung & Landrum, 2013; Stoa et al., 2022), and suggest specific pedagogical approaches you might consider incorporating to transform these potential obstacles into opportunities for deeper learning.

7.3.1 Synonyms

Synonyms occur when multiple words have the same or very similar meanings. Using redundant synonyms can massively increase the vocabulary required for scientific understanding, creating a learning barrier. The solution here is to select the least ambiguous and most informative term and to consistently use only that term (see Table 7.1). Once the concept has gained some purchase in the students' scientific lexicon, be sure to make students aware that there are synonyms and that they will hear alternate phrases once they leave your classroom. Here are three examples that occur early in the teaching of research methods and can add to confusion or a feeling that the field is overwhelming.

Table 7.1   Synonyms

Suggested vocabulary choice	Concept	Synonyms
Research hypothesis	The specific prediction about the relation between the variables of interest.	working hypothesis, alternative hypothesis, experimental hypothesis, competing hypothesis
§Between-groups	Design: participants experience one level of the independent variable	between, between-subjects, between-participants, independent groups, independent samples
§Within-group	Design: participants experience all levels of the independent variable	within, within-subject, within-participant, repeated measures,

Note: § identified as a challenging learning outcome (Stoa et al., 2022).
Source: Definitions adapted from Vogt & Johnson (2016), Dictionary.com (2025), and The Science Dictionary (2025).

7.3.1.1 Research hypothesis

In science, we make a specific prediction about the relationship between two variables. We also generate a null hypothesis stating that the variables will not share a relationship. The phrases 'working hypothesis,' 'alternative hypothesis,' and 'experimental hypothesis' are commonly used as synonyms for the research hypothesis. The term 'research hypothesis' is the best choice as it disambiguates, is not overly precise, and expresses appropriate confidence. Each of these synonyms is easily eliminated for use in an introductory research methods course: the term 'experimental hypothesis' is too specific as it implies experimental research (i.e., creating equivalent groups and manipulating the independent variable); the term 'alternative hypothesis' is too easily confused with other uses of the word alternate (i.e., alternate explanations); and the term 'working hypothesis' implies a more preliminary prediction.

7.3.1.2 Within-groups and between-groups designs

Participants will either experience all or only one level of the predictor variable. These designs are also called 'between and within,' 'between-subjects and within-subjects,' 'between-participants and within-participants,' or 'independent groups and repeated measures.' There are multiple reasonable solutions to this ambiguity; here are some points to consider. Include a noun; do not just abbreviate to 'between' and 'within.' Selecting parallel nouns may help students focus on the 'within-' and 'between-' portion of the vocabulary.

The *Publication Manual of the American Psychological Association* (2020) indicates that the noun 'subjects' is acceptable to describe these designs, though the word 'participants' may be more appropriate if the participants are human. Consider your students' experience with statistics and tolerance for synonyms. The phrase 'independent groups' may lead students happily toward the independent t-test, but it may also create confusion when using the term 'independent' to refer to the independent variable. Likewise, the phrase 'repeated-measures' may help students select a repeated-measures analysis of variance. However, as it does not have an obvious parallel, it may not be the best choice for introducing the research design.

7.3.2 Homonyms Within Science

Homonyms are words that are spelled or pronounced similarly but have different meanings. As with all languages, some words in the vocabulary of science have multiple meanings. The best solution to resolve these ambiguities is to find a viable synonym for one meaning or to add context by always using the homonym within a phrase (see Table 7.2).

Table 7.2   Homonyms with multiple scientific meanings

Word	Meanings
Correlation	Correlation coefficient: An inferential statistic that quantifies the nature and strength of the relationship between two variables. Correlational study: Both variables are measured. Not sufficient to determine causation.
Independent	Independent variables are manipulated by the researcher. Independent groups is an experimental design where participants experience one level of the independent variable. The occurrence of one event does not change the probability of another event.
Selection	Internal validity: The selection effect occurs if equivalent groups are not created. Equivalent groups are created through random assignment. If participants self-select into treatment condition, then the selection effect weakens internal validity. External validity: Sampling. Selection into the sample.
Positive and Negative	Description of correlations: $r < 0$ or $r > 0$ Errors: False positive (Type I) and false negative (Type II)

Source: Definitions adapted from Vogt and Johnson (2016) and The Science Dictionary (2025).

In practice, here is a more detailed analysis of three particularly demanding homonyms, accompanied by examples of targeted solutions.

7.3.2.1 Correlation

When a researcher uses the word 'correlation,' they could either be referring to a correlational study (i.e., one where no variable was manipulated) or to a correlation coefficient (i.e., an inferential statistic, abbreviated with the letter r that quantifies the nature and strength of the relationship between two continuous variables). There are good alternatives to describe correlation studies and findings (e.g., association), allowing us to reserve the use of 'correlation' for the correlation coefficient. And, for good measure, always finish the phrase rather than abbreviating it to a single ambiguous word.

On a related note, the warning 'correlation does not imply causation' introduces two distinct ambiguities. First, though it lacks sufficient context to signal which definition of 'correlation' is relevant, it must refer to correlational research, not correlation coefficients. In correlational research, equivalent groups were not created, and an independent variable was not manipulated, so the internal validity does not support a causal claim. That warning is unrelated to the inferential statistic used to quantify the relationship; an independent variable could be manipulated along a continuum, and a correlation coefficient could be calculated. Secondly, the nuance of the logic is easily misunderstood, and it could be heard to indicate that correlation rules out causation (Vogt & Johnson, 2016). A more helpful mantra for the novice learner is 'no causation without manipulation' (Holland, 1986). This not only removes the ambiguity over the word 'correlation' but also directs the student to the requirements of causal reasoning. Of course, no four-word mantra will capture all nuances of scientific reasoning; this mantra ignores the ability of statistical analyses (e.g., path analyses and structural equation modeling) to provide causal evidence in non-experimental research.

7.3.2.2 Independent

The word 'independent' has a frustrating amount of versatility. Independent variables are manipulated by the researcher in an experiment. Independent groups is a synonym for between-groups research designs. The independent samples t-test is used to compare group means. Two variables that are not related to each other can be referred to as statistically independent. As these are all necessary nuances, the solution to reduce ambiguity is to provide sufficient context and always use 'independent' as part of a phrase.

7.3.2.3 Selection

The term 'selection' creates confusion because it can refer to either (1) a threat to internal validity when participants choose their own conditions or (2) the process of recruiting participants into a sample, which primarily affects external validity (generalizability). These distinct meanings operate at different stages of the research process and affect different types of validity. To minimize confusion, instructors should clearly differentiate between these uses by consistently referring to 'participant recruitment' for sampling procedures and reserving 'selection' specifically for discussions of threats to internal validity. This precise language helps students understand that while we recruit participants into our sample, we must avoid letting them select their experimental conditions if we wish to make causal claims.

7.3.3 Homonyms with Lay Terms

Homonyms that share spelling and pronunciation with lay terms present perhaps the most significant barrier to learning scientific language (Anderson-Cook, 2010; Kaplan et al., 2009). Unlike other types of lexical ambiguity, these familiar-sounding words with incompatible scientific meanings can be particularly problematic because they lull students into a false sense of comprehension. When encountering these terms, students naturally assume they understand the word based on its everyday usage and may remain unaware that the scientific definition differs significantly (Liu et al., 2022; Zukswert et al., 2019). This misconception is especially dangerous because students may not recognize their knowledge gap, leading to compound misunderstandings as they attempt to integrate new information using incorrect definitions. Through reflection on my teaching experience, consultation with relevant literature, and feedback from colleagues at teaching conferences, I have compiled an extensive (though certainly not exhaustive) list of these problematic homonyms (see Table 7.3).

Below, I examine three particularly challenging examples that illustrate how everyday meanings can interfere with scientific understanding and offer strategies for addressing each.

7.3.3.1 Manipulate
A researcher manipulates a variable in an experiment by assigning different groups or conditions to experience different levels of that variable. This is one of the more dangerous homonyms, as 'manipulate' has strong negative connotations when used in lay terms, and those negative connotations have no place in science. In science, 'manipulation' indicates that the experimenter can change the level of a variable; the variable is under the experimenter's control. Taking this ambiguous vocabulary word further out of context, students frequently misspeak and state that 'participants were manipulated.' It seems imperative to ensure that students understand that variables are manipulated,

Table 7.3   Homonyms with scientific and lay meanings

Word	Lay meaning	Scientific meaning
†Average	Typical. Norm.	Mean. Central tendency.
Basic (Science)	Simple. Unoriginal. Lowest rank.	Focused on expanding knowledge not solving a specific applied problem.
†Bias	Unreasoned prejudice or hostility. To influence unfairly.	A systematic error or distortion.
§Blind	Loss of vision.	Unaware of the hypothesis or group membership.
Chance	Luck or fortune. Unpredictable.	Random variation. Same likelihood.
Coding	Writing computer science language.	Translating information into standard codes.
§Confederate	A soldier in the US Civil War.	A research assistant acting as if they were a participant.
†^Confidence	Full trust. Self-esteem. Boldness.	Level of certainty.
*§Confound	Confuse.	A variable whose effect cannot be separated from the predictor variable.
†*^‡Control	Restraint.	Isolating the effect of a variable. Eliminating other variables by using a control group (given no treatment) or matching participants.
§Critical (Thinking)	To criticize. To look for fault.	To critique. To evaluate. Essential.
Discriminate	To treat one group unfairly (e.g., racial stereotyping).	To tell the difference between two things.
†^§Error	A mistake.	Noise. The difference between the observed data and the true value.
†‡§Experiment	Mess around. Tentative test.	Research that requires creating equivalent groups, manipulating one variable, and observing the effect, thereby eliminating alternate explanations and supporting a determination of a causal relationship.

Word	Lay meaning	Scientific meaning
†*‡§Independent	Not influenced by others.	One event does not affect another event. A variable that is manipulated.
Interaction	An exchange between two people.	A pattern found in a factorial design where the effect of one predictor variable on the outcome variable differs depending on the level of the other predictor variable.
Journal	Write about personal experience. Blank notebook.	Publication with peer-reviewed articles.
Main Effect	The main finding, the main event.	The effect of one predictor variable in a factorial design (effect is used even if the predictor variable was measured and not manipulated).
^Manipulate	Mislead. Influence unfairly.	Change the level of a predictor variable.
†^Mean	To be cruel. To indicate.	Central tendency. Average.
†^Median	The strip in the center of the highway that separates lanes.	Central tendency. The middle value.
Negative	Bad. Denial. Refusing. Not helpful.	$r < 0$. Increases in one variable are associated with decreases in another. Inverse relationship.
Noise	Sound.	Error.
§Operational (Definition)	Working. Surgery.	Description of the procedure used to measure or manipulate a variable.
^§Outlier	Incorrect or wrong. Possibly misheard as outlaw.	Extreme value.
Positive	Good. Certain.	$r > 0$. Increases in one variable are associated with increases in another. Two variables that increase or decrease together.
†*‡§Random	Haphazard.	Not predictable (random event). Every member has an equal likelihood of being selected (random number, random assignment, random selection).
^Research	To look up information in a library.	To conduct an empirical study.
†^‡Significant	Important. Valuable.	Statistically significant. Reliable.

Word	Lay meaning	Scientific meaning
†Spread	To scatter. To put jam evenly on toast.	Variability. Range.
~^‡Theory	Hunch. Guess.	Integrated explanation of phenomenon

Note: Definitions adapted from Vogt & Johnson (2016), Dictionary.com (2025), and The Science Dictionary (2025).

Source: Terms collected from the author's experience and the following sources: * adapted from Anderson-Cook (2010); † adapted from Kaplan et al. (2009); ~ adapted from Rector et al. (2013); ‡ identified as a bottleneck concept (Gurung & Landrum, 2013); § identified as a potential pothole (Stoa et al., 2022); ^ suggested by participants at PsychTERMS (Cross, 2024)

not participants. Please contribute to the important work of disambiguating this homonym from the negative connotations and clarify its use in science.

7.3.3.2 Critical

In science, critical thinking is the pinnacle of careful analysis and evaluation. When engaging in critical thinking, we approach the evidence with an open mind, with intellectual honesty, and we engage all our powers of reasoning to assess the claim and the evidence carefully. Unfortunately, 'critical' has strong negative connotations in lay terms. To be critical is to look for fault and to judge too severely, to criticize. A solution is to add more context to this pesky homonym and encourage your students to 'think critically about internal validity.' 'Critique' is a closely related term with similar scientific and lay meanings. If an assignment directs a student to 'critique a claim,' many students will feel encouraged to only look for faults. A viable alternative for 'critique' is 'evaluate' (e.g., 'evaluate the strengths and limitations of this article.')

7.3.3.3 Theory

A scientific theory is a way of understanding the natural world that integrates the data and organizes our knowledge. In lay terms, however, the word 'theory' means a guess or a hunch that is not carefully considered or expected to be true. There is no readily available alternative here, so as with homonyms, the advice is to explicitly point out the different definitions.

7.3.4 Dual Homonyms

Another problem arises when the language of science incorporates both a homonym's lay and scientific definitions (e.g., 'The mean means the average,' 'The chance of scoring 90% is well below chance.') The best advice in these cases is to work to replace the lay term with a viable synonym. Here are three specific examples:

Mean: Replace the lay definition of 'mean' with 'indicate.'
Chance: Replace the lay definition of 'chance' with 'likelihood.'
Error: Replace the lay definition of 'error' with 'mistake.'

7.4 PEDAGOGICAL RECOMMENDATIONS

The examples throughout this chapter illustrate the prevalence and complexity of lexical ambiguity in research methods. To help instructors translate this awareness into effective teaching practice, the following recommendations synthesize evidence-based approaches for addressing vocabulary challenges:

1. **Select vocabulary deliberately.** Choose the least ambiguous terms when introducing concepts and use them consistently. When synonyms exist (as with 'research hypothesis'), explicitly identify your preferred term, use it exclusively while students learn the concept, and then expose them to the synonyms.
2. **Make ambiguity explicit.** Rather than avoiding problematic terms, acknowledge their multiple meanings directly. Contrast scientific and lay definitions for homonyms, showing students what a term means and does not mean in scientific contexts.
3. **Provide contextual scaffolding.** Always embed ambiguous terms within phrases that clarify their meaning (e.g., 'correlation coefficient' rather than simply 'correlation').
4. **Use visual aids.** As you encounter ambiguous terms in your lectures and assignments, build reference materials with your students. Consider developing visual models (like Figure 7.1) that help illustrate potential misinterpretations of key terms.
5. **Incorporate regular formative assessment.** Check for understanding of vocabulary specifically, not just concepts. Ask students to generate correct examples using ambiguous terms or to identify incorrect usage in research scenarios.
6. **Leverage ambiguity as a teaching tool.** Use instances of misunderstanding as opportunities to deepen comprehension rather than simply correcting errors. Encourage each student to explain in his, her, or their own words why certain interpretations are scientifically inaccurate.

These strategies, implemented consistently across lectures, readings, assignments, and assessments, can transform lexical ambiguity from a barrier to an

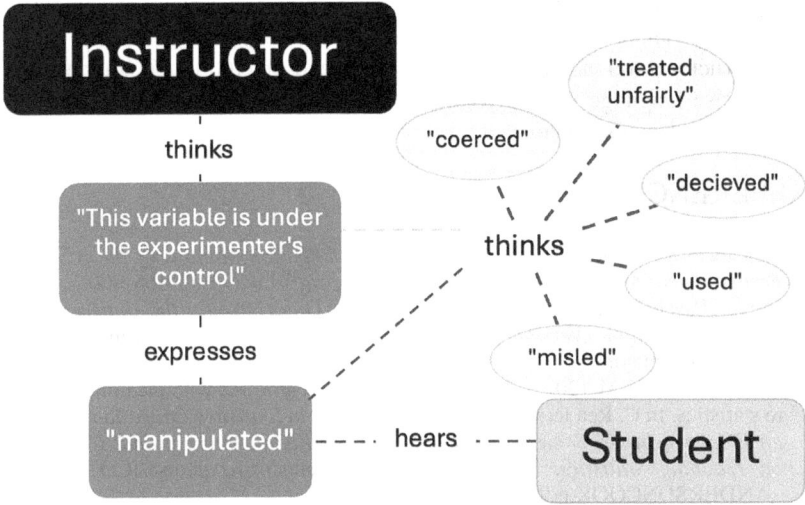

Note: Figure 7.1 depicts the disconnect between the instructor's intention (on the left) and the student's interpretation (on the right) that can be created by lexical ambiguity. The instructor's thoughts about 'manipulated' reference the scientific definition. The student, hearing the term 'manipulated,' may generate more common lay meanings of the word and may only very weakly tap into the scientific definition.
Source: Adapted from Rector et al. (2013).

Figure 7.1   Model of intention and interpretation of the word 'manipulated'

opportunity for developing scientific thinking. By treating vocabulary development as a central learning objective rather than an incidental outcome, instructors can significantly enhance students' ability to participate in scientific discourse.

7.5   CONCLUSION

Learning to speak science is complex and nuanced, requiring deliberate effort from both instructors and students. Research methods courses are a natural venue to focus students' attention on essential scientific vocabulary. To navigate the cognitive challenges of lexical ambiguity, students need repeated and consistent exposure to scientific terminology, with explicit attention drawn to potential confusion arising from homonyms and synonyms. By acknowledging these ambiguities, skilled teachers can transform potential misconceptions into opportunities for deeper understanding. While complete agreement on terminology and conceptual clarity may remain as elusive as 'eternal' validity, instructors who tackle lexical ambiguity head-on equip their students with the precise language needed to join scientific conversations and to begin to conduct their own science.

REFERENCES

American Psychological Association. (2020). *Publication Manual of the American Psychological Association* (7th Ed.). https://doi.org/10.1037/0000165-000

American Psychological Association. (2023). *APA Guidelines for the Undergraduate Psychology Major: Version 3.0.* https://www.apa.org/about/policy/undergraduate-psychology-major

Anderson-Cook, C. M. (2010). Hidden jargon: Everyday words with meanings specific to statistics. In C. Reader (Ed.), *Data and Context in Statistics Education: Towards an Evidence-Based Society. Proceedings of the Eighth International Conference on Teaching Statistics.* https://icots.info/documents/papers/icots8/ICOTS8_C202_ANDERSONCOOK.pdf?1402524973

Barwell, R. (2005). Ambiguity in the mathematics classroom. *Language and Education*, *19*(2), 117–125. https://doi.org/10.1080/09500780508668667

Beekhuizen, B., Armstrong, B. C., & Stevenson, S. (2021). Probing lexical ambiguity: Word vectors encode number and relatedness of senses. *Cognitive Science*, *45*(5), e12943. https://doi.org/10.1111/cogs.12943

Brookes, D. T., & Etkina, E. (2007). Using conceptual metaphor and functional grammar to explore how language used in physics affects student learning. *Physical Review Special Topics – Physics Education Research*, *3*(1), 010105. https://doi.org/10.1103/PhysRevSTPER.3.010105

Chi, M. T. H. (2005). Commonsense conceptions of emergent processes: Why some misconceptions are robust. *Journal of the Learning Sciences*, *14*(2), 161–199. https://doi.org/10.1207/s15327809jls1402_1

Cross, V. L. (2024, December). *Choose Your Words Wisely: Some Pitfalls in Scientific Vocabulary.* PsychTERMS, Virtual Conference. https://www.psychterms.com/

Dictionary.com. (2025). https://www.dictionary.com/

Gurung, R. A. R., & Landrum, R. E. (2013). Bottleneck concepts in psychology: Exploratory first steps. *Psychology Learning & Teaching*, *12*(3), 236–245. https://doi.org/10.2304/plat.2013.12.3.236

Gurung, R. A. R., & Stoa, R. (2020). A national survey of teaching and learning research methods: Important concepts and faculty and student perspectives. *Teaching of Psychology*, *47*(2), 111–120. https://doi.org/10.1177/0098628320901374

Gwilliams, L., Marantz, A., Poeppel, D., & King, J.-R. (2024). Top-down information shapes lexical processing when listening to continuous speech. *Language, Cognition and Neuroscience*, *39*(8), 1045–1058. https://doi.org/10.1080/23273798.2023.2171072

Holland, P. (1986). Statistics and causal inference. *Journal of the American Statistical Association*, *81*(396), 945–960. https://www.jstor.org/stable/2289064

Hyland, K., & Tse, P. (2007). Is there an "academic vocabulary"? *TESOL Quarterly*, *41*(2), 235–253. https://doi.org/10.1002/j.1545-7249.2007.tb00058.x

Kaplan, J. J., Fisher, D. G., & Rogness, N. T. (2009). Lexical ambiguity in statistics: What do students know about the words association, average, confidence, random and spread? *Journal of Statistics Education*, *17*(3), 6. https://doi.org/10.1080/10691898.2009.11889535

Kaplan, J. J., & Rogness, N. T. (2018). Increasing statistical literacy by exploiting lexical ambiguity of technical terms. *Numeracy*, *11*(1). https://doi.org/10.5038/1936-4660.11.1.3

Kaplan, J. J., Rogness, N. T., & Fisher, D. G. (2012). Lexical ambiguity: Making a case against spread. *Teaching Statistics*, *34*(2), 56–60. https://doi.org/10.1111/j.1467-9639.2011.00477.x

Kaplan, J. J., Rogness, N. T., & Fisher, D. G. (2014). Exploiting lexical ambiguity to help students understand the meaning of random. *Statistics Education Research Journal*, *13*(1), 9–24. https://doi.org/10.52041/serj.v13i1.296

Konold, C. (1995). Issues in assessing conceptual understanding in probability and statistics. *Journal of Statistics Education*, *3*(1), 3. https://doi.org/10.1080/10691898.1995.11910479

Lemke, J. (1990). *Talking Science: Language, Learning and Values*. Ablex Publishing Corporation.

Liang, X., Huang, F., Liu, D., & Xu, M. (2024). Brain representations of lexical ambiguity: Disentangling homonymy, polysemy, and their meanings. *Brain and Language*, *253*, 105426. https://doi.org/10.1016/j.bandl.2024.105426

Liu, Y., Medlar, A., & Głowacka, D. (2022). Lexical ambiguity detection in professional discourse. *Information Processing & Management*, *59*(5), 103000. https://doi.org/10.1016/j.ipm.2022.103000

Mason, R. A., & Just, M. A. (2007). Lexical ambiguity in sentence comprehension. *Brain Research*, *1146*, 115–127. https://doi.org/10.1016/j.brainres.2007.02.076

Parker, A. J., Taylor, J. S. H., & Rodd, J. M. (2024). Readers use recent experiences with word meanings to support the processing of lexical ambiguity: Evidence from eye movements. *Journal of Experimental Psychology: Learning, Memory, and Cognition*, *51*(7), 1157–1177. https://doi.org/10.1037/xlm0001418

Rector, M. A., Nehm, R. H., & Pearl, D. (2013). Learning the language of evolution: Lexical ambiguity and word meaning in student explanations. *Research in Science Education*, *43*(3), 1107–1133. https://doi.org/10.1007/s11165-012-9296-z

Reichardt, C. S. (2011). Criticisms of and an alternative to the Shadish, Cook, and Campbell validity typology. In H. T. Chen, S. I. Donaldson, & M. M. Mark (Eds.), Advancing Validity in Outcome Evaluation: Theory and Practice. *New Directions for Evaluation*, *130*, 43–53. https://doi.org/10.1002/ev.364

Rodd, J., Gaskell, G., & Marslen-Wilson, W. (2002). Making sense of semantic ambiguity: Semantic competition in lexical access. *Journal of Memory and Language*, *46*(2), 245–266. https://doi.org/10.1006/jmla.2001.2810

Rodd, J. M., Gaskell, M. G., & Marslen-Wilson, W. (2004). Modelling the effects of semantic ambiguity in word recognition. *Cognitive Science*, *28*(1), 89–104. https://doi.org/10.1207/s15516709cog2801_4

Sanker, C. (2019). Effects of lexical ambiguity, frequency, and acoustic details in auditory perception. *Attention, Perception, & Psychophysics*, *81*(1), 323–343. https://doi.org/10.3758/s13414-018-1604-x

Shadish, W. R., Cook, T. D., & Campbell, D. T. (2002). *Experimental and Quasi-Experimental Designs for Generalized Causal Inference*. Houghton Mifflin.

Stoa, R., Chu, T. L., & Gurung, R. A. R. (2022). Potential potholes: Predicting challenges and learning outcomes in research methods in psychology courses. *Teaching of Psychology, 49*(1), 21–29. https://doi.org/10.1177/0098628320979881

Talanquer, V. (2009). On cognitive constraints and learning progressions: The case of "structure of matter." *International Journal of Science Education, 31*(15), 2123–2136. https://doi.org/10.1080/09500690802578025

The Science Dictionary. (2025). https://www.thesciencedictionary.com/

Vogt, W. P., & Johnson, R. B. (2016). *The SAGE Dictionary of Statistics & Methodology: A Nontechnical Guide for the Social Sciences.* SAGE Publications. https://www.researchgate.net/publication/264274755_Dictionary_of_Statistics_Methodology_A_Nontechnical_Guide_For_The_Social_Sciences

Witzel, J., & Forster, K. (2014). Lexical co-occurrence and ambiguity resolution. *Language, Cognition and Neuroscience, 29*(2), 158–185. https://doi.org/10.1080/01690965.2012.748925

Zukswert, J. M., Barker, M. K., & McDonnell, L. (2019). Identifying troublesome jargon in biology: Discrepancies between student performance and perceived understanding. *CBE – Life Sciences Education, 18*(1), ar6. https://doi.org/10.1187/cbe.17-07-0118

8. Learning how to read primary literature: A 'Focus Article' activity for research methods in psychology

Nicole Alea Albada and Vanessa E. Woods

8.1 TEACHING STUDENTS HOW TO READ PRIMARY LITERATURE

Learning how to read and interpret primary literature, as is found in scientific journal articles, is central to developing scientific literacy (Goudsouzian & Hsu, 2023; Sato et al., 2014).[1] It is not an easy skill. However, it is foundational for understanding research methodology in psychological science (Ball & Pelco, 2006; Thieman et al., 2009), which is an expectation that the American Psychological Association has for undergraduate psychology majors (Goal 2 Scientific Inquiry & Critical Thinking; APA, 2023a). Reading and understanding primary literature not only enhances knowledge about the content of the discipline but also showcases norms experts use when writing about psychological research (Adler-Kassner & Wardle, 2022; Lerner, 2015; Woods et al., 2021). Students must be taught how to read primary literature. It is not intuitive, as disciplinary norm assumptions are implicit and thus require explicit scaffolding. For example, many students are not familiar with the idea that the term 'significant' may mean something besides important (Woods et al., 2021). The process of reading and interpreting empirical work is quite different from other forms of reading that students might have been exposed to, and understanding research is a discipline-specific exercise (Lerner, 2015; Woods et al., 2021). Research methods courses are often the first place in which students in undergraduate psychology programs are exposed to primary research articles. If the goal of instructors of research methods is to ensure that students can develop research literacy to meet the goals of scientific inquiry and critical thinking, scaffolding is important (APA, 2023a). We developed the activity described in this chapter, a 'Focus Article' activity, to meet this objective: to help undergraduate psychology students, with little or no exposure to primary literature in psychology, learn how to read and understand primary research.

To develop students' understanding, we have them focus on one specific article and work through understanding it with peers using heavy scaffolding (e.g., pre-recorded introductions to articles, detailed slide decks, worksheets) over the course of weeks. We created worksheets using best practices (APA, 2023b) to explicitly name the disciplinary norms and assumptions and to help students practice reading research as a psychological scientist would.

We considered four evidence-based pedagogical initiatives when developing this activity: (1) relevance – ensuring that students were reading topics that would feel applicable to them and thus more engaging (e.g., Gurung & Christopher, 2023); (2) agency – creating a sense of autonomy in the learning process by letting students choose an article to focus on for the reading activity (e.g., Reeve, 2012); (3) community – building connections among student peer groups to normalize the difficulty inherent in learning how to read primary literature (e.g., Frankowski, 2023); and (4) scaffolding – guiding students systematically through readings to model psychological science norms (e.g., Svinicki & Schallert, 2016). Each of these initiatives, as they apply to the Focus Article activity, is further described in the first four sections below. We then discuss the context in which we teach and who the students are in our research methods course, followed by a full description of how we created the Focus Article activity and implemented it into our courses. In the final two sections, we provide data from student feedback about their perceptions of the efficacy and usefulness of the Focus Article activity in meeting our intended aims, and discuss ways that others can incorporate this activity into their own research methods course.

8.1.1 Fostering Student Motivation with Relevant Readings

Students come to courses with a diversity of backgrounds, experiences, strengths, and motivations. This variability is a strength, but also makes it challenging as an instructor when trying to find primary research articles for students to read. It is difficult to know what might interest and motivate any individual student (Renninger & Hidi, 2015), and this might be particularly true in large-enrollment university courses (Cross et al., 2025). However, creating this relevance is imperative because student motivation and interests are related to enhanced learning and student success (Renninger & Hidi, 2015). Fortunately, student interest and motivation can be galvanized with engaging pedagogical practices (Mayer, 1998). Pedagogical practices that emphasize the relevance of material for students can increase motivation (e.g., Svinicki, 2004) and engagement, as well as foster interest (Gurung & Christopher 2023; Reeve 2012), and doing so seems to be particularly efficacious for marginalized communities (e.g. first-generation students; Pascarella et al., 2004).

One way to foster student motivation to read primary research articles would be to let what students find most relevant for them guide their reading decisions. Although this might have its advantages, the students likely do not have enough knowledge about the disciplinary practices of psychological science communication to independently find articles that are both relevant to them and good science (Sego & Stuart, 2015). It is also not likely to be scalable in terms of instruction, assessment, and scaffolding students in the reading process (Cross et al., 2025) if all students are reading a different article. To circumvent these potential problems, while still creating a meaningful and relevant Focus Article activity, the instructors for the course can narrow down topics and choose specific articles from those topics that they believe would most interest students and represent real-world topics of relevance to today's student generation.

8.1.2 Enhancing Student Agency by Allowing Reading Choice

Feeling agentic is a core human value that relates to self-efficacy and motivation (Bandura, 2006). Enhancing student agency in university settings comes in many forms (Deci & Ryan 2012), such as allowing students to self-pace their learning (e.g., Zimmerman, 2002) or giving them choice about the direction of the content in a course or topic for an activity (e.g., Patall et al., 2008). Student choice is linked to beneficial learning processes, such as enhanced metacognition and self-regulation; better learning outcomes, such as increased critical thinking and test performance; and increased student interest and persistence on tasks (see Stenalt & Lassesen, 2022 for a review). Thus, giving students opportunities for limited and structured choices seems important for a variety of student successes, which is why it was a core initiative incorporated into our Focus Article activity.

There is some evidence to suggest that giving too much choice in the learning process can be overwhelming for students, particularly novice learners who might not have enough baseline knowledge to enact their agency well (e.g., Lindgren & McDaniel, 2012). In large courses, too much choice for students can also be overwhelming for instructors, creating challenges when scaffolding activities or difficulties when developing rubrics and standardized grading schemes (Cross et al., 2025). Thus, in our Focus Article activity, students were able to choose from five different articles to read that were picked by the instructor. Narrowing down the articles in this way also allowed the instructors to create worksheets for each article.

8.1.3 Normalizing the Difficulty of Reading Articles by Creating Community

Finding ways to promote a comfortable and welcoming classroom climate that encourages students to actively engage with content and learn from each other is important to support student learning (Felten & Lambert, 2020), to help students feel a sense of belonging and identity as scientists (Carlone & Johnson, 2007; McDonald et al., 2019), and for college persistence (Hanauer et al., 2016). Creating a sense of community in large-enrollment research methods courses, in which science identity might first be forming, thus seems imperative. We attempted to accomplish this by having students work in the same small groups over the course of five weeks to complete the worksheets associated with each reading.

Working in groups has the additional benefit of showcasing for students how their peers might also be struggling with reading empirical articles for the first time (e.g., Frankowski, 2023). Research on Wise Interventions in Social Education and belonging interventions suggests that students can see struggle as a cue to non-belonging, which can result in them doubting their abilities in a course or in university (Laiduc & Covarrubias, 2022; Walton & Cohen, 2011). Normalizing struggle by hearing from peers' experiences (Alea Albada et al., in press, Laiduc & Covarrubias, 2022) can be a successful way of creating community in courses. Voicing confusion may be even less likely to occur when there are many peers listening, as in large-enrollment courses, but might be more common in small groups (Cross et al., 2025). Thus, having students work together in small groups to learn how to read primary literature can create a sense of community that helps to normalize struggle and foster a sense of belonging in science.

8.1.4 Scaffolding Reading to Teach Disciplinary Knowledge

Scaffolding student learning has a long tradition in education (Vygotsky, 1978). The scaffolding process is particularly important when teaching students how to read primary literature in university because it is an often overlooked skill that needs to be acquired. Ideally, it should be learned as early as possible in students' university careers (Griffiths & Davila, 2022), like in a research methods course. Scaffolding reading of primary research articles involves making the reading process and the disciplinary knowledge about the way that scientists write about their work visible. Puntambekar (2022) provides a review of types of scaffolds that can be used, such as material scaffolds, which might involve an instructor using prompts to guide students; and social scaffolds, which involve encouraging dialogue among peers when learning. We relied on these 'distributive scaffolding' processes (Puntambekar, 2022): moving from an individual student reading the article to group discussions about it, and providing article overview slides as well as worksheets with guiding questions that were completed over time. The goal is to bring everyone along on the same learning journey about reading primary literature together; it is inclusive and builds students' confidence (Nallaya & Kehrwald, 2013).

We developed an explanatory slide deck (individual support) and group worksheets to scaffold the reading of primary literature as part of the Focus Article activity. The themes of the worksheets were consistent and focused on helping students learn how to read primary research even though the topics for the readings were drastically different. The aim was to showcase for students, through the worksheet completed in small peer group collaborations, how psychologists think and write about research in order to teach the skill of reading research. The worksheets scaffolded the students' experience by considering:

1) how psychological researchers discuss and make inferences about problems to be addressed or motivations for a study;
2) how researchers link theory and previous research to formulate and rationalize hypotheses;
3) validity of study methodology;
4) interpretation of results of empirical research, and how inferences are made from statistical results to evaluate a theory and previous research; and
5) the importance of researchers acknowledging the limitations of their work, and how they move from conclusions to practical implications and future directions.

Thus, regardless of which article the students chose in terms of content, they were learning to ask and answer questions about the research in the same way.

8.2 LEARNING CONTEXT: THE UNIVERSITY, COURSE, STUDENTS, AND INSTRUCTORS

Before describing the Focus Article activity in detail, we wanted to describe the context in which students were learning how to read the empirical articles. Our institution is both a Hispanic-Serving Institution and an Asian American and Native American Pacific Islander-Serving Institution, making it a Minority-Serving Institution. Our student body is diverse in racial and ethnic makeup and also includes many transfer students (~ 33% of undergraduates), students who were first in their family to go to college (~ 33%), and students from different income backgrounds. The university is an R1, research-intensive institution and runs on the quarter system (ten instruction weeks per term).

Our department is focused on experimental psychology, and research methods is core to a student's undergraduate training. Most upper division courses have students read primary literature, and training students to properly read, understand, and critique research articles is key to their success in the major. The research methods course that the Focus Article activity was designed for is a required lower division prerequisite for an upper level course. The purpose of the course is to introduce the basics of research methods in psychology (e.g., psychology as a science, common research designs, measurement considerations) to pre-major students. Learning how to read primary research is explicitly stated as a learning objective on the syllabus and emphasized in early lectures and in lab sections. Students in the course are in their second (sophomore) year at our four-year institution, or have transferred into the university in their third year (junior), and have not necessarily had experience with reading primary literature. Reading primary literature is not required in our Introduction to Psychology course, which is the only prerequisite for our research methods course (there is no statistics prerequisite).

The research methods course typically has high enrollment (~ 200–250 students) and is offered every quarter. It has a 75-minute lecture twice per week, led by the instructor, and an associated weekly 110-minute lab section, led by graduate student teaching assistants. Lab sections have ~25 students. The Focus Article activity was implemented in the lab section during the first weeks of the quarter. Research methods is taught in person, and we are the two primary instructors for the course. Together, the two instructors have 19+ years of teaching experience and have jointly taught this research methods course for our department 22+ times. The second author developed the course for the department in 2017.

8.3 FOCUS ARTICLE ACTIVITY: DESCRIPTION AND IMPLEMENTATION

Details about the Focus Article activity are in the supplementary materials. The development and implementation of the activity were aimed at our goals of relevance, fostering student agency, and creating a sense of community, using a heavily scaffolded approach. Students were given five article options to choose from. These correspond to five subareas of psychology we thought would be most relevant for students: social, developmental, cognitive, neuroscience, and clinical. The subareas of psychology covered by the articles also correspond to our departmental faculty's research areas (with the exception of clinical psychology). A summary of the subarea and topic being addressed in each article is provided in Table 8.1. Each student, in the first week of the course, chose one article as their 'focus.' Students were then put into small peer groups (3–5 students) based on shared article interest. They stayed in the

Table 8.1 Summary of the Focus Article psychology subareas and full reference for articles

Subarea of psychology	Issue or question being addressed in article	Article reference
Social	What psychological factors influence people's attitudes toward pro-environmental actions?	Eom, K., Kim, H. S., & Sherman, D. K. (2018). Social class, control, and action: Socioeconomic status differences in antecedents of support for pro-environmental action. *Journal of Experimental Social Psychology, 77*, 60–75. https://doi.org/10.1016/j.jesp.2018.03.009
Cognitive	Can immersive virtual reality environments have a positive impact on engagement and learning for students?	Parong, J., & Mayer, R. E. (2018). Learning science in immersive virtual reality. *Journal of Educational Psychology, 110*(6), 785. https://doi.org/10.1037/edu0000241
Developmental	Do children use resource sharing as a cue to figure out who is friends with who?	Liberman, Z., & Shaw, A. (2017). Children use partial resource sharing as a cue to friendship. *Journal of Experimental Child Psychology, 159*, 96–109. https://doi.org/10.1016/j.jecp.2017.02.002
Clinical	What is the role of screening in reducing racial disparities in mental health?	Guo, S., Kim, J. J., Bear, L., & Lau, A. S. (2017). Does depression screening in schools reduce adolescent racial/ethnic disparities in accessing treatment? *Journal of Clinical Child & Adolescent Psychology, 46*(4), 523–536. https://doi.org/10.1080/15374416.2016.1270826
Neuroscience	How do hormonal changes across a cycle affect brain structure and function?	Taylor, C. M., Pritschet, L., Olsen, R., Layher, E., Santander, T., Grafton, S. T., & Jacobs, E. G. (2020). Progesterone shapes medial temporal lobe volume across the human menstrual cycle. *NeuroImage, 220*, 1–10. https://doi.org/10.1016/j.neuroimage.2020.117125

same groups for the Focus Article activity to build community and a support system. The topics and articles listed in Table 8.1 have been used for five years and still seem relevant to students.

We included individual and group scaffolding. First, the instructors developed a brief pre-recorded summary of the activity and articles for students to watch on their own through the course learning management system. The description of and link to the video were in the lab information announcement for the first week of the term as well. Second, we created a comprehensive slide deck that summarized each article by section (e.g., introduction, methods). This summary gave students a broad overview of each article prior to them choosing one, and a soft and scaffolded introduction to the research detailed in the paper. Third, students read only the one chosen article over a period of weeks. Thus, the reading task was divided into small, manageable segments, with explicit instructions each week of which pages of the article to read in order to avoid overwhelming students by requiring the entire article at once. Students read the assigned portion of the article prior to attending the lab section in which the peer collaborative learning would take place, which was the final scaffolded activity using the worksheets.

The worksheets were developed to highlight parts that are typical in all empirical articles. Thus, they flowed from introduction to discussion over the course of the four to five worksheets (depending on instructor). Students read the articles from beginning to end with the worksheets to scaffold their understanding of the research and the science. The worksheets had specific prompts (e.g., 'Reread the last sentence in the second paragraph...') that moved beyond the content of each article to consider the norms that exist in all empirical papers. Thus, the worksheets were developed to meet the following objectives:

1) to help students see how researchers discuss and make inferences about problems to be addressed or the motivation for a study;
2) to help students understand how they can use an article they are reading to find theory/previous work that was influential in the work's conceptualization, including showing students how synthesizing across research findings provides a rationale for research questions/hypotheses;
3) to evaluate the sample used in a study, begin to interpret and understand the procedures and measures of a study, and to learn how to use the formatting of a paper, its tables, subsections, etc., to help understand the research design and results;
4) to give students practice with reading and interpreting the results of empirical research, and demonstrating how researchers make inferences from the results of their studies back to theory and/or forward to a next research study;

5) to help students understand how psychological researchers make conclusions based on results and consider the practical implications of their research;
6) to understand that no study is perfect and how researchers consider the limitations of their research and/or potential ideas for future directions.

All of the worksheets were completed in peer groups during the lab section, with roles for each student sometimes assigned (depending on the instructor). They counted for 5% to 7% of students' lab-related grades in the course. Students would spend approximately 20–30 minutes in the lab section working together in the assigned small group to complete the worksheets. Students not able to attend the lab section were permitted to submit the worksheet individually for partial credit. Worksheets were graded for completion only.

8.4 FEEDBACK FROM STUDENTS ABOUT THE FOCUS ARTICLE ACTIVITY

To explore whether the Focus Article activity was meeting our intended aims of relevance, agency, and community, we conducted an anonymous mid-quarter feedback survey. The survey also asked students about their perceptions regarding the extent to which the activity helped them to better learn how to read empirical work. The survey was given in five different quarters, with six courses taught by Alea Albada and four courses taught by Woods (there are usually multiple offerings of the course in the same quarter). This provides variability in when students were taking the course and completing the Focus Article activity and who their instructor was. The survey was given the week after the activity was completed in the lab sections, with the entire article read and all worksheets completed. There were four questions in this survey, given in the following order:

1) To what extent do you feel that being able to choose which Focus Article to read throughout the quarter enhanced your *sense of self-directed learning* in the course?
2) To what extent do you feel that the Focus Articles helped you *engage more with learning how to read and understand empirical research*?
3) To what extent did working in groups for the Focus Article worksheets help you get to know your peers and *foster a sense of community* in the course?
4) To what extent did the Focus Article that you read throughout the quarter feel *relevant to a real-world problem*?

Responses were made on a 3-point Likert scale, ranging from 'not at all' to 'somewhat' to 'very much.' Response rates to the mid-quarter survey were about 40% on average. No additional student demographics related to the survey are available since it was anonymous. The data is summarized in Tables 8.2a, 8.2b, 8.2c, and 8.2d.

Table 8.2a Student responses to mid-quarter survey about the Focus Article activity. Survey question: Self-directed learning

Quarter % = response rate	Very much	Somewhat	Not at all
Winter 2023 (N = 67; 28%)	43%	52%	5%
Fall 2023 (N = 77; 31%)	40%	51%	9%
Winter 2024 (N = 181; 72%)	36%	57%	7%
Fall 2024 (N = 97; 38%)	57%	41%	2%
Winter 2025 (N = 66; 31%)	47%	42%	11%
AVG (SD)	45% (8%)	49% (7%)	7% (3%)

Table 8.2b Student responses to mid-quarter survey about the Focus Article activity. Survey question: Learning to read literature

Quarter % = response rate	Very much	Somewhat	Not at all
Winter 2023 (N = 67; 28%)	42%	51%	7%
Fall 2023 (N = 77; 31%)	36%	56%	8%
Winter 2024 (N = 181; 72%)	54%	45%	1%
Fall 2024 (N = 97; 38%)	49%	46%	5%
Winter 2025 (N = 66; 31%)	58%	39%	3%
AVG (SD)	48% (9%)	47% (6%)	5% (3%)

Table 8.2c Student responses to mid-quarter survey about the Focus Article activity. Survey question: Sense of community

Quarter % = response rate	Very much	Somewhat	Not at all
Winter 2023 (N = 67; 28%)	41%	49%	10%
Fall 2023 (N = 77; 31%)	42%	50%	8%
Winter 2024 (N = 181; 72%)	44%	45%	11%
Fall 2024 (N = 97; 38%)	44%	46%	10%
Winter 2025 (N = 66; 31%)	41%	42%	17%
AVG (SD)	42% (2%)	46% (3%)	11% (3%)

Table 8.2d Student responses to mid-quarter survey about the Focus Article activity. Survey question: Relevance to real world

Quarter % = response rate	Very much	Somewhat	Not at all
Winter 2023 (N = 67; 28%)	61%	37%	2%
Fall 2023 (N = 77; 31%)	36%	56%	8%
Winter 2024 (N = 181; 72%)	56%	41%	3%
Fall 2024 (N = 97; 38%)	55%	44%	1%
Winter 2025 (N = 66; 31%)	73%	22%	5%
AVG (SD)	56% (13%)	40% (12%)	4% (3%)

Note for Tables 8.1a–d: Values represent the percentage of students who responded to each point on the Likert scale (Very Much, Somewhat, Not at All). Survey questions correspond to the four questions (in order) described in the text.

The data displayed in Tables 8.2a–d is across the five quarters that the activity was used, with different instructors. The pattern is incredibly consistent. Students had an overwhelmingly positive response to the Focus Article activity in terms of meeting the intended aims. Focusing just on those instances in which students reported gaining 'very much' from the Focus Article activity, it is clear that, on average, 56% of the students reported that the assigned articles were relevant to a real-world problem, indicating that the articles seemed to serve the purpose of enhancing the relevance of psychological science. With regard to fostering agency as part of the learning process, 45% of students, on average across the five quarters, reported that being able to choose which article to read as part of the Focus Article activity greatly fostered their sense of self-directed learning in the course. Forty-two percent of students also very much agreed that the Focus Article worksheets completed in the lab section in small groups with peers enhanced their sense of community in the course. Finally, although we were not focused on measuring specific learning associated with the Focus Article activity, we were able to evaluate students' perceptions about whether the activity helped them learn how to read empirical research in psychology. Forty-eight percent of students reported that the Focus Article activity helped them to feel more engaged with and better understand how to read empirical research. Most of the additional responses indicated that students were 'somewhat' impressed with the relevance of the activity and its emphasis on helping students learn to read primary literature, as well as develop a sense of community and agency in their learning process. In fact, very few responses to the survey questions (4% to 11%) were below this neutral point, suggesting that very few students had negative views of the Focus Article activity's ability to meet its intended objectives. Overall, the majority of students saw value in the Focus Article activity and corresponding worksheet. Importantly, this value was not specific to one quarter with one instructor. The consistency in the pattern of responses across the various quarters is notable.

8.5 CONSIDERATIONS AND APPLICATION TO OTHER COURSES

The Focus Article activity seems most relevant to research methods courses where students are first learning how to read primary research articles and to think like psychological scientists. We structured the worksheets to focus on themes related to how psychologists think and write about research – rather than questions about the content of the work presented in each reading – which seems unique and applicable to a wide variety of courses. Teaching the framework that experts use when writing, including the process and considering scholarly thinking, sets the foundation for reading other research articles successfully in the future (Lerner 2015; Woods et al., 2021). Our descriptive data suggest that the Focus Article activity is successful in a lower division learning context. However, we can also envision this type of activity working well in other psychology research methods courses, where students are relative novices at reading primary literature. For example, in smaller enrollment courses, instructors might have the flexibility to allow each student to choose their own article to read and be able to vet articles for suitability. This would likely enhance the feelings of relevance that the students might have related to reading primary research. We believe, and the data collected seem to suggest, that providing a sense of community was important for students' engagement with the activity. We encourage future iterations of the Focus Article activity to retain this component.

The beauty of the Focus Article activity is that it can be easily adjusted for future iterations of the course. As students' interests change, instructors can update the articles that they read and the corresponding worksheets. Part of what made this activity successful is the highly structured and scaffolded way that students were introduced to the activity, and the focus on disciplinary norms in how to read and understand research in psychology. The extensive scaffolding via slideshow presentations that students could work through at their own pace, discussion about the topics in lab sections, and being allowed to slowly read through the articles over a period of weeks are essential to build students' abilities and confidence. Students were allowed time to let their knowledge of reading primary literature build, and we would suggest that future uses of this activity allow for this structured and distributed scaffolded approach. Further, this activity could be a useful way to infuse research methods into introductory psychology courses (Gurung et al., 2016), which is a goal many shy away from given that students taking introductory psychology typically would have little or no experience of reading primary literature in psychology. Future research about the Focus Article activity would benefit from taking into account the extent to which it links to students' performance on related outcomes, like a research writing assignment. It would also be useful to see if their knowledge about reading psychological research in a lower division research methods course transfers to upper division courses in which reading empirical work is required.

NOTE

1. Co-authors had equal contribution to the manuscript. Grant awarded to the second author to fund Focus Article activity development from the Reimagining Instruction for the Student Experience Teaching Institute, Office of Teaching & Learning, University of California, Santa Barbara.

REFERENCES

Adler-Kassner, L., & Wardle, E. A. (2022). *Writing Expertise: A Research-based Approach to Writing and Learning Across Disciplines.* WAC Clearinghouse. https://doi.org/10.37514/PRA-B.2022.1701

Alea Albada, N. Woods, V. E., German, T, & Ma de Sousa, A. Q. (in press). Gaining insight: Student's personal stories as a pedagogical tool in Introduction to Psychology. *Teaching Introduction to Psychology.* Elgar Guides to Teaching Series.

American Psychological Association (APA). (2023a). *APA Guidelines for the Undergraduate Psychology Major. Version 3.0.* https://www.apa.org/about/policy/undergraduate-psychology-major

American Psychological Association. (2023b). *The APA Guide to College Teaching.* https://www.apa.org/ed/precollege/undergrad/college-teaching-guide

Ball, C. T., & Pelco, L. E. (2006). Teaching research methods to undergraduate psychology students using an active cooperative learning approach. *International Journal on Teaching and Learning in Higher Education, 17*(2), 147–154. https://www.isetl.org/ijtlhe/pdf/IJTLHE38.pdf

Bandura, A. (2006). Toward a psychology of human agency. *Perspectives on Psychological Science, 1*(2), 164–180.

Carlone, H. B., & Johnson, A. (2007). Understanding the science experiences of successful women of color: Science identity as an analytic lens. *Journal of Research in Science Teaching: The Official Journal of the National Association for Research in Science Teaching, 44*(8), 1187–1218. https://doi.org/10.1002/tea.20237

Cross, V. L., Alea Albada, N., Ditta, A., Geller, E., Hendley, H., Paquette-Smith, M., Pilegard, C., & Woods, V. E. (2025) Scaling up *APA guidelines 3.0* for large-enrollment classes. *Scholarship of Teaching and Learning in Psychology, 11*(1), 113–121. https://psycnet.apa.org/doi/10.1037/stl0000426

Deci, E. L., & Ryan, R. M. (2012). Self-determination theory. In P. A. M. Van Lange, E. T. Higgins, & A. W. Kruglanski (Eds.), *Handbook of Theories of Social Psychology*, 416–436. Sage Publications.

Felten, P., & Lambert, L. M. (2020). *Relationship-Rich Education: How Human Connections Drive Success in College.* Johns Hopkins University Press.

Frankowski, S. D. (2023). Increasing participation in psychological science by using course-based research projects: Testing theory, using open-science practices, and professionally presenting research. *Teaching of Psychology, 50*(3), 291–297. https://doi.org/10.1177/00986283211024200

Goudsouzian, L. K., & Hsu, J. L. (2023). Reading primary scientific literature: Approaches for teaching students in the undergraduate STEM Classroom. *CBE – Life Sciences Education, 22*(3), es3. https://doi.org/10.1187/cbe.22-10-0211

Griffiths, N. E. E. L. A., & Davila, Y. C. (2022). Embedding scaffolded reading practices into the first-year university science curriculum. In K. Manarin (Ed.), *Reading Across the Disciplines*, 143–163), Indiana University Press.

Gurung, R. A., & Christopher, A. (2023). Teaching the foundations of psychological science. In J. Zumbach, D. A. Bernstein, S. Narciss,, & G. Marsico, G. (Eds.), *International Handbook of Psychology Learning and Teaching*, 421–435. Springer Nature Link.

Gurung, R. A., Hackathorn, J., Enns, C., Frantz, S., Cacioppo, J. T., Loop, T., & Freeman, J. E. (2016). Strengthening introductory psychology: A new model for teaching the introductory course. *American Psychologist, 71*(2), 112. https://doi.org/10.1037/a0040012

Hanauer, D. I., Graham, M. J., & Hatfull, G. F. (2016). A measure of college student persistence in the sciences (PITS). *CBE – Life Sciences Education, 15*(4), ar54. https://doi.org/10.1187/cbe.15-09-0185

Laiduc, G., & Covarrubias, R. (2022). Making meaning of the hidden curriculum: Translating wise interventions to usher university change. *Translational Issues in Psychological Science, 8*(2), 221–233. https://doi.org/10.1037/tps0000309

Lerner, N. (2015). Writing is a way of enacting disciplinarity. In L. Adler-Kassner & E. Wardle (Eds.), *Naming What We Know: Threshold Concepts of Writing Studies*, 40–42. Utah University Press.

Lindgren, R., & McDaniel, R. (2012). Transforming online learning through narrative and student agency. *Educational Technology & Society, 15*(4), 344–355. https://www.jstor.org/stable/10.2307/jeductechsoci.15.4.344

Linnenbrink-Garcia, L., Patall, E. A., & Pekrun, R. (2016). Adaptive motivation and emotion in education: Research and principles for instructional design. *Policy Insights from the Behavioral and Brain Sciences, 3*(2), 228–236. https://doi.org/10.1177/2372732216644450

Mayer, R. E. (1998). Cognitive, metacognitive, and motivational aspects of problem solving. *Instructional Science, 26*(1), 49–63. https://doi.org/10.1023/A:1003088013286

McDonald, M. M., Zeigler-Hill, V., Vrabel, J. K., & Escobar, M. (2019). A single-item measure for assessing STEM identity. *Frontiers in Education, 4*, 1–15. https://doi.org/10.3389/feduc.2019.00078

Moriarty, M. A. (2007). Inclusive pedagogy: Teaching methodologies to reach diverse learners in science instruction. *Equity & Excellence in Education, 40*(3), 252–265. https://doi.org/10.1080/10665680701434353

Nallaya, S., & Kehrwald, J. (2013). Supporting academic literacies in an online environment. *Journal of Academic Language and Learning, 7*(2), A79–A94.

Pascarella, E. T., Pierson, C. T., Wolniak, G. C., & Terenzini, P. T. (2004). First-generation college students: Additional evidence on college experiences and outcomes. *The Journal of Higher Education, 75*(3), 249–284. https://doi.org/10.1080/00221546.2004.11772256

Patall, E. A., Cooper, H., & Robinson, J. C. (2008). The effects of choice on intrinsic motivation and related outcomes: A meta-analysis of research findings. *Psychological Bulletin, 134*(2), 270–300.

Puntambekar, S. (2022). Distributed scaffolding: Scaffolding students in classroom environments. *Educational Psychology Review, 34*(1), 451–472.

Reeve, J. (2012). A self-determination theory perspective on student engagement. In S. L. Christenson, A. L. Reschly, & C. Wylie (Eds.), *Handbook of Research on Student Engagement*, 149–172. Springer.

Renninger, K. A., & Hidi, S. E. (2015). *The Power of Interest for Motivation and Engagement*. Routledge.

Sato, B. K., Kadandale, P., He, W., Murata, P. M., Latif, Y., & Warschauer, M. (2014). Practice makes pretty good: Assessment of primary literature reading abilities across multiple large-enrollment biology laboratory courses. *CBE – Life Sciences Education, 13*(4), 677–686. https://doi.org/10.1187/cbe.14-02-0025

Sego, S. A., & Stuart, A. E. (2015). Learning to read empirical articles in general psychology. *Teaching of Psychology, 43*(1), 38–42. https://doi.org/10.1177/0098628315620875

Stenalt, M. H., & Lassesen, B. (2022). Does student agency benefit student learning? A systematic review of higher education research. *Assessment & Evaluation in Higher Education*, *47*(5), 653–669. https://doi.org/10.1080/02602938.2021.1967874

Svinicki, M. D. (2004). *Learning and Motivation in the Postsecondary Classroom*. John Wiley & Sons.

Svinicki, M. D., & Schallert, D. L. (2016). Learning through group work in the college classroom: Evaluating the evidence from an instructional goal perspective. In M. B. Paulsen (Ed.), *Higher Education: Handbook of Theory and Research*, 513–558. Springer.

Thieman, T. J., Clary, E. G., Olson, A. M., Dauner, R. C., & Ring, E. E. (2009). Introducing students to psychological research: General psychology as a laboratory course. *Teaching of Psychology*, *36*(3), 160–168. https://doi.org/10.1080/00986280902959994

Vygotsky, L. S. (1978). *Mind in Society: The Development of Higher Psychological Processes*. Harvard University Press.

Walton, G. M., & Cohen, G. L. (2011). A brief social-belonging intervention improves academic and health outcomes of minority students. *Science*, *331*(6023), 1447–1451. https://doi.org/10.1126/science.1198364

Woods, V. E., Safronova, M., & Adler-Kassner, L. (2021) Guiding students towards disciplinary knowledge with structured peer review assignment. *Journal of Higher Education Theory and Practice*, *21*(4), 160–175. https://doi.org/10.33423/jhetp.v21i4.4216

Zimmerman, B. J. (2002) Becoming a self-regulated learner: An overview. *Theory Into Practice*, *41*(2), 64–70, https://doi.org/10.1207/s15430421tip4102_2

9. Engaging students in real and open science
Jordan R. Wagge

One of the most common experiences shared by undergraduate psychology students in the United States is engaging in research, either in a class or in collaboration with a faculty member. In a survey of department chairs from different types of institutions (2-year, 4-year, master's, doctoral), Perlman and McCann (2005) found that 98% of the responding departments *offered* some sort of research opportunity for their students, while 55% of the 2-year institutions and 73% of the 4-year institutions *required* some sort of research experience for their students. Norcross and colleagues (2016) found that independent research experiences are available in almost all (97%) psychology curricula at 4-year institutions, though very few (3%) require these experiences.

The educational benefits of doing undergraduate research in a research lab, in a course, or together with a faculty member are plentiful. For this reason, undergraduate research experiences are considered 'high-impact' practices (Blessinger & Hensel, 2020; Lopatto, 2010). These experiences have a range of both short- and long-term benefits for the student (e.g., content knowledge, persistence in STEM, increased self-efficacy) (Corwin et al., 2015). Additionally, doing research is seen as an essential experience for the graduate school (particularly doctoral) selection process (Novacek, 2016).

During my first few years as a teaching assistant at a graduate school, I remember reflecting on how the ideals I had formed about research (e.g., use participants' time well, adequately power your studies, use valid and reliable measures) often felt incompatible with the practicalities of individual student projects – for example, students (reasonably) lacked the expertise to use or write the most appropriate measures, I lacked the time (and also, often, expertise!) to adequately supervise all of them in doing so, and we all lacked the resources to get enough participants to adequately power our studies.

This wasn't just an issue in teaching – in general, the state of standard practice in psychological science throughout the 'aughts' (2000–2009) was often at odds with the 'shoulds' of good science (e.g., common use of the phrase 'marginally significant'; Bem (2004) recommending writing papers after completing 'fishing expeditions' with data rather than write the paper initially intended). The open science movement of the 2010s and beyond has in part been a response to these types of practices. Open science is a movement within scientific fields to make the process, results, and communication of science more transparent and accessible to individuals both within and outside of the scientific community (Center for Open Science, n.d.). There is a large movement to incorporate open science practices within educational training, both as good pedagogy and to ensure these practices become more common within the field (e.g., Azevedo et al., 2019).

Approaches to open science vary, but typically include aspects of good scientific practices such as preregistration and data sharing, using open source materials and software, and publishing in open-access journals. Importantly for this chapter, open science practices also include inclusivity in the research process with regard to research collaborators and participants.

This chapter is partially a product of my desire to realign my students' and my own research practices with those of the open science movement. My hope is that student projects align with these practices while being meaningful benefits to student learning.

This chapter proposes a shift away from isolated, student-led research projects toward collaborative, structured, and authentic research models aligned with open science principles. In this chapter, I will discuss how research projects are typically taught, what their benefits and challenges are, and how authentic research projects (defined as the type of research in which professionals engage, with the intention of contributing to the field) can confer additional benefits in the spirit of inclusive and open science. I then present a few models instructors can use to engage students in authentic research projects in their classes, labs, or independent studies.

9.1 UNDERGRADUATE RESEARCH PROJECTS: BENEFITS AND CHALLENGES

Research projects (defined as students engaging in multiple parts of the research process, such as conceptualization, data collection, and data analysis) are likely to be valuable for students. Undergraduate research is a high-impact practice, which refers to a practice that particularly benefits college students (Kuh, 2008; Lopatto, 2010) and can particularly benefit students from underrepresented or historically marginalized backgrounds when done with intention (Kinzie et al., 2021). Research projects can be used to directly meet a variety of APA 3.0 learning goals and outcomes, summarized in Table 9.1.

In addition to these goals and outcomes, research projects can be used to meet many of the others with some customization. For example, outcome 5.4 (within Goal 5) is 'Cultivate workforce collaboration skills' with an exemplar

Table 9.1 How research projects in psychology courses help meet APA undergraduate learning goals

APA Goal	Outcome	How research projects help meet outcomes	Example indicators and suggested class activities
Goal 1: Content Knowledge and Applications	Psychological science relies on empirical evidence and adapts as new data develop	Research is key to empirical efforts, and by participating in research by completing a project, students learn that this is how new knowledge in the field is acquired.	1.5A: 'Discuss the contributions that integrative themes make to the understanding and impact of psychological science.' Students' written reports could contain a discussion regarding what the knowledge acquired from their project implies in the context of the larger science.
Goal 2: Scientific Inquiry and Critical Thinking	2.1 Exercise scientific reasoning	Students make predictions about the outcomes of research related to human behavior and mental processes through hypotheses, and test those hypotheses.	2.1A: 'Distinguish psychological research concepts in a research study.' Students could complete annotated bibliographies of the readings for their literature review that ask them to identify concepts such as: hypothesis, operationalization, type of design, etc.
Goal 2: Scientific Inquiry and Critical Thinking	2.2 Interpret, design, and evaluate psychological research	Students completing projects actively design studies, collect and analyze data, and evaluate the strengths and limitations of their findings in light of existing research through written reports.	2.2D: 'Use replicable and open scientific practices.' Students could register projects on the Open Science Framework, where they also share anonymized data, analysis scripts, and precise methods.

APA Goal	Outcome	How research projects help meet outcomes	Example indicators and suggested class activities
Goal 2: Scientific Inquiry and Critical Thinking	2.4 Use statistics to evaluate quantitative research findings	Research reports include results sections.	2.4C: 'Communicate research findings using data visualizations.' Students could include appropriate graphs when presenting results from projects.
Goal 3: Values in Psychological Science	3.1 Employ ethical standards in research, practice, and academic contexts	Research reports require students to complete ethics reviews.	3.1C: 'Prepare a research proposal to submit to a designated ethical review process.' Students could prepare an IRB application for their institution based on their research (or for a proposed next project).
Goal 4: Communication, Psychological Literacy, and Technology Skills	4.2 Write and present effectively for different purposes	Students who write research reports are preparing information in a prescribed manner for a specific audience.	4.2D: 'Deliver complex communication projects that meet established conventions and professional guidelines.' Students could complete a full research report in APA style.

indicator for students to 'Collaborate effectively on team-based projects' (APA, 2023, p. 20). If a research project within a class is a team-based project, then this indicator can be easily met and assessed in that class.

It is important to know what aspects of research projects instructors typically adopt in their courses. Wagge and colleagues (2022) surveyed psychology instructors who teach research courses with projects and found that 97.27% of the projects included some sort of written report, while fewer included data collection (92.64%), data analysis (84.24%), class presentations (78.82%), or IRB applications (59.15%); this indicates that many students are not being exposed to all aspects of the research process within these courses. Instructors also ranked aspects of the research project they considered most important for students; writing and hypothesis generation were ranked at the top of the list, followed by data analysis, data collection, presenting, then IRB applications and data entry. There is some discrepancy here (e.g., IRB applications were required by the majority of the instructors but were found to be the least valuable experience), perhaps because some aspects of the research process are considered unimportant to learning but also unavoidable. At most institutions and in most programs, students need to complete IRB applications if they are going to collect data.

While research projects can have pedagogical benefits, they do present challenges to students and instructors. In a survey of research methods instructors, Ciarocco and colleagues (2017) found that instructors struggled to balance heavy course content with active learning and engagement, and that it was difficult for instructors to get students through the entire research process.

These findings suggest that modifications to more traditional research projects (defined as students conducting their own research) might be desirable for instructors seeking to achieve more balance without affecting student knowledge, attitudes, or outcomes. In fact, requiring students to complete their own projects from beginning to end might introduce unnecessary obstacles. Gurung and Stoa (2020) found that whether students conducted their own research projects predicted neither attitudes nor knowledge in research methods. Additionally, Stoa and colleagues (2022) surveyed psychology students to determine the most subjectively difficult concepts they encounter during research methods courses. Some of the most difficult concepts identified by their student sample included aspects of sound and rigorous research design – those related to validity, operational definitions, and experimental designs, suggesting that students might struggle the most with the concepts related to research planning and design. Difficulties understanding these concepts might affect not just the progress and rigor of a student's own project, but could also create downstream issues in their research process if they are unable to operationalize or interrogate the validity of their variables.

More traditional research projects in psychology are seen as valuable pedagogical experience by some, but they may not be considered scientifically rigorous (Frank & Saxe, 2012; Standing et al., 2014). Additionally, they may not have many uses beyond the bounds of a one-semester class. Wagge and colleagues (2022) found that surveyed instructors of psychology research courses mostly agreed that data from student projects contribute to knowledge within the classroom and that student-generated hypotheses are interesting. The instructors were less likely to agree that data contribute to knowledge beyond the classroom, that enough data is collected to make appropriate statistical conclusions, that student-developed methodology is rigorous, and that student research questions are typically grounded in theory. Instructors in the survey disagreed that students adequately review the literature prior to forming a research question or that data for students' projects are collected from a diverse population.

None of these findings are surprising when considering the practical issues related to a student completing a project within one college course, given the constraints related to time and resources. However, the responses from these instructors and students suggest that both instructors and students struggle to do *everything*, and that there are gaps between what is happening and what is possible with regard to contributions to the field as well as research quality (e.g., power, rigor); regardless of whether research eventually contributes to the literature, research quality is particularly important. Krishna and Peter (2018) present work that indicates students' endorsements of questionable research practices originate from their research supervisors. It is therefore important for student outcomes that research supervisors model and support best practices in research.

Given the option between more traditional projects or those that have similar pedagogical benefits *but also* contribute to the knowledge base in the field, some instructors might be interested in the latter. In the next section of this chapter, I will discuss some models for research projects that may support student learning and participation in undergraduate research experiences *in addition to* directing students' energies toward research that is well powered, more likely to be published, a more authentic representation of work that is done in the field, and/or contributes to the field in meaningful ways (e.g., replication). Importantly, adopting one of these models does not necessarily mean that instructors or students will need to do more work than a traditional project; this is an important area for future research. When considering what type of model to apply in a research course or lab, it might be helpful to consider how principles of open science could guide your decisions.

9.2 OPENING SCIENCE THROUGH AUTHENTIC RESEARCH

One way to bridge the gaps between what is happening and what is possible is by applying principles of open science and, instead of supervising traditional projects in your curriculum, inviting students to collaborate on authentic research projects.

Authentic research projects (Grahe, 2017; see also 'real-life research projects' discussed in Marley et al., 2022) are projects meant to contribute to the field in some way, in addition to (and not in lieu of) important pedagogical outcomes. I argue that facilitating authentic research projects with students in required courses fits into open science because they involve students as collaborators in conducting real research (e.g., research that is meant to contribute to the general knowledge base beyond the classroom). You are truly 'opening science' to folks who might have the most enthusiasm and need the most training and mentorship, and if you do it within a curriculum where it is required (i.e., not more work than a traditional project would have been), then you are doing it in an equitable way so that every student is invited.

Authentic research projects can be difficult to do in student-directed individual or group research projects for a few reasons: first, real research can be (and in most cases, should be) time consuming; for example, the instructor needs to be able to mentor each research project individually, particularly if the authentic research involves a community partner. Even in a class with ten students, if each student had their own project, it would be difficult to mentor real research in a way that doesn't drain all of your resources and time. A silver lining of student-led projects is that the questions are often so straightforward that the instructor does not have to be an expert in everything in order to assess the methodology, rationale, and rigor (at the same time, this might be a disadvantage – instructors cannot be experts in all of these things anyway, and so the feedback and research mentorship might not be quite as valuable as they would be otherwise).

Second, authentic studies need to be powered adequately, and this is difficult to fit into the timeline of a semester when you do not have funds or robust participant pools. This might be especially true at smaller teaching institutions with fewer students.

It is possible for instructors to give students several options, including individual projects *or* replication projects. This is a common model for research instructors and may be a little more palatable for departments where the consensus is that projects need to be student originated, since students would be responsible for 'originating' their choice to do a replication study. Additionally, choices give students a sense of autonomy and that autonomy can manifest in increased efficacy and engagement in the classroom (e.g., Deci et al., 1991). Giving students the choice also opens a conversation about the benefits of replication research versus novel research. Your experience might differ, but my experience is that giving too many options can sometimes lead to my own disorganization and stress, and I believe this negatively impacts the classroom experience for students much more than being told what their project will be about might. In the next section, I will present authentic research alternatives to the traditional research project that fit multiple needs (instructor, field, student) and remain student centered.

9.3 SOME MODELS FOR INCLUDING STUDENTS IN REAL RESEARCH

I believe that there are some ways standard psychology research projects could be improved. Standard psychology research projects aren't often grounded in theory, they are often underpowered, and they sometimes do not get presented outside of the classroom (Perlman & McCann, 2005; Wagge et al., 2022). While it is helpful for students to understand that there are methodologies that can be employed to answer practical questions – the types of questions likely to be asked by 200-level students in psychology – there is also tremendous benefit to students focusing on learning the skills of research through scientifically sound and professionally authentic projects.

9.3.1 Model 1: Do Your Own Research

One potential model for students to engage in authentic research is through working on the lines of research conducted by their professors (see LoSchiavo, 2018 for a description of the author's process in conducting a professional-grade class project). Students could benefit from doing the research in their instructor's area of expertise: when participating in this approach, students have access to an actual expert in that area, so they get to see how experts think about and study their own topics. Instructors may also benefit by overlapping their professional needs for scholarship and undergraduate research mentorship with what ends up being their primary role at teaching institutions like mine – teaching. If you can reach into the same 'bucket' in a way that benefits everyone and takes nothing away from the students, why not try it? Doing this in a class as a part of the students' curriculum would open up an area of real research for students that they otherwise might not have been able to engage in.

9.3.2 Model 2: Do Someone Else's Research, Again

One promising avenue for student research is to conduct replication research as part of the bachelor's and master's coursework. Quintana (2021) proposes that student projects should be focused on replication research rather than original research, focusing largely on issues related to power (having enough participants to detect an actual effect, if present) and the time constraints present with students' development and testing of original research questions. The author argues that conducting replication research can serve pedagogical functions while also contributing to knowledge in the field.

I agree that replications have the potential to serve both the field and the students. Until replication work is considered more 'glamorous' by scientific disciplines, there will always be a need for replications to be done by people who don't need to worry about what is more or less glamorous. The stakes are not very high for 200-level undergraduate students; if they don't get *this next article published*, then they don't have to worry about not getting promotions, tenure, keynote invitations, awards, or just the implicit acknowledgment from the field and colleagues that they are doing something new and exciting. At the same time, we need replications, and they need projects.

Additionally, there is a benefit to students replicating and using established methods developed by experts in the field. Flake and Fried (2020) identify several 'questionable measurement practices' (QMPs) that researchers often make, which impact our ability to make sense of data and research. One of these includes the creation of scales or measurements 'on the fly,' that is, without any regard to validity or psychometric properties. While there may be plenty of existing measurements with established psychometric properties, students may not know what these are and it may be difficult for instructors to oversee every student's on-the-fly measurement properties and suggest better measures where needed. Replications of more recent published work, while not immune from QMPs, will hopefully fare better than measurements created by novice researchers without deep knowledge of the field they are studying.

Also, despite what I just wrote above regarding students not needing publications, there really are many opportunities for students to present and publish replication research (Wagge, 2019). The Collaborative Replication and Education Project (CREP), which I'll discuss shortly, is one model students can use to run replication studies and then contribute them to a network-wide meta-analysis across student teams from other universities around the world. There are plenty of examples of publications of replication research that have either centered or involved students (e.g., Hawkins et al., 2018; Burns et al., 2019; Chen et al., 2021). These models could therefore help with students for whom publications really do matter, such as those who will apply to PhD programs in psychology.

CREP is a network of students and instructors who facilitate and conduct replications of recent high-interest work in psychology. The CREP team selects studies, communicates with the authors of original studies, curates materials, responds to student and instructor questions, provides guidance to teams completing studies, and most importantly conducts reviews of the projects both before and after data collection to ensure fidelity to the original study. Students and instructors who contribute can present their research at conferences and can also publish their work once the CREP meta-analysis is ready to be written. There are a few examples of these that have been published (e.g., Leighton et al., 2018) including two that were first-authored by students (Ghelfi et al., 2020; Hall et al., 2024). These contributions are then responded to in comments (e.g., Buckwalter & Friedman, 2024; Schmidt et al., 2024) or cited by other meta-analytic researchers (e.g., Lehmann et al., 2018), demonstrating the incremental nature of science and the value of students' contributions to the field.

CREP projects are continuously accepting new submissions, so there is no one time of year or month that contributors must decide to join. I personally use CREP projects in my research lab – we generally have two or three projects going on at any one time – and secondary data analysis projects in my class (which I'll describe later). When you do run a CREP project in your class, you can customize it: CREP projects can be initiated by the instructor or the student, review communication can happen with either, you can add extension hypotheses to your projects, or you can have the whole group working on the same project or divide it up between groups. One instructor has taught using CREP in large classes by having students act as participants in a first stage of research, and then as researchers with extension hypotheses in groups in a second stage (Urry et al., 2020). You can review the basic steps involved in completing a CREP project below in Table 9.2, and see Supplementary Materials for materials I have developed for my own class to complete CREP projects and associated empirical reports.

There are other popular models for doing replication research with students, such as Dr. Gilad Feldman's work organizing replication projects in social psychology and judgment and decision-making with his students in his CORE Team (CORE Team, 2025). The CORE Team has curated many resources for other folks interested in doing replication research, most of which could be easily adapted to fit an undergraduate research course, lab, or independent study. Additionally, Murphy and Greene (2023) conducted a collaborative replication of the famous 'lost in the mall' study with graduate students who contributed to a large data set, but also reported individualized aspects of the study in their projects. In their paper, they describe the process they used as well as their lessons learned, and this could also be adapted for the aforementioned purposes. A similar approach is reported by Jekel and colleagues (2020), along with

Table 9.2   Basic instructions and recommendations for completing CREP projects

Step	Required or recommended for CREP participation	Details and suggestions
1	Recommended	Teach students about the replication crisis in psychology (Diener & Biswas-Diener, 2025)
2	Recommended	Ask students to read about CREP – Wagge (2019)
3	Required	Read about available studies to replicate here: https://osf.io/flaue/
4	Required	Read the getting started guide here: https://osf.io/stdgm/
5	Required	Sign up for a study (see getting started guide above). This can be completed prior to the start of the semester if you want to choose a study for your students
6	Recommended	Have students read the study you selected
7	Recommended	Ask students to write/propose extension hypotheses for your study – see video (https://youtu.be/qrjglVuDFIM) of the 2023 summer workshop related to drafting effective DEIA-related extension hypotheses
8	Required	Prepare and submit CREP materials (see getting started guide above)
9	Required	Prepare and submit IRB application for your institution
10	Required	Once your project is reviewed, preregister the study and collect data (see getting started guide above)
11	Required	After data collection, revise your OSF page and submit for final CREP review
12	Recommended	Present your site's research at a conference
13	Recommended	Contribute to the CREP paper on your study

lessons learned and a guide for future instructors who would like to do something similar. Instructors do not need to be familiar with all of these projects in order to do any of them, so if you are on the fence about doing a replication project in your class, lab, or with thesis students, review one of these and see where it takes you. The wonderful thing about the open science community is that folks who do this work with students are motivated to share what they've done and help others walk the same path, so you may find a surplus of available materials online that could overwhelm your decision fatigue. My advice is to pick one, start with an independent study or lab, and then see how you could adapt it for a class.

9.3.3 Model 3: Find a Crowdsourced Project

There are several networks that regularly offer scaffolded, crowdsourced research opportunities for student contributors, and their timelines are often very sensitive to the needs of students and instructors. One of these projects is Psi Chi's Network for International Collaborative Exchange, or NICE (Cascalheira et al., 2023). This is an annual project sponsored by Psi Chi that involves data collection around the world to answer a research question with relevant cross-cultural components submitted by a research team. The project is highly scaffolded with supporting materials for instructors and students. NICE projects are conducted and then published in a timely manner, allowing for student participation and authorship. Information on Psi Chi's current NICE projects can be found on their website, https://www.psichi.org/page/research#collaborate.

Psi Beta (the Community College National Honor Society in Psychology) also offers an annual research project for community college students in Psi Beta, and has done so since 2008. Current research opportunities can be found on their website, http://psibeta.org (Psi Beta, n.d.). These research questions are often questions that community college students find interesting and relevant: the topic for the 2024–2025 research project is community college student stigma.

The Psychological Science Accelerator (PSA; Moshontz et al., 2018) is another standing project for students and instructors to join and contribute to that is grounded in the principles and processes of open science. Contributing teams complete collaboration agreements, are given research materials and links for data collection, and are invited to contribute to manuscripts that are almost always completed as registered reports prior to data collection. For some students (and instructors!), having authorship on a registered report can be handy while pursuing graduate school admission, the job market, and rank and tenure. PSA and CREP collaborated on a joint project from 2018 through 2024 (Hall et al., 2024), and found that it was difficult to balance the pedagogical needs of the CREP with the rigor of the PSA studies; for example, the centralized data collection procedures used by PSA mean that CREP students were not creating or implementing their own materials or procedures. This left fewer aspects of the research process open to students for learning experiences.

For more advanced undergraduates or graduate students, contribution to a PSA project would be an excellent use of time and energy, but it is primarily a scientific (not a pedagogical) network and therefore when there are conflicts of interest between these two roles, the scientific role will be (and should be) prioritized. I recommend the PSA for independent studies or research being conducted in a continuous lab, rather than within the confines of a semester necessary for class participation or thesis projects.

9.3.4 Model 4: Do a Secondary Data Analysis

I currently use secondary data analyses when teaching 200-level statistics and methods courses. At my institution, we have two courses that are offered in two continuous semesters: Psychological Statistics & Methods I & II. In the first part of the course, students conduct highly scaffolded literature reviews on a topic of interest to them while also learning the basics of data processing and description in jamovi (The jamovi project, 2025) or a similar free analysis program. In the second part of the semester, students conduct inferential statistical analyses (e.g., *t*-tests, correlations, ANOVAs) and also complete a research project. The past few times I have taught this course, we all use the same large data set with many variables of interest to choose from for the research project. I also use the same data set for demonstrations and assignments in jamovi (see Supplementary Materials for a sample list of assignments), so that students gain familiarity with the data set and its variables over the course of the semester.

Early assignments during the semester require students to summarize and discuss the data set we are using, while later assignments require them to explore some of the constructs from the data set in more detail and then eventually propose an analysis based on their reading of the literature and understanding of the data set. Because we use data that has already been gathered, there is no need to conduct an IRB review at my institution, which allows for more time during the semester to develop research ideas. Additionally, because I know this one data set in detail, as the instructor I can more effectively mentor students than I could if they were all conducting their own projects.

The two data sets I have used most often in my classes are the data from Terry and colleagues' SMARVUS (Statistics and Mathematics Anxieties and Related Variables in University Students) project (2023), and Grahe and colleagues' EaMMi2 (Emerging Adulthood Measured at Multiple Institutions 2) project (2018). Both of these projects published their data in data papers in the *Journal of Open Psychology Data* (n.d.). This journal is an excellent resource for data sets that students can use; because the purpose of the journal is to share data from projects, they often have better resources (e.g., codebooks) than open data sets in other journals. The work of both Terry et al. (2023) and Grahe et al. (2018) contain a large number of scales and a range of other variables and can be used for most types of analyses that would be covered in an undergraduate statistics course in psychology. The number of variables is not so large as to be overwhelming, but is large enough that most students in a course of 20 will develop their own unique research question and analytical method. Also, because both of these projects are related to things relevant to their lives (e.g., emerging adulthood and anxiety about taking a statistics course), students can engage in discussions about these constructs.

9.4 CONCLUSION

In conclusion, research projects in psychology have value for the student, but alternatives to traditional research projects might invite students to engage in real science that could also benefit the field. Many models of such projects exist and come with associated resources for both students and instructors.

Anecdotally, my students and I have all benefited from the application of these types of projects (specifically, CREP and secondary data analysis). While teaching using these approaches, I am able to focus on methodological rigor rather than attempting to understand the literature in 20+ different student projects each semester; because I already know the literature intimately and every student shares similarities across their work when completing these projects, I am able to offer faster, more well-developed feedback on student papers, allowing for more scaffolding of their projects.

My students completing replication projects are eligible to earn authorship in an eventual paper and present research at conferences. Many of them express great interest in understanding the replication crisis, as well as discussing its determinants and potential solutions (e.g., students completing replication projects in their courses). They frequently express joy in their course reflections and evaluations regarding their contributions to the field, highlighting that they appreciate models that allow students to do so.

For students completing secondary data analysis, having a well-powered study that does not require the collection of new data and allows them to have a professional conference-ready poster within a semester has also been helpful. Several students who have completed secondary data analysis projects with me are planning publications of their work, and others have asked if I could supervise additional secondary data analyses because they have new questions or want to be able to bring another project to a professional conference.

Ongoing research on CREP's effectiveness suggests that, compared to traditional projects, outcomes related to trust in science, science efficacy and belonging, and interest in science are statistically equivalent across these models, while critically thinking about psychology and open science concepts shows improvements from pre- to post-test uniquely for CREP students (Wagge, 2023). While more research is needed, this also means that there are many opportunities for further research related to outcomes for these projects, particularly within psychology.

REFERENCES

American Psychological Association. (2023). *APA Guidelines for the Undergraduate Psychology Major: Version 3.0.* https://www.apa.org/about/policy/undergraduate-psychology-major.pdf

Azevedo, F., Parsons, S., Micheli, L., Strand, J. F., Rinke, E. M., Guay, S., Elsherif, M. M., Quinn, K. A., Wagge, J. R., Steltenpohl, C. N., Kalandadze, T., Vasilev, M. R., Oliveira, C. M., Aczel, B., Miranda, J. F., Baker, B. J., Galang, C. M. O., Pennington, C. R., Marques, T., ... & FORRT. (2019). *Introducing a Framework for Open and Reproducible Research Training (FORRT)*. Open Science Framework. https://doi.org/10.31219/osf.io/bnh7p

Bem, D. J. (2004). Writing the empirical journal article. In J. M. Darley, M. P. Zanna, & H. L. Roediger III (Eds.), *The Complete Academic: A Career Guide* (2nd Ed.), 185–219. American Psychological Association.

Blessinger, P., & Hensel, N. H. (2020). Undergraduate research as a high-impact educational practice. In N. H. Hensel & P. Blessinger (Eds.), *International Perspectives on Undergraduate Research*, 1–18. Springer International Publishing. https://doi.org/10.1007/978-3-030-53559-9_1

Burns, D. M., Fox, E. L., Greenstein, M., Olbright, G., & Montgomery, D. (2019). An old task in new clothes: A preregistered direct replication attempt of enclothed cognition effects on Stroop performance. *Journal of Experimental Social Psychology*, *83*, 150–156. https://doi.org/10.1016/j.jesp.2018.10.001

Buckwalter, W., & Friedman, O. (2024). Robust evidence for knowledge attribution and luck: A comment on Hall et al. (2024). *Advances in Methods and Practices in Psychological Science*, *7*(4), 25152459241268220. https://doi.org/10.1177/25152459241268220

Cascalheira, C. J., Moussa Rogers, M., Irgens, M. S., Cuccolo, K., Edlund, J., Zlokovich, M. S., & ... Fitapelli, B. (2023, June 30). *Psi Chi's Network for International Collaborative Exchange* (NICE). https://doi.org/10.17605/OSF.IO/JUUPX

Center for Open Science. (n.d.). *What is Open Science?* https://www.cos.io/open-science

Chen, J., Hui, L. S., Yu, T., Feldman, G., Zeng, S., Ching, T. L., Ng, C. H., Wu, K. W., Yuen, C. M., Lau, T. K., Cheng, B. L., & Ng, K. W. (2021). Foregone opportunities and choosing not to act: Replications of inaction inertia effect. *Social Psychological and Personality Science*, *12*(3), 333–345. https://doi.org/10.1177/1948550619900570

Ciarocco, N. J., Strohmetz, D. B., & Lewandowski, G. W., Jr. (2017). What's the point? Faculty perceptions of research methods courses. *Scholarship of Teaching and Learning in Psychology*, *3*(2), 116–131. https://doi.org/10.1037/stl0000085

CORE Team. (2025). *Collaborative Open-science and Meta REsearch*. http://osf.io/5z4a8, https://mgto.org/core-team/

Corwin, L. A., Graham, M. J., & Dolan, E. L. (2015). Modeling course-based undergraduate research experiences: An agenda for future research and evaluation. *CBE–Life Sciences Education*, *14*(1), es1. https://doi.org/10.1187/cbe.14-10-0167

Deci, E., Vallerand, R., Pelletier, L., & Ryan, R. (1991). Motivation and education: The self-determination perspective. *Educational Psychologist*, *26*(3), 325–346. https://doi.org/10.1207/s15326985ep2603&4_6

Diener, E. & Biswas-Diener, R. (2025). The replication crisis in psychology. In R. Biswas-Diener & E. Diener (Eds.), *Noba Textbook Series: Psychology*. Champaign, IL: DEF publishers. http://noba.to/q4cvydeh

Flake, J. K., & Fried, E. I. (2020). Measurement schmeasurement: Questionable measurement practices and how to avoid them. *Advances in Methods and Practices in Psychological Science*, *3*(4), 456–465. https://doi.org/10.1177/2515245920952393

Frank, M. C., & Saxe, R. (2012). Teaching replication. *Perspectives on Psychological Science*, *7*(6), 600–604. https://doi.org/10.1177/1745691612460686

Ghelfi, E., Christopherson, C. D., Urry, H. L., Lenne, R. L., Legate, N., Ann Fischer, M., Wagemans, F. M. A., Wiggins, B., Barrett, T., Bornstein, M., de Haan, B., Guberman, J., Issa, N., Kim, J., Na, E., O'Brien, J., Paulk, A., Peck, T., Sashihara, M., ... & Sullivan, D. (2020). Reexamining the effect of gustatory disgust on moral judgment: A multilab direct replication of Eskine, Kacinik, and Prinz (2011). *Advances in Methods and Practices in Psychological Science*, *3*(1), 3–23. https://doi.org/10.1177/2515245919881152

Grahe, J. E. (2017). Authentic research projects benefit students, their instructors, and science. In R. Obeid, A. Schartz, C. Shane-Simpson, & P. J. Brooks (Eds.). *How We Teach Now: The GSTA Guide to Student-Centered Teaching*. http://teachpsych.org/ebooks/

Grahe, J. E., Chalk, H. M., Cramblet Alvarez, L. D., Faas, C. S., Hermann, A. D., & McFall, J. P. (2018). Emerging Adulthood Measured at Multiple Institutions 2: The Data. *Journal of Open Psychology Data*, *6*(1), 4. https://doi.org/10.5334/jopd.38

Gurung, R. A. R., & Stoa, R. (2020). A national survey of teaching and learning research methods: Important concepts and faculty and student perspectives. *Teaching of Psychology*, *47*(2), 111–120.

Hall, B., Schmidt, K., Wagge, J., Lewis, S. C., Weissgerber, S. C., Kiunke, F., Pfuhl, G., Stieger, S., Tran, U. S., Barzykowski, K., Bogatyreva, N., Kowal, M., Massar, K., Pernerstofer, F., Sorokowski, P., Voracek, M., Chartier, C. R., Brandt, M. J., Grahe, J. E., ... & Buchanan, E. M. (2024). Registered replication report: A large multilab cross-cultural conceptual replication of Turri et al. (2015). *Advances in Methods and Practices in Psychological Science*, *7*(4), 25152459241267902. https://doi.org/10.1177/25152459241267902

Hawkins, R. X. D., Smith, E. N., Au, C., Arias, J. M., Catapano, R., Hermann, E., Keil, M., Lampinen, A., Raposo, S., Reynolds, J., Salehi, S., Salloum, J., Tan, J., & Frank, M. C. (2018). Improving the replicability of psychological science through pedagogy. *Advances in Methods and Practices in Psychological Science*, *1*(1), 7–18. https://doi.org/10.1177/2515245917740427

Jekel, M., Fiedler, S., Allstadt Torras, R., Mischkowski, D., Dorrough, A. R., & Glöckner, A. (2020). How to teach open science principles in the undergraduate curriculum—The Hagen Cumulative Science Project. *Psychology Learning & Teaching*, *19*(1), 91–106. https://doi.org/10.1177/1475725719868149

Journal of Open Psychology Data. (n.d.). https://openpsychologydata.metajnl.com/

Kinzie, J., Silberstein, S., McCormick, A. C., Gonyea, R. M., & Dugan, B. (2021). Centering racially minoritized student voices in high-impact practices. *Change: The Magazine of Higher Learning*, *53*(4), 6–14. https://doi.org/10.1080/00091383.2021.1930976

Krishna, A., & Peter, S. M. (2018). Questionable research practices in student final theses – Prevalence, attitudes, and the role of the supervisor's perceived attitudes. *PLOS ONE*, *13*(8), e0203470. https://doi.org/10.1371/journal.pone.0203470

Kuh, G. D. (2008). *High-Impact Educational Practices: What They Are, Who Has Access to Them, and Why They Matter* (1st Ed.). American Association of Colleges & Universities.

Lehmann, G. K., Elliot, A. J., & Calin-Jageman, R. J. (2018). Meta-analysis of the effect of red on perceived attractiveness. *Evolutionary Psychology*, *16*(4), 1474704918802412. https://doi.org/10.1177/1474704918802412

Leighton, D. C., Legate, N., LePine, S., Anderson, S. F., & Grahe, J. (2018). Self-esteem, self-disclosure, self-expression, and connection on Facebook: A collaborative replication meta-analysis. *Psi Chi Journal of Psychological Research*, *23*(2), 98–109. https://doi.org/10.24839/2325-7342.JN23.2.98

Lopatto, D. (2010). Undergraduate research as a high-impact student experience. *Peer Review*, *12*(2), 27–30.

LoSchiavo, F. M. (2018). incorporating a professional-grade all-class project into a research methods course. *Frontiers in Psychology*, *9*. https://www.frontiersin.org/articles/10.3389/fpsyg.2018.02143

Marley, S. A., Siani, A., & Sims, S. (2022). Real-life research projects improve student engagement and provide reliable data for academics. *Ecology and Evolution*, *12*, e9593. https://doi.org/10.1002/ece3.9593

Moshontz, H., Campbell, L., Ebersole, C. R., IJzerman, H., Urry, H. L., Forscher, P. S., Grahe, J. E., McCarthy, R. J., Musser, E. D., Antfolk, J., Castille, C. M., Evans, T. R., Fiedler, S., Flake, J. K., Forero, D. A., Janssen, S. M. J., Keene, J. R., Protzko, J., Aczel, B., . . . Chartier, C. R. (2018). The psychological science accelerator: Advancing psychology through a distributed collaborative network. *Advances in Methods and Practices in Psychological Science*, *1*(4), 501–515. https://doi.org/10.1177/2515245918797607

Murphy, G., & Greene, C. M. (2023). Conducting inter-institutional collaborative replication studies as student projects. *The Irish Journal of Education / Iris Eireannach an Oideachais*, *46*, 1–14.

Norcross, J. C., Hailstorks, R., Aiken, L. S., Pfund, R. A., Stamm, K. E., & Christidis, P. (2016). Undergraduate study in psychology: Curriculum and assessment. *American Psychologist*, *71*(2), 89–101. https://doi.org/10.1037/a0040095

Novacek, D. M. (2016). How to get in: Applying to psychology grad school. *APS Observer*, *29*. https://www.psychologicalscience.org/observer/how-to-get-in-applying-to-psychology-grad-school

Perlman, B., & McCann, L. I. (2005). Undergraduate research experiences in psychology: A national study of courses and curricula. *Teaching of Psychology*, *32*(1), 5–14. https://doi.org/10.1207/s15328023top3201_2

Psi Beta. (n.d.). *Psi Beta's Annual National Research Project (2024–2025)*. https://psibeta.org/psi-betas-annual-national-research-project-2024-2025/

Quintana, D. S. (2021). Replication studies for undergraduate theses to improve science and education. *Nature Human Behaviour*, *5*, 1117–1118. https://doi.org/10.1038/s41562-021-01192-8

Schmidt, K., Haeffel, G. J., Levy, N., Moreau, D., Lee, S. T. H., Buchanan, E. M., Krafnick, A. J., Voracek, M., Pfuhl, G., Barzykowski, K., Kowal, M., & Wagge, J. (2024). A response to a comment on Hall et al. (2024). *Advances in Methods and Practices in Psychological Science*, *7*(4), 25152459241268249. https://doi.org/10.1177/25152459241268249

Standing, L. G., Grenier, M., Lane, E. A., Roberts, M. S., & Sykes, S. J. (2014). Using replication projects in teaching research methods. *Psychology Teaching Review*, *20*(1), 96–104.

Stoa, R., Chu, T. L. (A.), & Gurung, R. A. R. (2022). Potential potholes: Predicting challenges and learning outcomes in research methods in psychology courses. *Teaching of Psychology*, *49*(1), 21–29.

The jamovi project (2025). jamovi (Version 2.6) [Computer Software]. https://www.jamovi.org

Terry, J., Ross, R. M., Nagy, T., Salgado, M., Garrido-Vásquez, P., Sarfo, J. O., Cooper, S., Buttner, A. C., Lima, T. J. S., Öztürk, İ., Akay, N., Santos, F. H., Artemenko, C., Copping, L. T., Elsherif, M. M., Milovanović, I., Cribbie, R. A., Drushlyak, M.

G., Swainston, K., . . . Field, A. P. (2023). Data from an International Multi-Centre Study of Statistics and Mathematics Anxieties and Related Variables in University Students (the SMARVUS Dataset). *Journal of Open Psychology Data, 11*(1), 8. https://doi.org/10.5334/jopd.80

Urry, H. L., Garay, M., Hickey, P. C. C., Nour Eddine, S. N., Pagan, J., Rasmussen, R. E. E., ... Jones, R. H. H. (2020, May 31). Replication of De Neys, W., Rossi, S., & Houdé, O. (2013) at Tufts University (Spring, 2020). osf.io/k4pd2

Wagge, J. R. (2023, October 6). Just as good, if not better? Comparing outcomes for replication and traditional projects in research methods and statistics courses [Poster]. ACT (Annual Conference on Teaching), Portland, OR.

Wagge, J. R. (2019). Publishing research with undergraduate students via Replication Work: the Collaborative Replications and Education Project. *Frontiers in Psychology, 10.* https://doi.org/10.3389/fpsyg.2019.00247

Wagge, J. R., Hurst, M. A., Brandt, M. J., Lazarevic, L. B., Legate, N., & Grahe, J. E. (2022). Teaching research in principle and in practice: What do psychology instructors think of research projects in their courses? *Psychology Learning & Teaching,* 147572572211019. https://doi.org/10.1177/14757257221101942

PART III

Promoting and sustaining class engagement in psychological research methods

10. Using alternative teaching methods to promote student engagement in research methods courses

Bryan K. Saville

For the last several decades, there has been much discussion of the factors that lead students to succeed, or not succeed, in college (e.g., Chickering & Gamson, 1987; Hersh & Merrow, 2005). Not surprisingly, the factors that contribute to college student success are many, varied, and often difficult to isolate. Individual difference variables such as intelligence (Neisser et al., 1996), motivation (e.g., Linnenbrink & Pintrich, 2002), personality (Farsides & Woodfield, 2003), mindset (Dweck, 2006), and passion (Saville et al., 2018) all predict academic success. Conversely, other factors seem to hinder students' ability to succeed in college. Hersh and Merrow (2005), for example, noted that lack of rigorous pre-college preparation, a mismatch between what students want and get from college, and the common belief that college is simply job preparation all have a negative impact on students' success.

Most likely, some of these same factors affect students' performance in research methods courses. In addition, Saville (2008) discussed other factors that impact students' ability to succeed in research methods courses: their lack of interest (at least initially) in 'doing research,' their greater interest in other topics such as abnormal psychology and personality, and a misunderstanding of science in general and of psychology as a scientific endeavor.

In short, success in college, and more specifically success in research methods courses, is likely a multifactorial outcome that is not reducible to some singular trait or specific educational experience. Nevertheless, despite the notion that student success is a complicated construct to understand, researchers have repeatedly identified one mediating factor that seems to connect many of the aforementioned variables to student learning and success – and that factor is student engagement.

10.1 STUDENT ENGAGEMENT

The topic of student engagement can be traced back to the 1930s with the early work of Ralph Tyler, who observed that the amount of time students spent 'on task' was a significant contributor to student learning (see Groccia, 2018). Three decades later, in the 1960s and 1970s, student engagement became an even more prominent part of the educational lexicon with the seminal work of Alexander Astin and Arthur Chickering (Kuh, 2001). In an early longitudinal study on student engagement, Astin (1975) found that nearly every factor that predicted whether students would drop out of college – from place of residence to athletic involvement to faculty-student interactions – could be understood in terms of engagement: the more students were engaged in their college experience, the less likely they were to drop out. Since Astin's early influential work, a plethora of studies has shown that student engagement is predictive of college student learning and success (see Astin, 1993; Chickering & Gamson, 1987; Pascarella & Terenzini, 1991). Moreover, interest in student engagement has only grown in the intervening years, leading Gibbs (2014) to label it 'the latest buzzword' in higher education.

In the years that have passed since Tyler, Astin, and Chickering's early work, researchers have continued to examine not only how student engagement contributes to students' college experiences but also exactly what student engagement entails. Although there has been healthy debate about the construct of student engagement (e.g., Appleton et al., 2008; Carini et al., 2006; Groccia, 2018; Steele & Fullagar, 2009; Wolf-Wendel et al., 2009), Astin (1984/1999) provided a useful starting point for understanding just what student engagement is: Student engagement refers to 'the amount of physical and psychological energy that the student devotes to the academic experience' (1984/1999, p. 518). Although students' subjective experiences are an important part of engagement, Astin ultimately concluded that 'it is not so much what the individual thinks or feels, but what the individual does, how he or she behaves' (1984/1999, p. 519).

Astin also suggested that all 'engagement behaviors' can be placed into one of three categories: student-student interactions, student-teacher interactions, and time on task. In other words, students who interact more with their peers and teachers and who spend more time doing academic (and other college-related) activities are more engaged and, consequently, more likely to succeed during their time in college. This engagement might include going to class consistently, spending several hours per day studying, asking and answering questions in class, getting involved in a research team, attending educational seminars, and participating in various student organizations. Students who 'behave' in these ways are, by definition, more engaged than students who do fewer of those things, even if the latter students spend time thinking about and enjoying their college experiences. And, importantly, behaving in these ways is likely to produce the positive changes in student learning outcomes that typically define 'learning.'

Astin further outlined five postulates of his theory of student engagement: (1) engagement refers to both physical and psychological energy and can be directed both narrowly – say, by studying for a research methods exam – and broadly – say, by joining a professor's research team; (2) engagement lies on a continuum and can change over time; (3) engagement is both quantitative (e.g., how many hours a student studies) and qualitative (e.g., is a student reading 'deeply' or just skimming the words); (4) learning and development are directly related to the quantity and quality of engagement; and (5) the efficacy of any educational practice is a function of its ability to increase student engagement.

Ultimately, Astin's theory, along with the work of others who study student engagement, has important implications for teachers as they consider how to construct their research methods courses. In short, if teachers can find ways to increase how much their students interact with one another, interact with their teachers, and spend more time on task, they can potentially help their students learn and succeed at a higher level than they would otherwise.

There are likely many ways that research methods teachers can increase the extent to which their students are engaged. For example, teachers could incorporate classroom activities (e.g., Saville, 2008; Ware & Johnson, 2013) that encourage or even require students to engage more with the material and with one another, thus increasing time on task and student-student interactions. Teachers could also use personal response systems, or 'clickers,' during their lectures to keep students more attentive (see Morling et al., 2008). Likewise, assigning activities outside of class could increase time on task. Finally, teachers could simply make a more concerted effort to engage with their students, both formally and informally (e.g., Buskist & Saville, 2004; Wilson, 2006), thereby increasing student-teacher interactions. In short, there are likely myriad ways that teachers could positively influence their students' engagement, thereby improving their learning.

Even though these suggestions will likely result in more student engagement, there is another, possibly more systematic way to increase student engagement in research methods courses. And that is by adopting alternative, evidence-based teaching methods that introduce contingencies designed specifically to increase student-student interactions, student-teacher interactions, and time on task.

10.2 ALTERNATIVE TEACHING METHODS

Ultimately, there are numerous alternative methods that teachers could use to provide a more systematic approach to increasing student engagement. Below I highlight a few methods that have been studied specifically in the context of psychology classrooms. This list is not intended to be exhaustive and provides but a glimpse into how teachers can introduce alternative teaching methods into their research methods courses. Although several of the following methods have their roots in non-psychology disciplines, they hold promise for increasing learning in research methods courses given that (1) they promote student-student interactions, student-teacher interactions, and time on task; and (2) their efficacy has been examined empirically.

Before describing these alternative teaching methods, though, I feel it is important to mention one caveat first. Very often, students who have been exposed mostly to traditional, lecture-based teaching methods (see Benjamin, 2002) are resistant to change. They wonder, 'If I can get a good grade by listening to lectures and taking notes, why are you asking us to do something different?' To counter this concern, teachers would do well to spend some time at the start of the semester (and also at various times throughout the semester) explaining to students why they have chosen to use these alternative methods (see, e.g., Saville, 2013). This might entail not only describing the methods in detail but also presenting data showing that these methods have produced positive outcomes in terms of student learning and enjoyment. I have found that providing this context to students can go a long way toward getting them 'on board' early in the semester.

10.2.1 Flipped Classrooms

Although various forms of 'flipped' classrooms have existed since at least the 1960s (e.g., Keller, 1968; Mazur, 1997), the concept of the flipped classroom was (re)introduced by Lage et al. (2000), who described the use of 'inverted' classrooms in their introductory microeconomics course.

A flipped classroom is a classroom in which typical in-class components (e.g., lectures) are moved out of class and replaced with active learning strategies. For example, as Lage et al. (2000) described, prior to class, students might be tasked with reading course material and then getting further review in the form of a prerecorded lecture, PowerPoint slides, a YouTube video, or a podcast episode. Once in class, the teacher might spend a small amount of time answering questions about the material students reviewed before class. After this mini-lecture, students then engage in discussions with their teacher and classmates or participate in other activities that require them to engage further with the material to which they were exposed outside of class. These activities might include answering review questions, completing assignments in small groups, or conducting relevant experiments to further clarify course concepts. Lage et al. (2000) found that both students and teachers viewed the use of flipped classrooms favorably and noted the many benefits of using such a format (e.g., more opportunities to interact with other students and the teacher).

Since Lage et al.'s (re)introduction of the inverted, or flipped, classroom over 20 years ago, it has found its way into many different disciplines, including psychology (see Hussey et al., 2015). In one study using a flipped format, Talley and Scherer (2013) compared exam scores in two sections of an undergraduate physiological psychology course. One section followed a more traditional format (i.e., most classes consisted of lectures), whereas the other section followed a flipped format. In the flipped classroom, students viewed prerecorded lectures on synaptic transmission outside of class and then used class time for practice testing and review. Students in the flipped classroom also constructed presentations in which they 'lectured' about the material they had learned. Talley and Scherer (2013) found that final course grades were about one letter grade higher, on average, in the flipped classroom condition. Students also reported that they perceived the flipped format as helping them to better understand the course material.

In the context of a research methods course, teachers could 'flip' their classrooms by having students watch various prerecorded lectures on experimental design outside of class and then use class time to design an experiment, collect data, and analyze the results. Similarly, teachers could have students read about American Psychological Association (APA) style outside of class and then use class time for writing and additional instruction. Likewise, teachers could have students review material on a specific concept, say random sampling, outside of class and then use class time to complete an activity (e.g., Smith's 1999 activity on sampling, which entails examining whether the distribution of M&Ms in a 'fun-size' pack is the same as the distribution when packs are combined). Ultimately, flipped classrooms provide a great opportunity for teachers to use more active learning strategies to enhance students' understanding of research methods concepts (see Saville, 2008; Ware & Johnson, 2013). And importantly, when carefully constructed, flipped classrooms are likely to increase student-student and student-teacher interactions as well as time on task.

10.2.2 Interteaching

Interteaching is a relatively new teaching method that has its roots in the psychology of learning (Boyce & Hineline, 2002). The theoretical basis for interteaching suggests that modifying the antecedents and consequences of student behavior will decrease undesired behavior and produce a shift toward the more desired behaviors that define 'learning' (e.g., Skinner, 1954/1999). The general procedure for interteaching works as follows (see Boyce & Hineline, 2002 and Saville, 2024 for additional detail). Prior to each class period, the teacher provides students with a preparation (prep) guide consisting of 8–12 items (each of which might contain one or more related questions) covering a specified reading assignment. The questions are typically designed to get students to analyze, apply, and synthesize course material (see Supplementary Material for a sample prep guide). Prior to class, students read and complete the prep guide questions. Once in class, after hearing a short clarifying lecture, students form pairs and discuss their answers to the prep guide items. While students are discussing the material, the teacher moves among pairs, answers questions, and guides students through their discussions, if necessary. Once students are done with their discussions, they submit a record sheet on which they list items from the prep guide that were difficult to understand. The teacher then uses this information to construct a clarifying lecture that begins the next class period, lasts approximately one-third of the session, and focuses on the information that most students asked to review. This lecture time might also provide an opportunity for teachers to include activities that help students to better understand difficult concepts (Saville, 2008; Ware & Johnson, 2013). Following this lecture, students form pairs and discuss the next prep guide.

Since its introduction over 20 years ago, a growing body of research has shown that interteaching tends to produce better student learning outcomes than more traditional teaching methods (for reviews, see Hurtado-Parrado et al., 2022; Querol et al., 2015; Saville, 2024; Saville et al., 2011). For example, in one early study, Saville and colleagues (2006; see also Saville et al., 2005) compared interteaching to lectures in two sections of an undergraduate psychological research methods course. Students in one section experienced the course material via interteaching while the other section heard lectures. Saville et al. (2006) then alternated the teaching methods several times during the semester, counterbalancing the order across sections. Saville et al. (2006) found that students in the interteaching condition consistently scored higher on exams (approximately 10 percentage points, on average) than students in the lecture condition. Moreover, students reported that they enjoyed interteaching more than lecture.

Since those early studies, researchers have found that interteaching transfers nicely to online formats, works well in a variety of disciplines, and is viewed favorably by students (see Saville, 2024 for a recent review). Maybe most importantly, interteaching has produced consistent improvements in student learning outcomes, likely because it has a positive effect on student-student interactions, student-teacher interactions, and time on task (see, e.g., Mason, 2012, and Saville, 2024).

10.2.3 Just-in-Time Teaching

Another teaching method that teachers could use to increase student engagement is Just-in-Time Teaching (JiTT; Novak et al., 1999). Although originally developed for use in physics courses, JiTT has since found its way into multiple disciplines, including biology, chemistry, economics, geology, math, and psychology. With JiTT, teachers provide students with questions – sometimes called 'warm-ups' or 'pre-class questions' (PCQs) – prior to each class. These PCQs are intended to guide students through a particular reading assignment and typically include a few multiple-choice questions and a short-answer or essay question. Students submit their answers to the PCQs anywhere from 1–24 hours before class, typically via a class management system (e.g., Canvas or Blackboard). The teacher then examines students' answers to see what they seem to understand or misunderstand and creates a clarifying lecture 'just in time' for class. Specifically, this lecture entails the teacher reviewing students' answers to the PCQs, showing examples of both 'good' and 'bad' answers. This lecture is typically accompanied by a discussion that involves students and helps them correct any misunderstandings they might have and solidify their knowledge of course concepts. In addition to the PCQs and in-class discussion, teachers might include other cooperative-learning activities that require student interaction and help students better understand the course material. Subsequent PCQs are then constructed based on what students already know and what they need to know moving forward.

To date, a growing body of research has shown that JiTT can promote student learning compared to more traditional teaching methods (Jia et al., 2023). Most of these studies have been conducted in disciplines other than psychology (e.g., Formica et al., 2010). In the field of psychology, Benedict and Anderton (2004) compared JiTT and lectures in two sections of an undergraduate psychological statistics course. Students in the JiTT condition submitted their answers to PCQs online and then discussed the answers with their teacher during class sessions. Students in the lecture condition took reading quizzes at the start of each class and then heard a lecture about the assigned material. Benedict and Anderton found that students in the JiTT section scored significantly higher on a final exam than students in the lecture condition. In addition, students in the JiTT group positively evaluated the method and noted that it had helped them learn the material.

In research methods courses, teachers could use the JiTT format in myriad ways. Like Benedict and Anderton (2004), teachers could have students review material outside of class and then submit answers to PCQs. Class time could then be used to review answers, provide further clarification, and engage in discussion. Likewise, teachers could reserve class time for demonstrations, writing, or study design. Again, there are many possible ways to design a

JITT-inspired course. Regardless, the use of JiTT is likely to have a positive impact on student engagement.

10.2.4 Problem-Based Learning

A fourth teaching method that has been examined extensively and in the context of psychology classes is problem-based learning, or PBL. PBL was first developed in the 1960s for use in medical schools where students were tasked with finding solutions to issues they encountered in clinical case studies. With PBL, teachers construct 'real-world' problems for students to solve. For example, a teacher in a research methods (or abnormal psychology) course might ask students to design a study to see if a given therapy helps clients suffering from social anxiety. Such an 'ill-defined' problem might require students to learn about research methods, social anxiety, classical conditioning (which often forms the basis for effective counterconditioning therapies), ethics, and so on. Students then work, both individually and collaboratively, using course (and potentially non-course) material to come up with valid solutions to the problem. During the process, the teacher acts as a facilitator or guide rather than as a primary source of information. This facilitation usually occurs during meetings or class sessions when students can ask questions as they are working to solve their problem. Importantly, there may be several possible solutions to a problem, and students must provide rationale for why they approached the problem the way they did. Students might present their results in the form of a comprehensive paper, class presentation, or other format. Ultimately, a main premise of PBL is that learning problem-solving skills that transfer to other contexts is just as, if not more, important than learning specific course content, which is likely to change across time (e.g., Connor-Greene, 2005).

Although researchers have examined PBL extensively outside of psychology (Albanese & Mitchell, 1993; Dochy et al., 2003), there have been fewer studies in the context of psychology courses. Nevertheless, studies of PBL in psychology courses have produced positive outcomes. In one such study, Hays and Vincent (2004) used PBL in three graduate-level psychology courses (forensic psychology, applied psychology, and ethics). Students worked in small groups to examine problems relevant to their particular course. At the end of the course, students answered questions pertaining to their perceptions of PBL and how it compared to more traditionally taught courses. In sum, students reported that PBL enhanced student and faculty interactions, critical thinking skills, comprehension of course content, research methods skills, and oral presentation skills.

Connor-Greene (2002) also evaluated the use of PBSL (problem-based *service* learning) in multiple sections of an undergraduate abnormal psychology course. In PBSL, students apply problem-based learning in a community service learning project – in this case, creating community resources for identifying and treating various psychiatric disorders. Connor-Greene described the evolution of the PBSL project across four semesters and identified ways to improve student accountability as well as the overall efficacy of the PBSL process. Students reported that they enjoyed the implementation of PBSL and that it helped them not only to better understand the course material but also to be more aware of other issues that surround psychological disorders (e.g., empathy toward those diagnosed with a disorder). A large majority of students also stated that the PBSL project should continue to be used in future classes.

Although PBL and PBSL have not been examined extensively in psychology, they nevertheless seem nicely suited for use in research methods courses (but see Saville, 2008, for a discussion of how PBL could be incorporated into a research methods course). Given that there are often many ways to examine a research question, or 'solve a problem,' teachers could construct a handful of questions for students to analyze. One example of a PBL topic might be: 'Design a study to see if an intervention based on cognitive dissonance theory could reduce texting while driving in college students.' Students could then work in small groups outside of class to progress toward a possible answer to this question. Class time could be used to 'check in' with teachers, who would provide guidance on what steps students would need to take next to solve their 'problem.' This process would continue until students have produced a favorable answer to their research question. Additional class time could then be used to have students present their results, work on an APA paper, or even construct another research study based on the answer they found for their original question. Moreover, if students had a way to work with college personnel on this problem, it could become a PBSL-based project.

10.2.5 Team-Based Learning

A final method that teachers might consider is team-based learning, or TBL (Michaelsen et al., 2004). With TBL, students are placed into small groups, or teams, of 5–7 students at the start of the semester. The teacher divides the course into units, of which there are typically 5–7 in a traditional semester. Prior to each unit, students prepare by reading course material or reviewing other sources of content (e.g., listening to a podcast) before class. Once in class, students take an individual multiple-choice quiz on the assigned materials. They then take the quiz again as a team, which requires them to discuss the answers and come to consensus on their choices. Teams then receive immediate feedback on the quiz. After receiving this feedback, the team can 'challenge' an answer they got wrong by writing a rebuttal if they feel their answer was correct. Based on the overall class performance on the quizzes, the teacher then gives a short clarifying lecture that covers the material most students seemed to misunderstand. The rest of the unit time (which may include multiple classes) consists of different team-based application activities designed to help students better understand the course material and to build cohesion, both with teammates and with the teacher. A final component of TBL is peer evaluation, which students do several times during the semester. The purpose of the peer evaluations is to increase the chances that each member of a team is engaged and contributing to the other members' learning experiences.

In one study on TBL, Travis et al. (2016) randomly assigned 29 sections of an introductory psychology course (involving approximately 1,100 students) to either TBL or lecture. Students in the TBL sections completed the activities described above (e.g., pre-class preparation, individual and team quizzes, application activities) while students in the lecture condition simply heard lectures about the course material. All students then took a midterm exam and a final exam. Travis et al. (2016) found that students in the TBL condition performed better on both exams and especially on exam questions that pertained to material covered in the application exercises.

In another study, Jakobsen et al. (2014) compared course performance in two sections of an undergraduate developmental psychology course, one of which was lecture based and the other of which implemented TBL. Students in both sections took individual 'readiness' quizzes at the start of each unit. Jakobsen et al. (2014) found that scores on the readiness quizzes were not significantly different, suggesting that students in both sections were spending equivalent time outside of class on the course material. But Jakobsen et al. also found that students in the TBL section outperformed students in the traditional lecture condition in overall course performance. Importantly, Jakobsen et al. (2014) found that the differences were due to different rates of course attendance – students in the TBL section had a higher rate of attendance than students in the lecture section. Jakobsen et al. (2014) suggested that the difference in course performance was because students in the TBL condition were more engaged in class – ultimately spending more time on task and interacting more with their peers and teacher – than students in the lecture condition.

Although the results of TBL studies have been mixed, two recent meta-analyses found that TBL has produced better outcomes than more traditional teaching methods (Liu & Beaujean, 2017; Swanson et al., 2019), providing support for the notion that TBL might be a useful way to improve student learning via student engagement.

In research methods courses specifically, teachers could incorporate TBL by having students first read material or listen to a prerecorded lecture outside of class. Once in class, students could take the typical assessments and then get a brief clarifying lecture about material. As mentioned previously, additional class time could be used for writing, designing a study, collecting data, or participating in demonstrations designed to explain certain course concepts.

10.3 CONCLUSION

In sum, each of the methods described above has been shown to improve student learning outcomes, an important component of college student 'success.' And although empirical evidence is just starting to accumulate (Jakobsen et al., 2014; Mason, 2012), one reason these methods likely produce positive outcomes is that they increase student-teacher interactions, student-student interactions, and time on task – in other words, student engagement. As such, teachers hoping to increase student engagement in their research methods courses would do well to consider adopting one of these alternative teaching methods.

Finally, as I noted earlier in this chapter, regardless of which method teachers might choose to employ in their classrooms – whether lecture-based or one of the alternative methods described above – it is important to remember, as Astin (1984/1999) noted, that finding ways to engage students should be a primary goal for teachers. In addition, because students might initially balk at the use of alternative methods, it is important for teachers to explain thoroughly to students why they are using these methods (see Saville, 2013). Taking the time to create rapport with students (Buskist & Saville, 2004) will likely go a long way to creating a trusting environment in which students are more likely to engage in a way that will ultimately enhance their success in research methods courses and beyond.

REFERENCES

Albanese, M. A., & Mitchell, S. (1993). Problem-based learning: A review of literature on its outcomes and implementation issues. *Academic Medicine, 68,* 52--81. https://doi.org/10.1097/00001888-199301000-00012

Appleton, J. J., Christenson, S. L., & Furlong, M. J. (2008). Student engagement with school: Critical conceptual and methodological issues of the construct. *Psychology in the Schools, 45,* 369–386. https://doi.org/10.1002/pits.20303

Astin, A. W. (1975). *Preventing Students From Dropping Out.* Jossey-Bass.

Astin, A. W. (1984/1999). Student involvement: A developmental theory for higher education. *Journal of College Student Personnel, 40,* 518–529. (Reprinted from *Journal of College Student Development, 25,* 297–308, 1984).

Astin, A. W. (1993). *What Matters in College?: Four Critical Years Revisited.* Jossey-Bass.

Benedict, J. O., & Anderton, J. B. (2004). Applying the Just-in-Time Teaching approach to teaching statistics. *Teaching of Psychology, 31,* 197–199.

Benjamin, L. T., Jr. (2002). Lecturing. In S. F. Davis & W. Buskist (Eds.), *The Teaching of Psychology: Essays in Honor of Wilbert J. McKeachie and Charles L. Brewer,* 57–67. Lawrence Erlbaum.

Boyce, T. E., & Hineline, P. N. (2002). Interteaching: A strategy for enhancing the user-friendliness of behavioral arrangements in the college classroom. *The Behavior Analyst, 25,* 215–226. https://doi.org/10.1007/BF03392059

Buskist, W., & Saville, B. K. (2004). Rapport-building: Creating positive emotional contexts for enhancing teaching and learning. In B. Perlman, L. I. McCann, & S. H. McFadden (Eds.), *Lessons Learned, Vol. 2: Practical Advice for the Teaching of Psychology*, 149–155. American Psychological Society.

Carini, R. M., Kuh, G. D., & Klein, S. P. (2006). Student engagement and student learning: Testing the linkages. *Research in Higher Education, 47*, 1–32. https://doi.org/10.1007/s11162-005-8150-9

Chickering, A. W., & Gamson, Z. F. (1987). Seven principles for good practice in undergraduate education. *American Association for Higher Education Bulletin, 39*, 3–7.

Connor-Greene, P. A. (2002). Problem-based service learning: The evolution of a team project. *Teaching of Psychology, 29*, 193–197. https://doi.org/10.1207/S15328023TOP2903_02

Connor-Greene, P. A. (2005). Problem-based learning. In W. Buskist & S. F. Davis (Eds.), *The Handbook of the Teaching of Psychology*, 70–77. Blackwell. https://doi.org/10.1002/9780470754924.ch12

Dochy, F., Segers, M., Van de Bossche, P., & Gijbels, D. (2003). Effects of problem-based learning: A meta-analysis. *Learning and Instruction, 13*, 533–568. https://doi.org/10.1016/s0959-4752(02)00025-7

Dweck, C. S. (2006). *Mindset: The New Psychology of Success*. Random House.

Farsides, T., & Woodfield, R., (2003). Individual differences and undergraduate academic success: The roles of personality, intelligence, and application. *Personality and Individual Differences, 34*, 1225–1243. https://doi.org/10.1016/S0191-8869(02)00111-3

Formica, S. P., Easley, J. L., & Spraker, M. C. (2010). Transforming common-sense beliefs into Newtonian thinking through Just-In-Time Teaching. *Physical Review Special Topics – Physics Education Research, 6*, 020106. https://doi.org/10.1103/PhysRevSTPER.6.020106

Gibbs, G. (2014). Student engagement, the latest buzzword. *Higher Education Times*. https://www.timeshighereducation.com/news/student-engagement-the-latest-buzzword/2012947.article

Groccia, J. E. (2018). What is student engagement? *New Directions for Teaching and Learning, 2018* (154), 11–20. https://doi.org/10.1002/tl.20287

Hays, J., & Vincent, J. P. (2004). Students' evaluation of problem-based learning in graduate psychology courses. *Teaching of Psychology, 31*, 124–127.

Hersh, R. H., & Merrow, J. (Eds.) (2005). *Declining by Degrees*. Palgrave Macmillan.

Hurtado-Parrado, C., Pfaller-Sadovsky, N., Medina, L., Gayman, C. M., Rost, K. A., & Schofill, D. (2022). A systematic review and quantitative analysis of interteaching. *Journal of Behavioral Education, 31*, 157–185. https://doi.org/10.1007/s10864-021-09452-3

Hussey, H. D., Richmond, A. S., & Fleck, B. (2015). A primer for creating a flipped psychology course. *Psychology Learning & Teaching, 14*, 169–185. https://doi.org/10.1177/1475725715592830

Jakobsen, K. V., McIlreavy, M., & Marrs, S. (2014). Team-based learning: The importance of attendance. *Psychology Learning & Teaching, 13*, 25–31. https://doi.org/10.2304/plat.2014.13.1.25

Jia, S. S., Li, C., & Cui, X. S. (2023). The impact of Just-in-time Teaching model on nursing students' learning in the background of "Internet+": A meta-analysis. *Nursing Communications, 7*, e2023002. https://doi.org/10.53388/IN2023002

Keller, F. S. (1968). "Good-bye teacher..." *Journal of Applied Behavior Analysis*, *1*, 79–89. https://doi.org/10.1901/jaba.1968.1-79

Kuh, G. D. (2001). Assessing what really matters to student learning: Inside the National Survey of Student Engagement. *Change*, *33*, 10–17. https://doi.org/10.1080/00091380109601795

Lage, M. J., Platt, G. J., & Treglia, M. (2000). Inverting the classroom: A gateway to creating an inclusive learning environment. *Journal of Economic Education*, *31*, 30–43. https://doi.org/10.1080/00220480009596759

Linnenbrink, E. A., & Pintrich, P. R. (2002). Motivation as an enabler for academic success. *School Psychology Review*, *31*, 313–327. https://doi.org/10.1080/02796015.2002.12086158

Liu, S. N. C., & Beaujean, A. A. (2017). The effectiveness of team-based learning on academic outcomes: A meta-analysis. *Scholarship of Teaching and Learning in Psychology*, *3*, 1–14. https://doi.org/10.1037/stl0000075

Mason, L. L. (2012). Interteaching to increase active student responding and differentiate instruction. *Behavioral Technology Today*, *7*, 1–15.

Mazur, E. (1997). *Peer Instruction: A User's Manual*. Prentice Hall. https://doi.org/10.1063/1.881735

Michaelsen, L. K., Knight, A. B., & Fink, L. (2004). *Team-Based Learning: A Transformative Use of Small Groups in College Teaching*. Stylus.

Morling, B., McAuliffe, M., Cohen, L., & DiLorenzo, T. M. (2008). Efficacy of personal response systems ("clickers") in large, introductory psychology classes. *Teaching of Psychology*, *35*, 45–50.

Neisser, U., Boodoo, G., Bouchard Jr, T. J., Boykin, A. W., Brody, N., Ceci, S. J., ... & Urbina, S. (1996). Intelligence: Knowns and unknowns. *American Psychologist*, *51*, 77–101. https://doi.org/10.1037/0003-066X.51.2.77

Novak. G. M., Patterson, E. T., Gavrin, A. D., & Christian, W. (1999). *Just-in-Time Teaching: Blending Active Learning with Web Technology*. Prentice-Hall.

Pascarella, E. T., & Terenzini, P. (1991). *How College Affects Students: Findings and Insights From Twenty Years of Research*. Jossey-Bass.

Querol, B. I. D., Rosales, R., & Soldner, J. L. (2015). A comprehensive review of interteaching and its impact on student learning and satisfaction. *Scholarship of Teaching and Learning in Psychology*, *1*, 390–411. https://doi.org/10.1037/stl0000048

Saville, B. K. (2008). *A Guide to Teaching Research Methods in Psychology*. Blackwell.

Saville, B. K. (2013, January). Interteaching: Ten tips for effective implementation. *APS Observer*, *26*. https://www.psychologicalscience.org/observer/interteaching-ten-tips-for-effective-implementation

Saville, B. K. (2024). Research and application for interteaching in higher education. In A. DeSouza & D. Crone-Todd (Eds.), *Behavior Analysis in Higher Education: Teaching and Supervision*, 145–174. Vernon Press.

Saville, B. K., Bureau, A., Eckenrode, C., & Maley, M. (2018). Passion and burnout in college students. *College Student Journal*, *52*, 105–117.

Saville, B. K., Lambert, T., & Robertson, S. (2011). Interteaching: Bringing behavioral education into the 21st century. *The Psychological Record*, *61*, 153–166.

Saville, B. K., Zinn, T. E., & Elliott, M. P. (2005). Interteaching versus traditional methods of instruction: A preliminary analysis. *Teaching of Psychology*, *32*, 161–163. https://doi.org/10.1207/s15328023top3203_6

Saville, B. K., Zinn, T. E., Neef, N. A., Norman, R. V., & Ferreri, S. J. (2006). A comparison of interteaching and lecture in the college classroom. *Journal of Applied Behavior Analysis, 39,* 49–61. https://doi.org/10.1901/jaba.2006.42-05

Skinner, B. F. (1954/1999). The science of learning and the art of teaching. *Harvard Educational Review, 24,* 86–97. (Reprinted in *Cumulative Record, Definitive Edition,* 179–191, 1999. B. F. Skinner Foundation).

Smith, R. A. (1999). A tasty sample(r): Teaching about sampling using M & Ms. In L. T. Benjamin, B. F. Nodine, R. M. Ernst, & C. B. Broeker (Eds.), *Activities Handbook for the Teaching of Psychology, 4,* 66–67). Washington, DC: American Psychological Association. https://doi.org/10.1037/e513682017-001

Steele, J. P., & Fullagar, C. J. (2009). Facilitators and outcomes of student engagement in a college setting. *Journal of Psychology, 143,* 5–27. https://doi.org/10.3200/JRLP.143.1.5-27

Swanson, E., McCulley, L. V., Osman, D. J., Scammacca Lewis, N., & Solis, M. (2019). The effect of team-based learning on content knowledge: A meta-analysis. *Active Learning in Higher Education, 20,* 39–50. https://doi.org/10.1177/1469787417731201

Talley, C. P., & Scherer, S. (2013). The enhanced flipped classroom: Increasing academic performance with student-recorded lectures and practice testing in a "flipped" STEM course. *Journal of Negro Education, 82,* 339–347. https://doi.org/10.7709/jnegroeducation.82.3.0339

Travis, L. L., Hudson, N. W., Henricks-Lepp, G. M., Street, W. S., & Weidenbenner, J. (2016). Team-based learning improves course outcomes in introductory psychology. *Teaching of Psychology, 43,* 99–107. https://doi.org/10.1177/0098628316636274

Ware, M. E., & Johnson, D. E. (2013). *Handbook of Demonstrations and Activities in the Teaching of Psychology: Volume I: Introductory, Statistics, Research Methods, and History.* Psychology Press.

Wilson, J. H. (2006). Predicting student attitudes and grades from perceptions of instructors' attitudes. *Teaching of Psychology, 33,* 91–95. https://doi.org/10.1207/s15328023top3302_2

Wolf-Wendel, L., Ward, K., & Kinzie, J. (2009). A tangled web of terms: The overlap and unique contribution of involvement, engagement, and integration to understanding college student success. *Journal of College Student Development, 50,* 407–428. https://doi.org/10.1353/csd.0.0077

11. The 'Students as Partners' framework in teaching research methods

Sangeeta Gupta, Ethan Fireside and Alyssa Peters

Research methods classes are often regarded as one of the more challenging and least appealing components in traditional psychology programs, as observed both anecdotally and more formally via the literature (Papanastasiou & Zembylas, 2008). Despite understanding their importance and relevance (Turner et al., 2018), students frequently approach these courses with apprehension, viewing these classes as a necessary but dreaded hurdle in their academic journey (Gurung & Landrum, 2013; Gurung & Stoa, 2020). However, when framed as a collaborative and participatory process, research methods can transform from a dreaded obstacle into an avenue for meaningful exploration and intellectual growth. This chapter discusses the 'Students as Partners' (SaP) framework (Healey et al., 2016; Matthews et al., 2018) to rethink how research methods classes are taught. The SaP approach emphasizes collaboration and shared responsibility, fostering an environment where students are not passive recipients of knowledge but active co-creators of their learning experience (Cook-Sather, 2014; Cook-Sather et al., 2014). By involving students in decision-making processes, instructors shift the focus from grades and task completion to curiosity, critical thinking, and intrinsic motivation. The SaP model supports key learning outcomes identified in American Psychological Association (APA) Goal 2: Scientific Inquiry and Critical Thinking, particularly goals 2.1 (exercising scientific reasoning) and 2.2 (designing and evaluating psychological research), by engaging students as active contributors to the research process.

This chapter is itself an example of the SaP framework in practice. The author team consists of a faculty member in collaboration with two undergraduate students, whose contributions reflect not only their perspectives as learners but also their active roles as researchers and co-authors. This process has highlighted the potential of partnership to empower students, bridge the gap between theory and practice, and create opportunities for authentic engagement in academic work. Drawing on existing literature and practical strategies, this chapter outlines specific methods for implementing the SaP approach in research methods courses.

While this chapter focuses on examples from a small in-person research methods class of roughly 25 students, the SaP approach is adaptable to most college courses, emphasizing that students bring valuable insights, skills, and perspectives to the learning process when given the opportunity to do so. By fostering a sense of ownership and shared responsibility, this approach not only enhances student engagement but also prepares them for the collaborative and iterative nature of academic and professional research. Additionally, it aligns closely with APA Goal 4.1 and builds our students' capacity to interact effectively with others. The following chapter provides a framework for educators seeking to adopt this approach and inspire a deeper, more meaningful connection to research methods among their students.

11.1 THE ROLE OF MOTIVATION

Understanding why this approach works requires looking more closely at the role of motivation in learning. Research in educational psychology has regularly studied the role of motivation in achieving positive learning outcomes (Bailey & Phillips, 2016; Kusurkar et al., 2013). Highly motivated students tend to remain engaged longer, acquire knowledge in more coherent forms, and apply what they have learned more effectively (Saeed & Zyngier, 2012). Motivation has been linked to a range of beneficial academic outcomes, including stronger performance and greater persistence in the face of academic challenges (Jang et al., 2009; Ryan & Deci, 2000).

Central to understanding motivation in education is Self-Determination Theory (SDT) which distinguishes between intrinsic and extrinsic motivation (Deci & Ryan, 1994; Ryan & Deci, 2000, 2017). When students are intrinsically motivated and driven by personal interest, curiosity, or the inherent satisfaction of learning, they engage in deeper learning processes that foster long-term academic success. In contrast, students motivated primarily by external rewards, such as grades or praise, often rely on surface-level learning strategies. For example, they might cram information the night before a test or memorize definitions without fully grasping the underlying concepts. This approach often results in fragmented knowledge that lacks meaningful connections, making it difficult for students to apply what they have learned to new problems or retain the information over time. Consequently, while surface-level learners may perform adequately on immediate assessments, they frequently struggle with long-term retention and the transfer of knowledge to real-world contexts.

On the other hand, intrinsic motivation supports active engagement, critical thinking, and meaningful learning; elements essential in a field like research methods, where deep understanding and application are key (Ryan & Pintrich, 1997). However, this type of motivation is not guaranteed, especially in courses that students often take as a requirement rather than out of interest. Research methods, while foundational for psychology majors, is frequently viewed as a 'have-to-take' course rather than a 'want-to-take' course (Earley, 2014). This perceived lack of autonomy can hinder motivation and limit engagement. According to SDT, such perceptions can undermine students' sense of autonomy, a core psychological need that supports intrinsic motivation. When students feel that their actions are externally controlled and dictated by rigid rubrics, instructor-led assignments, or prescriptive tasks, they are less likely to engage deeply or persist through challenges (Jang et al., 2010; Reeve, 2002). In contrast, environments that support student autonomy by offering meaningful choices, acknowledging student perspectives, and connecting learning to students' goals have been shown to enhance motivation, engagement, and learning outcomes (Niemiec & Ryan, 2009).

Therefore, instructional approaches that explicitly support and nurture intrinsic motivation are especially important in research methods instruction. One such approach is the SaP model (Cook-Sather et al., 2014), which directly engages students as collaborators in the learning process and aligns closely with the psychological needs outlined in SDT: autonomy, competence, and relatedness (Deci & Ryan, 1994).

11.2 STUDENTS AS PARTNERS APPROACH AND MOTIVATION

The SaP approach reshapes the traditional dynamics of research methods courses by positioning students as active collaborators in the learning process. Within this model, students and faculty co-create aspects of the course experience, such as via collaborative course design, shared decision-making, and a focus on process over product. By actively involving students in the teaching and learning process, SaP helps fulfill the three core psychological needs identified by SDT: *autonomy, competence, and relatedness* (Deci & Ryan, 1994).

11.2.1 Autonomy

Autonomy is fostered when students are given meaningful choices in their learning, such as selecting research topics that align with their interests, determining due dates for project components, and co-creating rubrics. This sense of agency contrasts with traditional lecture-based research methods courses, which often prescribe rigid structures that can stifle engagement. Research has shown that when students perceive their learning as self-directed, they are more likely to persist in challenging tasks and develop deeper conceptual understandings (Morris, 2019).

11.2.2 Competence

Competence is cultivated through active participation in the research process. In a SaP framework, students take on meaningful roles in designing, conducting, and reflecting on research, often with formative feedback and opportunities for iteration. Rather than just learning about research methods, they practice them, often in messy and unpredictable contexts. This active engagement builds skill and confidence, reinforcing students' belief in their ability to conduct meaningful research, which in turn fuels further motivation (Lopatto, 2007).

11.2.3 Relatedness

Relatedness is reinforced when students feel they are part of a collaborative, supportive learning environment, something that is often missing in traditional research methods courses where power imbalances and a focus on correctness can create anxiety or disengagement (Papanastasiou & Zembylas, 2008). When students work in genuine partnership with each other and with faculty, they are more likely to feel seen, valued, and connected. This sense of belonging is strongly linked to motivation and engagement (Freeman et al., 2007) and it helps create the conditions for deeper learning. When research methods courses are intentionally designed to support these needs, students are more likely to engage meaningfully with the material, think critically about research, and develop a lasting appreciation for the research process (Ryan & Deci, 2000, 2020).

11.3 INCORPORATING STUDENT PARTNERSHIPS INTO ASSESSMENT

11.3.1 Rubric Creation and Self-Assessment

One way to promote student autonomy and competence in research methods courses is through rubric co-creation and self-assessment. Clearly defined and unambiguous rubrics play a critical role in enhancing student learning by providing transparent expectations and consistent criteria for evaluation (Reddy & Andrade, 2010). Traditional grading structures often position students as passive recipients of instructor feedback, where faculty unilaterally define success criteria and students strive to meet these externally imposed standards (Panadero, 2017). This approach can undermine both autonomy and relatedness, and it often emphasizes correctness over growth. In contrast, a SaP-informed approach to assessment positions students as co-creators of evaluative criteria, inviting them to help shape rubrics, identify learning goals, and participate in self- and peer-assessment. This practice fosters a sense of ownership, enhances transparency, and helps students internalize course expectations (Andrade & Du, 2005; Panadero & Jonsson, 2013; Panadero et al., 2023).

As part of their final research paper in the course, students are required to write a literature review that introduces the topic, synthesizes relevant findings, and provides a rationale for their proposed study. To scaffold this complex task, students engage in a rubric-building exercise that encourages critical thinking about what makes a literature review effective and how it differs from related but simpler assignments, such as an annotated bibliography.

Rubric creation steps:

1. Step 1: In the previous semester, students selected a key empirical article relevant to their group project. They explored its cited sources and completed an annotated bibliography summarizing and evaluating several related studies. To create rubrics, students revisit that annotated bibliography and compare it to the literature review section in their original key article. In small group discussions, they identify the differences between an annotated bibliography (which tends to treat sources individually) and a synthesized literature review (which weaves sources together in a logical manner to build an argument). This step helps them shift from a summary-based mindset to a synthesis-based one.
2. Step 2: Working from the key article and its literature review section, each student individually analyzes the structure of that review. They take notes on items such as how the research question is introduced, how studies are grouped or contrasted, how the authors use transitions and synthesis, and how the authors introduce the current study.
3. Step 3: Within their research groups, students share the component lists they generated during Step 2. The instructor then facilitates a whole-class discussion using guiding prompts to focus their attention on what criteria to look for in a literature review. In our research methods class, we have found the following criteria to be most helpful based on student feedback: clarity of argument, synthesis of sources, logical arguments, rationale for study, academic tone, formatting. While students are not required to use these exact criteria, they often find it helpful to have a starting point.
4. Step 4: Within their groups, students select the criteria they believe are most important for evaluating a manuscript-level literature review and develop clear guidelines for each level of performance: 'Excellent,'

'Satisfactory,' and 'Needs Improvement.' For instance, when defining 'Use of Evidence,' they can consider questions such as how many sources are used, how sources are integrated, how much (and what kind of) detail is provided about each source, how citations support the overall argument, and how sources are critically evaluated. Using these reflections, students collaboratively write concrete descriptors that distinguish each performance level, such as what 'Excellent Use of Evidence' looks like compared to 'Satisfactory' or 'Needs Improvement.' The groups then repeat this process for other criteria like 'Clarity of Argument,' 'Organization,' and 'Writing Style,' ultimately creating a draft rubric that can guide their completed literature review.

5. Step 5: After groups create their draft rubric with guidelines for each criterion and performance level, the instructor provides detailed feedback to help refine clarity, consistency, and fairness and adds and adjusts criteria to ensure alignment with the learning objectives of the assignment. Following this revision, each group converts their rubric into a grade contract by specifying exactly how many criteria at each performance level correspond to final course grades. For instance, a recent group submitted this grade contract for their literature review:

A = 90% of criteria rated Excellent, with no criteria rated Needs Improvement

B = 70% of criteria rated Satisfactory or better, with no more than one criterion rated Needs Improvement

C = 50% of criteria rated Satisfactory or better, with up to three criteria rated Needs Improvement

F = More than three criteria rated Needs Improvement

In scholarly publishing, authors develop an understanding of what constitutes an excellent publishable manuscript by critically reading published articles and learning from editorial guidelines and reviewer feedback. Similarly, this classroom activity engages students in making these often implicit standards more explicit, helping them internalize what a high-quality literature review entails and how to critically evaluate their work. By collaboratively developing evaluation criteria and rubrics, students gain insight into the elements that elevate a manuscript from satisfactory to excellent. This approach embodies the SaP framework by involving students directly in shaping assessment criteria rather than passively receiving them. Through this partnership, students experience greater autonomy, develop competence through critical reflection and peer dialogue, and strengthen relatedness by working closely with peers and instructors.

11.3.2 Student Self-Assessment

Beyond co-creating rubrics, self-assessment is another powerful tool that reinforces the SaP approach in research methods courses. Self-assessment involves students evaluating their own work to deepen learning and promote metacognition. Encouraging students to reflect critically on their progress not only enhances autonomy but also fosters a deeper understanding of research concepts by identifying strengths and areas for growth (Andrade, 2019). Encouraging students to assess their progress promotes metacognition, helping them identify strengths and areas for growth while deepening their understanding of research concepts. This emphasis on reflection echoes principles from the ungrading movement, which advocates for feedback-rich, student-centered assessment practices that prioritize learning over point accumulation (Earley, 2014). Self-assessment also enhances critical thinking. By evaluating their own research designs or data analysis, students engage with key concepts and develop skills for independent inquiry. Research shows that when combined with structured reflection, self-assessment boosts intrinsic motivation and promotes deeper learning (Bourke, 2015; Fagerholm et al., 2024).

In the context of research methods, students often submit draft components of their final papers, such as literature reviews, methods sections, or data analyses, and then engage in a structured revise-and-resubmit process. Early self-evaluations help students set personalized goals and measure their progress, while revisiting these reflections after revisions strengthens their sense of agency. This iterative process mimics the scholarly publication cycle, where authors respond to reviewer feedback and refine their manuscripts, thus providing authentic insight into academic practices.

To be effective, self-assessment should encourage metacognition and provide opportunities for students to revise and refine their work, fostering a more active and invested approach to both individual and collaborative learning. This process supports the development of critical reflection skills and helps students take ownership of their learning. In practice, students engage in several key activities, such as rubric-based evaluations and self-reflections, that prompt meaningful analysis of their progress and guide future improvements. The following is an example of how self-assessment can be used when students are working on their IRB proposals.

Note: Previous class sessions have already discussed ethical principles and informed consent procedures, and have created rubrics and guidelines, providing a foundation for the submissions that follow.

1. Step 1: Alongside the initial draft, students complete a short reflection identifying which sections they feel most confident about and which areas they believe need improvement. This encourages goal-setting and fosters early awareness of their strengths and challenges.
2. Step 2: Using the collaboratively created rubric, students assess their own drafts. They assign themselves a tentative score for each criterion and include a brief written justification. For example, students might say: 'I gave myself a 'Satisfactory' in the Risk Assessment category because I identified potential risks but need to clarify how they'll be minimized.' This encourages students to internalize evaluation criteria and think critically about how their work measures up, reinforcing their role as co-assessors in the learning process.
3. Step 3: Students exchange proposals and complete a rubric-based evaluation of a peer's work. They write brief feedback notes for each section and discuss where their assessments aligned or diverged. While self-assessment fosters personal accountability and reflection, peer review enhances learning by exposing students to diverse perspectives and feedback. In research methods courses, peer review mimics the collaborative nature of academic research, shifting assessment from instructor-driven to community-focused. Research shows peer review improves both the quality of student work and understanding of course material (Odom et al., 2009; Orjuela-Laverde & Chen, 2015). It also builds collaboration skills and confidence in giving and receiving feedback, which is crucial in academia and other professional settings. Combining self-assessment with peer review promotes an iterative learning process, encouraging continuous improvement similar to academic publishing.
4. Step 4: After completing peer review, students submit their draft along with their self- and peer-assessments to the instructor. The instructor provides detailed feedback focusing on the expectations of the assignment and the agreed-upon rubric. This input helps students understand higher level expectations and identifies any gaps or misconceptions, in addition to providing the benefit of multiple lines of feedback.
5. Step 5: Students use all the accumulated feedback to create a detailed revision plan with their group. This step reinforces metacognitive skills and encourages students to take ownership of their learning by planning specific improvements before submitting their revised IRB proposals. They also get the autonomy to decide which feedback (if any) to incorporate, fostering critical evaluation and active decision-making in their revision process.

11.3.3 Revise and Resubmit

An important aspect of the SaP approach is creating opportunities for students to develop a mastery mindset. One effective way to foster this is by incorporating opportunities for revision and resubmission of work. Often, students may submit an assignment and then set it aside without further reflection. By allowing them to revise and resubmit, we encourage ongoing learning and reinforce the idea that learning is a continuous process, extending beyond the initial submission (Soysa et al., 2013).

Implementing resubmission reframes the review process as part of the mastery learning experience. Instead of simply identifying mistakes, this approach fosters intrinsic motivation and reduces the pressure to produce 'perfect' work (Armacost & Pet-Armacost, 2003). When students engage in discussions about what constitutes 'A-quality' work, they become motivated to improve and resubmit, striving for their desired grades. This practice builds intrinsic motivation and self-efficacy as students collaborate with instructors and peers to adjust and enhance their work. It is important to reflect on the mindset we want to cultivate in our students. Allowing only a single final submission can reinforce a fixed mindset, where students view their first draft as their final capability. In contrast, encouraging a growth mindset – one that believes students can continually develop their knowledge and skills – empowers them to see revisions as opportunities for growth rather than failures (Tila & Levy, 2023). To implement revision and resubmission in the research methods classroom in alignment with the SaP principles, we implemented two complementary strategies: a feedforward approach and a structured 'Letter to Reviewer' model.

Feedforward begins with students reviewing all feedback received from instructors and peers, using a forward-looking lens to guide their revisions (Carver, 2017). Unlike traditional feedback, which often focuses on identifying what went wrong, feedforward encourages students to think about how they can improve moving forward. The key shift is from a retrospective lens ('What's wrong with this?') to a solution-focused perspective ('How can I improve upon this?').

This approach emphasizes specific, actionable suggestions for refining their work, such as clarifying unclear sections, strengthening arguments, or improving data presentation. It also encourages students to reflect on the feedback in a way that promotes ownership and agency. This helps students decide which suggestions to incorporate and how to prioritize revisions based on their goals and understanding.

Feedforward can be integrated through guided reflection prompts or structured peer discussions. For example, students might be asked to identify two strengths in their draft that they want to maintain or enhance and two areas of improvement highlighted by feedback with concrete strategies to address them. These reflective activities not only support meaningful revision but also deepen students' metacognitive awareness and foster a sense of agency in their learning process.

Research shows that feedforward enhances motivation by reducing anxiety around errors and reframing revisions as opportunities for learning rather than punishment (Sadler et al., 2023).

By encouraging this proactive and reflective mindset, feedforward aligns perfectly with the SaP philosophy, positioning students as active partners in the learning process, rather than passive recipients of judgment.

To extend this approach and more closely mirror the iterative nature of scholarly research, students submit their revised work accompanied by a 'Letter to Reviewers.' This letter functions as a structured space for students to articulate how they addressed major feedback points and to justify their revision choices. Much like in academic publishing, this process encourages transparency, accountability, and thoughtful engagement with their work.

Writing the letter supports students in developing critical reflection and communication skills, as they must consider not only what they changed but why. Additionally, students are given the option to opt out of implementing certain instructor or peer feedback if they can justify their decision. End-of-year student evaluations frequently describe this process as extremely empowering and transformational, with many appreciating that it felt like their voice and judgment were genuinely respected in an academic setting. This process also reinforces the idea that revision is not a sign of failure but an essential and expected part of deep learning. Pairing feedforward with this letter transforms the revision process into a collaborative, empowering experience consistent with SaP's emphasis on shared responsibility and continuous learning.

11.3.4 Incorporating Student Partnerships into the Course Structure

A fundamental aspect of the SaP approach is fostering student ownership not only over their learning but also over how the course progresses. This means structuring the course so that students are active collaborators in managing key elements like deadlines, project choices, and ongoing teamwork. Rather than enforcing rigid instructor-imposed timelines and decisions, we integrate partnership principles into key aspects of the course structure, including:

1. Collaborative due dates: While the final project deadline is fixed, student groups negotiate deadlines for major components such as literature reviews, data collection, or analyses based on their collective calendars and workload. They are provided with a comprehensive list of all components that need to be completed for the final project. Together, we review and discuss realistic time estimates for each item, tweaking deadlines

based on group progress and workload. Students understand that if one step is delayed, it will inevitably cause future tasks to be rushed. Students quickly understand managing these consequences is their responsibility. This collaborative planning encourages proactive time management, accountability, and negotiation skills while keeping everyone aligned with the overall course timeline.
2. Project and analysis decision-making: Groups are given the autonomy to select studies to replicate through the Collaborative Replication and Education Project, evaluating feasibility given constraints like programming skills and the ability to obtain sufficiently large sample sizes. They collaboratively design a 'replication plus' study, making decisions about methodology, data analysis, and ethical considerations. This authentic choice fosters deeper engagement, critical thinking, and ownership of their scientific process.
3. Weekly lab meetings: Research groups hold structured lab meetings where they take minutes, documenting each member's current tasks, specific goals for the upcoming week, and any literature or resources they are reviewing. These minutes also capture challenges or troubleshooting discussions that arise during the meeting. This process ensures reflection and accountability and keeps everyone aligned on progress. By regularly recording and reviewing these details, students develop habits of clear communication, project management, and collaborative problem-solving. The instructor monitors these minutes to provide targeted guidance and to support reflection on the research process, fostering continuous improvement consistent with SaP principles. Please see Supplementary Material for guidelines used in class for lab meeting minutes.

11.4 SUMMARY

This chapter has outlined how the SaP approach can elevate student engagement and outcomes in research methods courses. By integrating practices such as rubric self-creation, collaborative due dates, peer review, self-assessment, and the opportunity to revise and resubmit work, we can create a learning environment that fosters intrinsic motivation, enhances academic performance, and prepares students for the collaborative, iterative work they will encounter in future careers. These strategies not only support students' academic success but also empower them with the tools and confidence necessary to excel both in their studies and in their future endeavors.

11.4.1 Reflections from Student Authors

I entered my research methods class with minimal interest in psychological research, and exited the class with hopes to turn my research into a career. I appreciated how the class provided a true replication of the research and publication process in a low-stakes environment. My media literacy also improved dramatically. What may be more motivating to other students is that I was able to learn real analytical skills worthy of being listed on my resume, something I believe many college students would be interested in.

(Ethan Fireside)

During my research methods course, I had the opportunity to collaborate with a group of students who shared my interests. Being able to contribute to the selection of our semester-long research focus fostered a sense of investment and enthusiasm in my team. This experience not only deepened my appreciation for research but also shifted my perspective – I had never anticipated being drawn to research, yet this project highlighted its significance. As a result, I am now considering how research can play a role in my future career.

(Alyssa Peters)

REFERENCES

Andrade, H. L. (2019). A critical review of research on student self-assessment. *Frontiers in Education, 4.* https://doi.org/10.3389/feduc.2019.00087

Andrade, H. L., & Du, Y. (2005). Student perspectives on rubric-referenced assessment. *Practical Assessment, Research & Evaluation. 10*(1), 3. https://doi.org/10.7275/g367-ye94

Armacost, R. L., & Pet-Armacost, J. (2003). Using mastery-based grading to facilitate learning. *33rd Annual Frontiers in Education, 1,* T3A_20-T3A_25. https://doi.org/10.1109/FIE.2003.1263320

Bailey, T. H., & Phillips, L. J. (2016). The influence of motivation and adaptation on students' subjective well-being, meaning in life and academic performance. *Higher Education Research & Development, 35*(2), 201–216. https://doi.org/10.1080/07294360.2015.1087474

Bourke, R. (2015). Liberating the learner through self-assessment. *Cambridge Journal of Education, 46*(1), 97–111. https://doi.org/10.1080/0305764X.2015.1015963

Carver, M. (2017). Limitations of corrective feedforward: A call for resubmission practices to become learning-oriented. *Journal of Academic Writing,* 1–15. https://doi.org/10.18552/joaw.v7i1.237

Cook-Sather, A. (2014). Student-faculty partnership in explorations of pedagogical practice: A threshold concept in academic development. *International Journal for Academic Development, 19*(3), 186–198. https://doi.org/10.1080/1360144X.2013.805694

Cook-Sather, A., Bovill, C., & Felten, P. (2014). *Engaging Students as Partners in Learning and Teaching: A Guide for Faculty.* Jossey-Bass.

Deci, E. L., & Ryan, R. M. (1994). Promoting self-determined education. *Scandinavian Journal of Educational Research, 38*(1), 3–14. https://doi.org/10.1080/0031383940380101

Earley, M. A. (2014). A synthesis of the literature on research methods education. *Teaching in Higher Education, 19*(3), 242–253. https://doi.org/10.1080/13562517.2013.860105

Fagerholm, N., Lotsari, E., Nylén, T., Käyhkö, N., Nikander, J., Arki, V., & Kalliola, R. (2024). Self-assessment in student's learning and developing teaching in geoinformatics – case of Geoportti self-assessment tool. *Journal of Geography in Higher Education, 48*(3), 414–444. https://doi.org/10.1080/03098265.2023.2251021

Freeman, T. M., Anderman, L. H., & Jensen, J. M. (2007). Sense of belonging in college freshmen at the classroom and campus levels. *The Journal of Experimental Education, 75*(3), 203–220. https://doi.org/10.3200/JEXE.75.3.203-220

Gurung, R. A. R., & Landrum, R. E. (2013). Bottleneck concepts in psychology: Exploratory first steps. *Psychology Learning & Teaching, 12*(3), 236–245. https://doi.org/10.2304/plat.2013.12.3.236

Gurung, R. A. R., & Stoa, R. (2020). A national survey of teaching and learning research methods: Important concepts and faculty and student perspectives. *Teaching of Psychology, 47*(2), 111–120. https://doi.org/10.1177/0098628320901374

Healey, M., Flint, A., & Harrington, K. (2016). Students as partners: Reflections on a conceptual model. *Teaching & Learning Inquiry: The ISSOTL Journal, 4*(2). https://doi.org/10.20343/teachlearninqu.4.2.3

Jang, H., Reeve, J., & Deci, E. L. (2010). Engaging students in learning activities: It is not autonomy support or structure but autonomy support and structure. *Journal of Educational Psychology, 102*(3), 588–600. https://doi.org/10.1037/a0019682

Jang, H., Reeve, J., Ryan, R. M., & Kim, A. (2009). Can self-determination theory explain what underlies the productive, satisfying learning experiences of collectivistically oriented Korean students? *Journal of Educational Psychology, 101*(3), 644–661. https://doi.org/10.1037/a0014241

Kusurkar, R. A., Ten Cate, Th. J., Vos, C. M. P., Westers, P., & Croiset, G. (2013). How motivation affects academic performance: A structural equation modelling analysis. *Advances in Health Sciences Education, 18*(1), 57–69. https://doi.org/10.1007/s10459-012-9354-3

Lopatto D. (2007). Undergraduate research experiences support science career decisions and active learning. *CBE Life Sciences Education, 6*(4), 297–306. https://doi.org/10.1187/cbe.07-06-0039

Matthews, K. E., Dwyer, A., Hine, L., & Turner, J. (2018). Conceptions of students as partners. *Higher Education, 76*(6), 957–971. https://doi.org/10.1007/s10734-018-0257-y

Morris, T. H. (2019). Self-directed learning: A fundamental competence in a rapidly changing world. *International Review of Education, 65*(4), 633–653. https://doi.org/10.1007/s11159-019-09793-2

Niemiec, C. P., & Ryan, R. M. (2009). Autonomy, competence, and relatedness in the classroom: Applying self-determination theory to educational practice. *Theory and Research in Education, 7*(2), 133–144. https://doi.org/10.1177/1477878509104318

Odom, S., Glenn, B., & Cannella, K. (2009). Group peer review as an active learning strategy in a research course. *International Journal of Teaching and Learning in Higher Education, 21*(1), 108–117.

Orjuela-Laverde, M., & Chen, L. R. (2015). Peer review as an active learning strategy in a large first year course. *Proceedings of the Canadian Engineering Education Association.* https://doi.org/10.24908/pceea.v0i0.5908

Panadero, E. (2017). A review of self-regulated learning: Six models and four directions for research. *Frontiers in Psychology*, *8*, 422. https://doi.org/10.3389/fpsyg.2017.00422

Panadero, E., & Jonsson, A. (2013). The use of scoring rubrics for formative assessment purposes revisited: A review. *Educational Research Review*, *9*, 129–144. https://doi.org/10.1016/j.edurev.2013.01.002

Panadero, E., Pérez, D. G., Ruiz, J. F., Fraile, J., Sánchez-Iglesias, I., & Brown, G. T. L. (2023). University students' strategies and criteria during self-assessment: Instructor's feedback, rubrics, and year level effects. *European Journal of Psychology of Education*, *38*(3), 1031–1051. https://doi.org/10.1007/s10212-022-00639-4

Papanastasiou, E. C., & Zembylas, M. (2008). Anxiety in undergraduate research methods courses: Its nature and implications. *International Journal of Research & Method in Education*, *31*(2), 155–167. https://doi.org/10.1080/17437270802124616

Reddy, Y. M., & Andrade, H. (2010). A review of rubric use in higher education. *Assessment & Evaluation in Higher Education*, *35*(4), 435–448. https://doi.org/10.1080/02602930902862859

Reeve, J. (2002). Self-determination theory applied to educational settings. In E. L. Deci & R. M. Ryan (Eds.), *Handbook of Self-Determination Research* (pp. 183–203). Rochester, NY: University of Rochester Press

Ryan, A. M., & Pintrich, P. R. (1997). "Should I ask for help?" The role of motivation and attitudes in adolescents' help seeking in math class. *Journal of Educational Psychology*, *89*(2), 329–341. https://doi.org/10.1037/0022-0663.89.2.329

Ryan, R. M., & Deci, E. L. (2000). Self-determination theory and the facilitation of intrinsic motivation, social development, and well-being. *American Psychologist*, *55*(1), 68–78. https://doi.org/10.1037/0003-066X.55.1.68

Ryan, R. M., & Deci, E. L. (2017). Self-determination theory: Basic psychological needs in motivation, development, and wellness. *The Guilford Press*. https://doi.org/10.1521/978.14625/28806

Ryan, R. M., & Deci, E. L. (2020). Intrinsic and extrinsic motivation from a self-determination theory perspective: Definitions, theory, practices, and future directions. *Contemporary Educational Psychology*, *61*, 101860. https://doi.org/10.1016/j.cedpsych.2020.101860

Sadler, I., Reimann, N., & Sambell, K. (2023). Feedforward practices: A systematic review of the literature. *Assessment & Evaluation in Higher Education*, *48*(3), 305–320. https://doi.org/10.1080/02602938.2022.2073434

Saeed, S., & Zyngier, D. (2012). How motivation influences student engagement: A qualitative case study. *Journal of Education and Learning*, *1*(2), 252. https://doi.org/10.5539/jel.v1n2p252

Soysa, C. K., Dunn, D. S., Dottolo, A. L., Burns-Glover, A. L., & Gurung, R. A. R. (2013). Orchestrating authorship: Teaching writing across the psychology curriculum. *Teaching of Psychology*, *40*(2), 88–97. https://doi.org/10.1177/0098628312475027

Tila, D., & Levy, D. (2023). Increasing students' growth mindset and learning perception by allowing online revision and resubmission in a community college. *Social Education Research*, 23–38. https://doi.org/10.37256/ser.5120243499

Turner, R., Sutton, C., Gray, C., Stevens, S., & Swain, J. (2018). Student experiences of research methods education in college-based higher education. *Research in Post-Compulsory Education*, *23*(3), 348–367. https://doi.org/10.1080/13596748.2018.1490089

12. Redirecting the focus of an online research methods course: Engaging the disengaged

Jisook Park and Darin Challacombe

Younger generations are showing a keener interest in psychology as evidenced by a 72.37% increase in psychology degrees earned in the past two decades (US Department of Education, National Center for Education Statistics, 2022a). The number of graduate students earning master's degrees in psychology also increased by 26.79% between 2010 and 2021 (US Department of Education, National Center for Education Statistics, 2022a). Students' increased interest in mental health, psychological well-being, and psychological factors impacting their daily lives could partially explain why psychology is a highly sought-after major for Generation Z.

Psychology course objectives are cascaded down by the American Psychological Association (APA) *Guidelines For The Undergraduate Major* to develop capacity for scientific inquiry and critical thinking skills and enhance values in psychological science (APA, 2023). The intentional and assessable program outcomes aimed at cultivating scientific mindsets are useful to generate learning outcomes that match national standards for undergraduate programs. The APA has similar guidelines for graduate students (APA, 2018), which are critical in order for students to be trained as scientist-practitioners and engage in evidence-based practice (Hilgard et al., 1947). Aligned with the APA guidelines, undergraduate and graduate research methods courses teach students to think critically, analyze the validity of claims, and apply the scientific method to the information they come across on a daily basis.

As such, integrating research methods courses into the psychology curriculum is consistent with best practices in teaching psychology (Richmond et al., 2022). It is also an effective way to equip psychology students with the knowledge of scientific principles in studying psychology. The understanding and appropriate use of the scientific method are both the underpinnings and core of psychological science (Gurung et al., 2016). Unfortunately, despite the clear significance of a scientific research methods course, the scientific method often imposes a burden on students and instructors (Ciarocco et al., 2017). The disengagement of students in research methods courses is a well-known challenge (Gurung et al., 2016; Strohmetz et al., 2023; Stoa et al., 2022). Moreover, the negative perception of the course at the undergraduate level seems to recur at the graduate level. While there has been a focus on research methods courses, little attention has been paid to master's students completing these courses online. This chapter overviews a few challenges when teaching graduate-level research methods courses and discusses a few suggestions to engage disengaged master's students who take this course online. While focused on graduate students, the same principles can be applied to students in undergraduate courses.

12.1　SIGNIFICANCE OF A RESEARCH METHODS COURSE

APA expects psychology students, both undergraduate and graduate, to demonstrate knowledge of psychology as a science, its core domains, and its research methods (APA, 2018). APA also expects psychology master's students to engage in innovative applications to solve problems based on evidence and employ research interventions when interacting with individuals from diverse sociocultural backgrounds. Adhering to the APA guidelines, most psychology graduate curricula require at the minimum a research methods and behavioral statistics course sequence. Offering these courses is expected and required of a high-caliber master's program. Rossen and Oakland (2008) shared evidence of an increase in the number of research methods courses offered in graduate programs.

One of the key outcomes of a research methods course is to educate students on the basic structures and principles behind research methods, conforming to the scientist-practitioner model (Hilgard et al., 1947; Stoa et al., 2022). A research methods course exposes students to scientific principles and methodologies utilized to examine psychological constructs and teaches students to understand the scientific procedure found in the literature and theories in psychological studies. The strengths of including a research methods course in the curriculum for a psychology master's degree become clear when completing a program evaluation (Stoa et al., 2022). Numerous studies also found enhanced understanding of the foundation of psychological science and the practice of important skills after taking a research methods course (Ciarocco et al., 2017; Strohmetz et al., 2023).

12.2 BARRIERS TO ENGAGEMENT IN A RESEARCH METHODS COURSE

Despite apparent benefits, a research methods course presents challenges to students (Strohmetz et al., 2023; Stoa et al., 2022). Students are not particularly excited about the course content (Rajecki et al., 2005). The fundamental objective of the scientist-practitioner model of graduate training is the reciprocal development of students' research and clinical skills. Conversely, master's students in clinical programs often show a disproportionate focus on clinical skills, which is expected given their career aspirations. Students often lack intrinsic interest in research methods because of the added component of statistics (Rajecki et al., 2005) and they do not see the practical utility of the course. However, knowledge in research methods is the core foundation behind evidence-based practice and data-driven decisions for practitioners.

Secondly, theoretical and abstract subject matters discussed in research methods, along with complex study design elements, often add barriers to student learning (see Cross, Chapter 7, this volume). There is often a higher emphasis or focus on the scientist model in research methods courses to train a scientist-practitioner model (Beck et al., 2014; Campbell et al., 2018; Peluso et al., 2010). Empirical, quantitative research methods are largely considered the gold standard in psychology and, unsurprisingly, controlled experimental procedures and designs are discussed in class. Despite the value of these methods, the theoretical assumptions, constructs, and terminology used in the dominant research methods courses might feel foreign to many students. The seemingly foreign nature of research methods could explain student disengagement in the course. Graduate students' preconceived notions and anxiety toward a research methods course may stem from uncertainty regarding course materials and the negative experiences or lack of concept mastery in their undergraduate research methods course (Ciarocco et al., 2017; Murtonen, 2015).

Lastly, there are intrinsic limitations of an online research methods course. Due to swift changes that had to be made during the COVID-19 pandemic, nearly every university has some experience in online education (Crespi & Amico, 2023; Gurung & Plaza, 2024). With increased popularity of online education (Castro & Tumibay, 2021), more advanced degree programs in applied psychology are offered online (Kraiger et al., 2022). Approximately 2.31 million graduate students have engaged in some type of online education and 1.28 million graduate students had completed their graduate education exclusively online in 2019–20 (US Department of Education, National Center for Education Statistics, 2022b). This is all to say that while online learning remains popular and offers significant flexibility to students, it does come with its challenges.

Isolation, feedback without any personal connections, and lack of (or limited) face-to-face synchronized interactions or hands-on projects are challenging for students in online modalities. For example, due to practical constraints in online research methods courses, it is difficult to utilize individual (or team) project-based teaching, hands-on activities, and data analysis and results based on firsthand data collection, though research shows these activities increase student engagement (Gurung & Stoa, 2020).

We noted similar challenges when teaching online research methods courses at Fort Hays State University (FHSU). Students struggle to connect with the course topics. Students' anxiety, frustration, and disinterest in research methods would often lead to negative learning experiences in class. However, we can improve student experiences by being intentional about integrating research with students' interests. This will open the door to finding pedagogical methods to remove barriers and engage the disengaged students without changing the core learning objectives. Rethinking the core values of a research methods course so that its practical value is more evident is expected to allow students to seek out their own research opportunities as well. As an example of incorporating best practices in teaching research methods online, we provide the case study of our program at FHSU. We first briefly describe our context and then discuss a few effective teaching strategies of our program.

12.3 FSHU ONLINE GRADUATE PROGRAM

Founded in 1902, FHSU is a regional comprehensive public university in Kansas. The total enrollment was 16,922 students in 2024 (13,183 undergraduate students; 45.63% full-time students; 52.97% White). The Department of Psychology offers a bachelor's degree in psychology and master's degrees in clinical and school psychology. The department has a long tradition of science-based teaching and evidence-based practice training that aligns with the APA guidelines. Launched in 2012 (school psychology) and 2021 (clinical psychology), FHSU online master's psychology programs have served approximately 300 students.

The graduate research methods course in the Psychology Department is designed to cultivate scientific mindedness in students – future practitioners – in the capacity they will most likely utilize research in their careers. These skills include scientific reasoning to evaluate the appropriateness of a study design and to understand the merits of psychological research when explaining behavior or solving problems. Both in-person and online research methods courses employ the same learning objectives and core assignments aligned with APA guidelines (see Table 12.1).

The online research methods course prioritizes preparing students to be proficient consumers of research who understand the information and

Table 12.1 Fort Hays State University (FHSU) online psychology graduate research methods objectives and corresponding key assignments

Number	Course objective	Key assignments
1	Define advanced concepts and principles of experimental methods in psychology, evaluate psychological information using scientific reasoning, and critique psychology literature and research as it applies to experimental methods.	Five article review assignments Critique faulty hypotheses Peer review two assignments from classmates
2	Relate psychological research techniques and skills to personal career goals.	Write literature review and methods section for proposed research Locate and describe two published research measures
3	Develop skills appropriate for professional presentations.	20-minute recorded presentation over annotated bibliography
4	Design empirical psychological research for a selected topic.	Design a research study
5	Integrate ethical decisions with experimental methods.	Completion of CITI online ethical research training Write ethically sound methods section for proposed research

critically evaluate findings within the existing literature. The course delivers content asynchronously and includes assessments and assignments to ensure comprehensive learning of research methods (e.g., application problems, article critique, and annotated bibliography). Course materials are designed to be more applicable to student interest, and assignments are placed into the context of their target work environment (viz., clinical and school psychology). Students are trained to evaluate limitations and advantages of the selected design in research that targets the development of research comprehension skills (see Supplementary Material). All assignments are intentionally chosen to strengthen the scientist-practitioner model and to apply a knowledge base and scientific thinking skills to enhance professional identity. For our program, statistics and research methods are taught in two separate courses, though statistics is briefly mentioned near the end of the research methods course in a way that reinforces methodological design.

12.4 EFFECTIVE TEACHING STRATEGIES FOR ONLINE RESEARCH METHODS COURSES

Research methods courses are meant to help students start thinking and processing information like scientists (Strohmetz et al., 2023). These courses facilitate greater critical thinking skills, help students develop study protocols inclusive of ethical considerations (Anderson et al., 2022), foster the grit required for operating within the research space, and guide them to make evidence-based decisions in their professional fields. In the literature, there are several suggested structures to help facilitate the growth of this research grit in graduate students. These structures include focusing on the adult learning model, using peer reviews, and being considerate of ethical concerns in research. For example, as illustrated below, several of these structures were outlined to improve student learning in an online research methods course.

12.4.1 Adult Learning Process

Chilton et al. (2019) suggested that the reinforcement of Caputi's (2010) Adult Learning Model was a key element in their nursing graduate research methods courses. Specifically, students learn best when the content is relevant to their professional lives. This theory is supported by other adult learning designs (Holtslander et al., 2012) but application to the real world is something that has always been challenging in research methods courses, especially since many students will not conduct their own research.

As most of our intended students are future practitioners and will most likely take on consumers-of-research roles, the FHSU online research methods course was structured around allowing students to both appreciate and critique research. This was a central focus of this course so as to enhance student learning outcomes with consideration for the needs of the students we serve (Brown, 2003). One of the ways that our program facilitates appreciation and critiques of research is through article review and annotated bibliography assignments. The annotated bibliography is segmented into smaller sections to make it accessible for students to complete by the end of the semester. Throughout the semester, students learn how to review and critique a series of research articles, focusing on methodologies, implications, and limitations of studies. Students practice targeted article reading and review literature in their selected area of personal or professional interest (e.g., National Association of School Psychologists ten domains of practice).

The five article critique assignments make up 20% of the final grade, and we provide students with a choice of three articles for each of the five assignments. Throughout the semester, students are required to get more granular in their critique, eventually evaluating whether the research method chosen was the best and if there were ethical concerns with the study (see Supplementary Material). The article critique assignments require students to correctly identify the designs, evaluate the merits of such designs when conducting research, and explain how the designs can be used to predict behavior or be applied to the understanding of psychological problems.

These article critique assignments teach students to review research in any format and evaluate whether the study design was appropriate as it relates to the research findings and conclusions. It also fosters the culture of research by allowing students the opportunity to review other research that may be outside the scope of their program. We have carefully curated articles showing different research designs that may inspire curiosity in students. Anecdotally, students have submitted course feedback that stated these article assignments were instrumental in shaping their views of other research methods and were helpful in preparing for comprehensive exams. Students also shared that this assignment was helpful in order to see how various research designs are utilized, acknowledging the value of research applied to their field.

12.4.2 Peer Reviews

Socratic learning methods, where students learn through questions and reflection, have been found to be effective in graduate-level teaching. Pelfrey and Bubolz (2014) approached the Socratic course design for graduate-level criminal justice students completing a research methods course. They found students who were active in writing and critiquing other students' work reported greater learning from the course. We also found similar benefits by utilizing peer reviews on other students' assignments (see Supplementary Material). Twice during the semester, students complete an assignment and upload it for grading by the instructor. They are also required to upload the same assignment for peer review. The assignment has four steps: 1) the student uploads their assignment into the peer review system; 2) the system automatically and anonymously assigns the assignment to another peer; 3) the peer is required to review and provide feedback on the assignment; and 4) the original student is required to review and comment on the usefulness of the peer-reviewed comments. The peer reviewer is graded on their critique. Since all students participate, students gain exposure to both sides of the peer review process and benefit from it (Patchan et al., 2016).

Over the past several years, many students have reported their initial intimidation about the peer review assignment. However, the student feedback has been largely positive. This assignment has the added benefit of fostering diplomacy and grace and facilitates students' understanding of the feedback process. Students saw what it is like to review their peers' assignments, and what it is like to give and receive feedback. Since the feedback is coming from other students, it sometimes created a more raw or visceral reaction. The one receiving the peer feedback can respond in gradients from outright rejection to embraced acceptance. Either way, students learn that in the research space, they can be challenged by different opinions or receive feedback that is difficult to embrace. Peer feedback is found to be an effective tool to encourage revisions and improvement in student writing, and instructors can give specific instructions on peer review (e.g., positive feedback accompanied by localized areas for revision) to encourage implementation of feedback (Patchan et al., 2016).

12.4.3 Self-Initiated Research

Our course is structured to help students take interest in a culture of research. This begins by allowing students to think creatively in a proposed research paper, a form of self-initiated research. This is integral to fostering a research curiosity as students are initially not limited by anything but their ideas of interest.

Self-initiated research is largely dependent upon understanding how to review literature by utilizing databases. Robinson and Uys (2023) found students needed more guidance in using the library, although finding information online seems to be a natural task for current students. One of the key assignments in our program is locating seminal studies for a chosen measure and finding supporting evidence for its psychometric soundness. This helps students to strategically use the library database and better appreciate the development and uses of the measure.

Furthermore, we deliberately encourage students to seek out research opportunities. Several years ago, a student reached out about conducting research on women sex offenders. This student had previously been connected through employment with a woman's correctional facility and found both research questions and a theory while completing course assignments. We worked with the student to shore up the ethical considerations and put them in touch with some of the correct individuals in order to help them move to the next step. With additional guidance, the student was able to pursue this research on their own based on the information they learned in the course and practical usefulness of the material.

12.4.4 Guided Research

A culture of research means mentorship both in and out of the classroom. We foster this by showcasing both student and faculty research, and we connect interested students with faculty who conduct research that parallels the student's interests. Faculty often emphasize that firsthand research is valuable experience for graduate students throughout the course and encourage their involvement in guided research.

About four years ago, a student approached one of the authors about getting more involved in research. This student was a first-generation, remote experimental graduate student interested in doing research beyond what the program required. We had been working on a project regarding attraction preferences of males who have sex with other males. Our interest in this subject came about when we saw data from a non-scientific survey with over 4,000 participants. There was common interest between the student and faculty researcher to better understand the process, and, if it were possible, for predictive analysis to be made. We had previously received approval and conducted a similar survey to critically study unscientific claims made regarding the data.

Before meeting via Zoom, we shared background information on the project and a few of the key references to this research area with the student. During the initial meeting, it was clear the student was well prepared and had the skills to find relevant sources as well as make methodological design changes and suggestions for the survey questions. The student had done his own research and was able to take more initiative with his ideas once he was guided through the research process. These were beyond what he would have learned from just attending the graduate-level research methods courses, but the student's background and experience allowed the research partnership to grow. The student and his mentor made the changes to the design and worked together to run the statistics after data collection. The student suggested a few different statistical tests to help better interpret the data, which allowed him to utilize the statistical knowledge earned in class. The student took the lead and presented the research at a Kansas-based conference in March 2021. The student approached the faculty member to co-author the manuscript, which was eventually published. The simple virtual introduction led to a presentation and publication for a young graduate student. This research would have never happened if the graduate student had not been encouraged to conduct his own research. And this introduction would have never happened had the other faculty members not known we were currently involved in research. This is an example of a culture of research initiated from the course.

12.4.5 Ethical Consideration in Research

In our program, we purposefully discuss ethical issues near the middle of the research methods course after students develop an understanding of various study designs and components. Understanding of ethics is an important part of developing study protocols (Anderson et al., 2022). Regardless of the field, students need to have more than a cursory understanding of the Belmont Report and other ethics specifics (Ponnaiah et al., 2022). With this in mind, our focus is on training students to become well-versed in research risk assessment, rather than limiting research ideas when they focus on the ethics of research. We believe that this way allows students to broaden their research ideas. If research were first approached through the lens of black-and-white ethics, it is likely many social psychology experiments that involved deception would not have been conducted.

12.4.6 Culture of Research

Fostering a culture of research is not about a singular element – it must be cultivated even after completing the course. A student with a great understanding of research protocols may struggle with balancing them alongside ethical considerations, and a student with excellent writing skills may be challenged by receiving a negative review on an article submission. All researchers have struggled at times during their careers, and we created our course objectives with the aim of helping students feel empowered and excited to do research after taking the course. Germain et al. (2018) relayed their own journeys as graduate students in approaching online research. There are many fields where students are only beginning to explore, and it is important for faculty to help shepherd students to explore areas that they have not yet traversed.

How does this work? It requires all those involved in the student's academic pathway to be research champions for students. Faculty could show commitment and passion when teaching a research methods course, be involved in their own research, and encourage students to be part of their research. It is only when this happens that students will learn and be mentored beyond the classroom.

12.5   CONCLUSION

A research methods course might never be a student's favorite, and an online learning modality adds additional challenges. The first challenge is motivating master's students to see the practical value of research methodology in their profession. Another challenge is to connect the learning to real-life application in order to engage students in the course. In this chapter, we examined how one university's online graduate-level psychology program addressed these challenges. While the approaches themselves were not necessarily novel, we have tailored our graduate research methods course to help minimize some of these struggles and maximize the practical utility of the course for our students with the intent to engage the disengaged and foster a culture of research. Based on the adult learning model, we shepherded students to find evidence of how research is utilized in their field of interest, practice systematic research critique and the scientific peer-review process, and develop their own research project they can adopt in their professional field. Both formal and informal student feedback indicated positive acceptance. The use of these approaches is supported in past studies and warrants further empirical validation in today's online learning context.

The greater goal is to share the culture of research where the systematic method of research is recognized and practiced in students' professional field. This culture will be strengthened if students are engaged with the instructor to collaborate on research projects after the course. If student-led research projects are shared with their peers, the disconnect between course material and its application is expected to be reduced, which in turn could increase student engagement in the course. These purposeful, goal-driven instructional approaches in an online research methods course could be promising teaching strategies for engaging students as well as contributing to their professional growth.

REFERENCES

American Psychological Association. (APA) (2018). *APA Guidelines On Core Learning Goals for Master's Degree Graduates in Psychology.* https://www.apa.org/pubs/reports/masters-goals-guidelines

American Psychological Association. (2023). *APA Guidelines for the Undergraduate Major: Version 3.0.* https://www.apa.org/about/policy/undergraduate-psychology-major

Anderson, L., Neil-Sztramko, S. E., Alvarez, E., Jack, S. M., Thabane, L., Scott, F., & Apatu, E. (2022). Development and evaluation of a research methods course in protocal writing for learners in a master of public health program. *The Canadian Journal for the Scholarship of Teaching and Learning, 13*(1). https://doi.org/10.5206/cjsotlrcacea.2022.1.10670

Beck, J. G., Castonguay, L. G., Chronis-Tuscano, A., Klonsky, E. D., McGinn, L. K., & Youngstrom, E. A. (2014). Principles for training in evidence-based psychology: Recommendations for the graduate curricula in clinical psychology. *Clinical Psychology: Science and Practice, 21*(4), 410–424. https://doi.org/10.1111/cpsp.12079

Brown, D. M. (2003). Learner-centered conditions that ensure students' success in learning. *Education, 124,* 99–107.

Campbell, L. F., Worrell, F. C., Dailey, A. T., & Brown, R. T. (2018). Master's level practice: Introduction, history, and current status. *Professional Psychology: Research and Practice, 49*(5–6), 299–305. https://doi.org/10.1037/pro0000202

Caputi, L. (2010). *Teaching Nursing: The Art and Science* (2nd Ed.). College of DuPage Press.

Castro, M. D. B., & Tumibay, G. M. (2021). A literature review: Efficacy of online learning courses for higher education institution using meta-analysis. *Education and Information Technologies, 26*(2), 1367–1385. https://doi.org/10.1007/s10639-019-10027-z

Chilton, J., He, Z., Fountain, R., & Alfred, D. (2019). A process for teaching research methods in a virtual environment. *Journal of Professional Nursing, 35*(2), 101–104. https://doi.org/10.1016/j.profnurs.2018.10.002

Ciarocco, N. J., Strohmetz, D. B., & Lewandowski, G. W. (2017). What's the point? Faculty perceptions of research methods courses. *Scholarship of Teaching and Learning in Psychology, 3*(2), 116–131. https://doi.org/10.1037/stl0000085

Crespi, T. D., & Amico, M. C. (2023). Virtual graduate education? Possibilities and probabilities for a virtuous PhD degree. *Eye on Psi Chi Magazine, 28*(1), 30–35. https://doi.org/10.24839/2164-9812.Eye28.1.30

Germain, J., Harris, J., Mackay, S., & Maxwell, C. (2018). Why should we use online research methods? Four doctoral health student perspectives. *Qualitative Health Research, 28*(10), 1650–1657. https://doi.org/10.1177/1049732317721698

Gurung, R. A. R., Hackathorn, J., Enns, C., Frantz, S., Cacioppo, J. T., Loop, T., & Freeman, J. E. (2016). Strengthening introductory psychology: A new model for teaching the introductory course. *American Psychologist, 71*(2), 112–124.

Gurung, R. A. R., & Plaza, D. (2024). *Higher Education Beyond COVID* (1st Ed.). Routledge.

Gurung, R. A. R., & Stoa, R. (2020). A national survey of teaching and learning research methods: Important concepts and faculty and student perspectives. *Teaching of Psychology, 47*(2), 111–120. https://doi.org/10.1177/0098628320901374

Hilgard, E. R., Kelly, E. L., Luckey, B., Sanford, R. N., Shaffer, L. F., & Shakow, D. (1947). Recommended graduate training program in clinical psychology: Report of the committee on training in clinical psychology of the American Psychological Association. *American Psychologist, 2*, 539–558.

Holtslander, L. F., Racine, L., Furniss, S., Burles, M., & Turner, H. (2012). Developing and piloting an online graduate nursing course focused on experiential learning of qualitative research methods. *Journal of Nursing Education, 51*(6), 345–348. https://doi.org/10.3928/01484834-20120427-03

Kraiger, K., Fisher, S., Grossman, R., Mills, M. J., & Sitzmann, T. (2022). Online I-O graduate education: Where are we and where should we go? *Industrial and Organizational Psychology, 15*(2), 151–171. https://doi.org/10.1017/iop.2021.144

Murtonen, M. (2015). University students' understanding of the concepts empirical, theoretical, qualitative and quantitative research. *Teaching in Higher Education, 20*(7), 684–698. https://doi.org/10.1080/13562517.2015.1072152

Patchan, M. M., Schunn, C. D., & Correnti, R. J. (2016). The nature of feedback: How peer feedback features affect students' implementation rate and quality of revisions. *Journal of Educational Psychology, 108*(8), 1098–1120. https://doi.org/10.1037/edu0000103

Pelfrey, W. V., & Bubolz, B. F. (2014). Hybridizing Socrates: A hybrid approach to teaching graduate research methods. *Journal of Criminal Justice Education, 25*(1), 34–53. https://doi.org/10.1080/10511253.2013.798422

Peluso, D. L., Carleton, R. N., & Asmundson, G. J. G. (2010). Clinical psychology graduate students' perceptions of their scientific and practical training: A Canadian perspective. *Canadian Psychology / Psychologie Canadienne, 51*(2), 133–139. https://doi.org/10.1037/a0018236

Ponnaiah, M., Bhatnagar, T., Ganeshkumar, P., Bhar, D., Elumalai, R., Vijayageetha, M., Abdulkader, R. S., Chaudhuri, S., Sharma, U., & Murhekar, M. V. (2022). Design and implementation challenges of massive open online course on research methods for Indian medical postgraduates and teachers – descriptive analysis of inaugural cycle. *BMC Medical Education, 22*(1), 369. https://doi.org/10.1186/s12909-022-03423-6

Rajecki, D. W., Appleby, D., Williams, C. C., Johnson, K., & Jeschke, M. P. (2005). Statistics can wait: Career plans activity and course preferences of American psychology undergraduates. *Psychology Learning & Teaching, 4*(2), 83–89. https://doi.org/10.2304/plat.2004.4.2.83

Richmond, A. S., Boysen, G. A., & Gurung, R. A. R. (2022). *An Evidence-Based Guide to College and University Teaching: Developing the Model Teacher.* Routledge.

Robinson, Z., & Uys, T. (2023). Determinants of graduate economics student preparation in an online environment. *Cogent Education, 10*(1), 2179835. https://doi.org/10.1080/2331186X.2023.2179835

Rossen, E., & Oakland, T. (2008). Graduate preparation in research methods: The current status of APA-accredited professional programs in psychology. *Training and Education in Professional Psychology, 2*(1), 42–49. https://doi.org/10.1037/1931-3918.2.1.42

Strohmetz, D. B., Ciarocco, N. J., & Lewandowski, G. W. (2023). Why am I here? Student perceptions of the research methods course. *Scholarship of Teaching and Learning in Psychology, 11*(2), 273–283. https://doi.org/10.1037/stl0000353

Stoa, R., Chu, T. L., & Gurung, R. A. R. (2022). Potential potholes: Predicting challenges and learning outcomes in research methods in psychology courses. *Teaching of Psychology, 49*(1). https://journals.sagepub.com/doi/10.1177/0098628320979881

US Department of Education, National Center for Education Statistics. (2022a). Degrees in psychology conferred by postsecondary institutions, by level of degree and sex of student: Selected academic years, 1949–50 through 2020–21. Table 325.80.

US Department of Education, National Center for Education Statistics. (2022b). Number and percentage of graduate students enrolled in distance education or online classes and degree programs, by selected characteristics: Selected academic years, 2003–04 through 2019–20. Table 311.32.

13. Bridging the gap between research and civic engagement through a case study of a culturally responsive research methods course

Lauren Mathieu-Frasier and Reiko Habuto-Ileleji

Psychological research lays the foundation for knowledge about the mind and behavior of individuals, distinguishing itself as a science rather than an intuitive practice. Psychological research did not formally study the role of cultural perspectives before the 1930s. Clark and Clark's (1947) historic work on racial identity development led efforts to diversify psychological research. Driven by the Civil Rights Movement in the 1950s and 1960s, psychologists began to seek out the inclusion of people of color (POC) to fully understand the complexities of their lived experiences. While slow, progress did emerge with the recruitment of diverse participants leading to a better understanding of the impact of culture and race on psychological processes. Today, the role of culture and the fact that human diversity abounds are explicit parts of the American Psychological Association's *Guidelines for the Undergraduate Psychology Major: Version 3.0* (APA, 2023) and the APA Introductory Psychology Initiative's student learning outcomes. This chapter aims to describe an interdisciplinary collaborative research project's alignment with culturally responsive research (CRR) and outline how the undergraduate advanced research methods course aligns with the APA's *Guidelines 3.0* and the transferable skills described in APA's *The Skillful Psychology Student* (APA, 2023; Naufel et al., 2018).

13.1 HISTORICAL REVIEW OF DIVERSITY IN PSYCHOLOGICAL RESEARCH

Historically, most psychological research studies recruited only White participants, designated by the traditional WEIRD (White, Educated, Industrialized, Rich, Democratic) acronym. While the diversity of research participants increased, researchers remained predominantly White. If researchers, particularly White psychologists, impose their worldview and values on research design and interpretation, knowledge of underrepresented groups suffers from skewed outcomes and interpretation of results, further stigmatizing or reinforcing negative stereotypes.

The famous Marshmallow Test from the 1970s underscores the need to not only recruit participants from diverse backgrounds but also consider sociocultural factors when interpreting results. Originally conducted with a sample of mostly White preschoolers attending the Stanford Bing Nursery School, located on Stanford University's campus, psychologists presented a single marshmallow to preschool students, providing the option of eating one immediately or waiting 15 minutes to eat two. Results implied that children who delayed gratification of eating the single marshmallow instead of waiting for 15 minutes for the incentive of a second were more likely to demonstrate self-control, suggesting more positive outcomes later in life. Based on this logic, those who were unable to delay gratification lacked self-regulatory skills needed to become successful (Mischel et al., 1972).

Contrasting the original interpretation, using archival data from the National Institute of Child Health and Human Development Study of Early Child Care and Youth Development, Watts et al. (2018) explored data on children who had been administered a delay-of-gratification test at around four years old. While statistically controlling for socioeconomic status, cognitive ability, and home environment, the predictive power of delayed gratification on academic achievement and behavior was significantly weaker. Rather than interpreting results through a deficit perspective that focuses on what groups lack or internal shortcomings rather than systematic barriers to explain the results, researchers in this study concluded that some children might prioritize an immediate reward due to uncertainty about the future or a potential mistrust in authority figures' promise of attending to their needs. Consequently, Benjamin et al. (2020) surveyed 113 participants from the original Bing Nursery School study when they were in their 40s and found that delay of gratification as a preschooler did not predict various aspects of their financial well-being (i.e., net worth and educational attainment). By intentionally analyzing data from a diverse group of participants, researchers can potentially uncover knowledge that would not be discovered, including nuances in interpretation that would not emerge from a limited sample. Recognizing the key conclusions between the studies underscores the importance of deliberately designing a study with sociocultural contexts in mind and acknowledging diversity in experience, while challenging overly simplistic interpretations often associated with reinforcement of stereotypes.

Of psychological studies that recorded race between 1974 and 2018, Roberts et al. (2020) noted that 42% of the participants were White, 48% were POC, and 10% were unspecified. Recruiting participants from diverse backgrounds represents necessary but minimal movement toward diversifying the knowledge psychological science provides. Despite most participants identifying as POC, minimizing the heterogeneity of the broader classification of POC leads to exaggerated generalizations, misinterpretations, and identifying cultural differences interpreted as deficits. To protect against these risks, researchers can apply CRR practices.

13.2 CULTURALLY RESPONSIVE RESEARCH

Culturally responsive pedagogy, initially described in Ladson-Billings' (1995) seminal article, highlighted teachers of successful African American students. Based on the author's observations and interpretations, she outlined four tenets of culturally responsive pedagogy: teachers' belief in students, viewing teaching as a continuously developing art form, students and teachers seeing themselves as members of the community, and creating teaching opportunities as a way to give back to the community. As a natural advancement from Ladson-Billings (1995), characteristics of a culturally responsive researcher were established, which included:

1. 'is socioculturally conscious;'
2. 'is able to operate from an asset-based framework, seeing all participants' backgrounds as opportunities for research;'
3. 'sees themself as a change agent responsible for creating environments for all participants to be successfully heard;'
4. 'is able to creatively navigate varied participants' communication styles and preferences in order to co-construct knowledge;'
5. 'utilizes the individual participant's story to expand and build their research knowledge base and, we would add, acknowledges the personal perspectives of their identity;'
6. 'seeks the good through research;'
7. 'is reflexive throughout the research process; and'
8. 'cultivates culturally responsive, relationally reflexive research practices' (Lahman, 2022, para. 5)

CRR incorporates and respects cultural values and perspectives while emphasizing community collaboration; ethnic sensitivity; and culturally appropriate study design, implementation, interpretation, and dissemination (Berryman et al., 2013; Gilbert et al., 2023; Roehr et al., 2022). Transformative research, a concept originally coined by Mertens (2017), noted how personal and societal issues should be intertwined to address issues of oppression and discrimination.

Applicable to CRR, Lahman (2022) argues the emphasis of CRR is not on the 'cultural' aspect but on the 'responsive' aspect, as this indicates meaningful engagement with the community. Throughout the process of the research design and dissemination, rather than aiming to use the research process to change and transform, CRR shifts the focus to a commitment of respect for and honor of the community (Berryman et al., 2013; Etherington, 2007). Due to the complexity and variation in research, monolithic strategies to apply CRR principles do not exist (Gilbert et al., 2023). Rather, attentive considerations are needed to enhance research so that it becomes more responsive to the community's needs.

13.3 ALIGNMENT WITH *APA GUIDELINES 3.0*

The process described in our case study directly addresses *APA Guidelines 3.0*, satisfying many of the pedagogical challenges of teaching the research methods class. The *APA Guidelines 3.0* are a set of educational goals and outcomes for undergraduate psychology majors designed to prepare students for professional careers. Six goals (content knowledge and application, scientific inquiry, values in psychological science, communication, psychological literacy and technology, and personal and professional development) correspond to outcomes with foundation indicators for introductory and baccalaureate programs intended to be used by institutions of any size. The course was intentionally designed with the *Guidelines 3.0*'s goals, embedding each of the core competencies, so that students not only engaged in meaningful research but also built workplace readiness skills (APA, 2023).

While addressing all five goals, scientific inquiry, ethical and social responsibility, and professional development were explicitly addressed in this course. Students engaged in discussions with guests and among peers to address complex research challenges, including the core topic, survey selection, and ongoing community support. After reflecting on diversity-related issues, students were empowered to make modifications and adjustments when new information was learned from those of Japanese heritage. Consistent with the *Guidelines 3.0*'s goal of encouraging ethical and social responsibility and behavior to promote strong communities, the unique projects conducted in this class (website development and a philanthropy project) allowed continued engagement with diverse populations (APA, 2023). Furthermore, through firsthand accounts, students began to understand the complexity of sociocultural contexts on the brink of losing their heritage language and culture (practices passed down from family or ancestral background) while developing a multipronged approach to find solutions. Similarly, another of *Guidelines 3.0*'s goals tasks students with refining project management skills. Throughout the academic year, students collaborated within small groups to coordinate a large multi-component project. Understandably, coordinating this project didn't always go as planned; however, students remained flexible and created alternative strategies to meet the goal of supporting families in Indiana who are at risk of losing their heritage culture and language.

13.4 BACKGROUND AND STRUCTURE OF THE STUDENT-LED RESEARCH PROJECT

To provide context about the project, the first author, a psychology instructor, facilitated the small advanced research methods class, while the second author, a Japanese instructor, guided a Japanese language learning class on translating selected study materials. Throughout this chapter, we will be using the term 'individuals of Japanese heritage' intentionally to reflect that not all Japanese consider themselves to be American; nor will some consider themselves to be Japanese. 'Heritage' refers to the language or culture passed down from one's family or ancestral background. Focusing solely on individuals of Japanese heritage in Indiana was an intentional decision, as families living in a predominantly White conservative state may differ in their connection to their cultural heritage as compared to those living in states in which there are enclaves of individuals of Japanese heritage.

Seven students from the Department of Psychological Science were selected to enroll in a 3-credit-hour, 400-level advanced research methods course that spanned the entire academic year. Students were required to complete the introductory research methods class. By instructing students to learn from one another, decide on directions for the project, and make mistakes in a safe environment, this project was generally student led. Rather than using a prescribed course schedule to guide the semester, general due dates for the study materials – review of research, completion of the survey, and IRB submission – were the only guidelines for the pace of the class. Meetings remained flexible to accommodate student interest and unanticipated challenges. Throughout the year, students engaged in CRR, broadening their perspective on psychological challenges faced by those of Japanese heritage in Indiana while also advancing their research skills. Considering the complexity regarding the length of the project and cross-disciplinary approach, each semester had different goals with corresponding student learning outcomes.

BOX 13.1 STUDENT LEARNING OUTCOMES

Course objective: The purpose of the proposed project is to provide students with a high-impact learning opportunity to help conduct a research study about communication and create tangible materials to provide to those of Japanese heritage in Indiana. To meet these goals, students will be expected to:

First Semester

- Integrate knowledge from scholarly research and guest speakers' experiences to create a study relevant to the community;
- Submit study materials to the Institutional Review Board;
- Utilize basic principles of science communication to share psychology-related information with students in the Modern Languages and Classics Department;
- Synthesize empirical research about shared language erosion and language brokering in a written literature review.

Second Semester

- Create conclusions by combining examples, facts, or theories from more than one field of study or perspective;
- Analyze survey results based on established hypotheses;
- Apply study findings to inform the creation of website content;
- Design a website for sharing the results of the study and appropriate resources for those of Japanese heritage in Indiana using UX Design principles.

13.5 FIRST SEMESTER: GUIDING STUDENTS IN DESIGNING CULTURALLY RESPONSIVE RESEARCH

CRR prioritizes meaningful engagement with community stakeholders throughout the research process and emphasizes the co-construction of knowledge. Instead of simply including diverse participants, CRR acknowledges values and lived experiences. The goal is to partner with communities in ways that are respectful, reciprocal, and responsive to their needs (Lahman, 2022; Roehr, 2022). Research methods instructors are tasked with introducing students to unfamiliar abstract concepts and supervising students' first research project while navigating time and resource limitations. Oftentimes, research methods instructors address diversity by highlighting the need for a representative sample or through assigning readings from POC authors. Considering the goal of CRR is to not only recruit individuals of diverse backgrounds but to authentically understand their needs, research methods instructors can implement CRR values within their own course to further align with *Guidelines 3.0*'s philosophical principle of psychology being an 'inclusive discipline.'

Kasouaher et al. (2021) acknowledge that a crucial initial step in CRR is to build academic partnerships and train researchers on culturally responsive practices. Before getting students to understand the nuances of cultural research, we faculty first had to educate ourselves. For the first author, who is not of Japanese heritage, this included learning more about Japanese culture and values. We learned about these CRR practices at the beginning of the project and throughout the academic year, beginning with understanding our own culture. Understanding our own personal worldview serves as a prerequisite to creating an awareness of others' cultures and experiences. Since we are immersed in our own culture, inherent challenges exist due to the limitations of understanding others' cultural backgrounds (Lahman, 2022). A lack of sociocultural awareness that a person's worldview is not universal but rather influenced by life experiences, race, gender, social class, and culture, causes egocentrism. These assumptions often lead to distortions in research findings (Villegas & Lucas, 2007). Whereas psychology instructors often highlight that perceptions are driven through a personal filter, this recognition is even more important in the research methods class where students need to realize that their own cultural biases can impact what they consider robust research or valid findings. Students must understand how their cultural assumptions can influence what they perceive as valid research, which in turn can affect how they design and interpret psychological studies involving diverse populations. When considering the population of interest, research on cultural implications requires an intentional shift in focus to avoid assumptions about intragroup diversity (Roehr et al., 2022).

Connecting with a gatekeeper of the community (who serves as the liaison between the stakeholders and the student researchers) prior to the start of the semester allowed time to build rapport and a confidence that the researcher/community relationship would be reciprocal. The second author, who is of Japanese heritage, served as a gatekeeper between the research project and the community. Among other key aspects of the study, she ensured respectful engagement.

To teach students about how to design CRR, the class met with community members, which provided valuable opportunities to learn about their lived experiences. This instructional choice emphasized the importance of grounding the research in the community. We created meaningful relationships to avoid using the community simply to benefit our own academic needs. Equally important, students learned about communication directly from Japanese community members' personal stories. During these interactions, students summarized the published scholarship on this topic with Spanish-speaking families – a population with which most of this line of research is conducted – to collaboratively theorize if the same results would apply to individuals of Japanese heritage in Indiana. This process allowed students to evaluate if similar patterns might apply to individuals of Japanese heritage. One visitor, a Japanese mental health professional, not only discussed mental health in this community but also spoke about their own experiences living in Japan, the challenges of moving to the United States, and communication within their own bilingual families. Another, who was biracial – Japanese and White – shared their story about differences in communication challenges based on birth order in their family. These stories helped shape the direction of the research, demonstrating the benefit of not using scholarship as the only source of information and reinforcing the value of individuals' perspectives and lived experiences (Villegas & Lucas, 2007). As Kasouaher et al. (2021) notes, collaborative efforts between researcher and community are needed to select a relevant topic that is of importance to both stakeholders. By receiving firsthand accounts of the community members' challenges faced in childhood and adolescence, students combined research concepts with personal accounts to help understand real-life problems.

While meeting with community members and reading research, students engaged in self-reflection activities aimed at understanding the similarities and differences between their own and Japanese culture. An activity conducted by the second author provided roleplay prompts to students. Without sharing the prompt, students were provided with one of two vignettes (see the online Supplementary Material). Group A was prompted to roleplay American communication styles – ask personal questions, engage in intense eye contact, smile a lot, and move closer to the speaker, while Group B was instructed to roleplay Japanese communication styles – avoid eye contact, answer personal questions with contrite answers, refrain from reciprocating questions, and look visibly uncomfortable with others' invasion of their personal space. After 15 minutes, the instructor debriefed students about their reactions to this exercise, leading to a more extended discussion about cultural values, communication, and integration into a culture. Another activity included a direct comparison between normative American and Japanese personal and societal values, using a sliding scale between eight dichotomous values (e.g., hierarchical vs. egalitarian, public vs. private). When debriefed, students supported their perspective based on specific examples from the community members. Notably, when there was a discrepancy between students' ratings, they compared guests' views, continuing to acknowledge the diversity within the population.

In addition to meeting with community members, students reviewed relevant research, leading to discussions of scholarship and identification of the gaps in research while referencing the community members' accounts. After sufficient research review, students collaboratively developed a comprehensive list of potential variables to study in shared language erosion and language brokering: the core topics of the study. After remarking on the number of variables and the potential length of the survey, the group systematically eliminated several, focusing on those most supported by the research and the most relevant based on their discussions with community partners. As part of an in-class activity, they brainstormed testable hypotheses. Then, a few weeks later, this list was revisited to narrow it down to a few key hypotheses. To support their growth in research and ownership of the project, each student identified a specific hypothesis from that list to analyze the data and disseminate the research. Examples of student-selected hypotheses included: 1) Role reversal found within language brokering is associated with worsened child behavior; and 2) Shared language erosion is more prevalent in families who are more established in the United States based on their desire to return to Japan, immigration status, and number of years in the United States.

After condensing the variables of interest, a challenge related to CRR remained; the research team needed to intentionally select the study materials that would be reliable and valid in this population. Acknowledging that a direct translation of the survey would not determine equivalency, researchers needed to ensure cultural and linguistic relevancy through piloting or using previously established reliable surveys (Roehr et al., 2022). Addressing how cultural context contributes to psychometric properties of a study, we used validated versions of the key variables (e.g., perceived stress, sense of belonging) to avoid imposing our individualistic society's value system.

Students were assigned to small groups in line with their own preferences. In the groups, students worked to contribute to a significant portion of the research study. The small group projects focused on: 1) writing a comprehensive literature review; 2) creating materials to communicate the psychological concepts to the Japanese-language students; 3) submitting the IRB application; and 4) building the survey in Qualtrics. Through these assignments, students gained hands-on experience to further develop their research skills previously learned in an introductory research methods class. Table 13.1 outlines these projects and the corresponding CRR values.

13.6 SECOND SEMESTER: DATA ANALYSIS, PROJECT DISSEMINATION, AND COMMUNITY PARTNERSHIP

In the second semester, the psychology students selected another small project to lead. The options included data analysis, website development, written content of the website, or a philanthropy project. To collaborate and support the community, the class created a website and participated in a student philanthropy project. Students built a sustainable website, which future students would be able to update, sharing the results of the study and resources to benefit those of Japanese heritage (Kasouaher et al., 2021). Because of their growing awareness about the importance of maintaining heritage culture and language in a conservative Midwestern state, students bridged the gap between research and real-world implications by acting as grant-makers and learning

Table 13.1 First semester student-led projects

	Project	Pedagogical purpose	CRR application
Group 1	Written literature review of 8–10 scholarly sources	Reviewed the literature and introduced the foundational concepts before meeting with community members.	Guests' lived experiences and stories served as sources of information in co-creating the direction of the study. Students and guests discussed scholarship as it related to their own experiences to determine relevancy and importance of these topics to those of Japanese heritage.
Group 2	Creation of science communication materials	Due to the interdisciplinary collaboration between the psychology and Japanese departments, psychology students created science communication materials (infographics and videos) to translate research-specific jargon which the Japanese-language students would need for translating portions of the survey.	Since a direct translation of a survey does not imply equivalency, it was important that students in the Japanese class learned general survey concepts – construct validity, order effects, and importance of using validated surveys – rather than creating their own questions or editing the language used. Without reliable and valid surveys, we risk imposing our values and perspectives on participants.
Group 3	Submit IRB application	Students were guided through the IRB application process to gain hands-on experience in ethical principles of working with a vulnerable population.	While preparing the IRB application, students considered ways to ethically and respectfully conduct research with individuals who are not proficient in English.
Group 4	Build survey in Qualtrics	While creating the survey, students expanded their proficiency working in Qualtrics, ensuring that the survey was functional in English and Japanese.	Students considered strategies for creating a survey for all participants to be successfully heard regardless of their language preference.

from non-profits, culminating in a university-sponsored donation to one of these organizations. Table 13.2 outlines these projects.

13.7 STUDENT REFLECTIONS

Integrating CRR into a small advanced research methods course provides students with an opportunity to develop transferable skills. According to *The Skillful Psychology Student* (Naufel et al., 2018), psychology education promotes five overarching skills: cognitive, communication, personal, social, and technological. These competencies were reflected in students' end-of-course reflections, demonstrating how CRR-based research experiences can promote both academic and professional growth.

Student 1:
I am walking away from this project not only with a better understanding of research, but also awareness of differences between cultures, respect for Japanese people and their culture, skills I can apply to my own life, and a new outlook…

Student 2:
As a psychology and data analytics student, I see each of the skills I gained, cross-cultural communication, interdisciplinary collaboration, and research, as valuable and plan to continue using them in my academic and professional career.

Arguably, the most important outcome of the course was students' interest in advocacy. While students learned about the psychological challenges of losing one's heritage language, they applied this knowledge to pressing societal needs, reflecting the *Guidelines 3.0*'s integrative theme of using psychological knowledge to 'change lives, organizations, and communities in a positive way' (APA, 2023). Through the philanthropy project, students learned from several non-profit organizations that promote the preservation of Japanese culture and language in different ways. Some organizations had a broad reach to a general audience, and others were structured and stable non-profits with secure funding from Japan. Ultimately, students selected a small non-profit Japanese language school that not only teaches K-12 students the Japanese language and culture but also helps children navigate cultural challenges, including how to respond to questions from peers at school or handle situations that may make them feel othered.

At the time of this class, an opportunity arose to consider the societal and policy shifts occurring in the state. The Indiana House Education Committee introduced a bill proposing to eliminate Indiana's Certificate of Multilingual Proficiency (CoMP) program. The CoMP provides high school students with the opportunity to earn a certificate and an annotation on their transcripts demonstrating their achievement in an 'Intermediate High Level' of proficiency in

Table 13.2 Second semester student-led projects

	Project	Pedagogical purpose	Connection to CRR
Group 1	Build a sustainable website of resources and study results	Students designed a website and applied research methods principles to survey community members about the functionality and content.	This project modeled research transparency and how to 'seek the good through research' by encouraging the creation of a website to share research findings and relevant resources with the community. Students engaged stakeholders in the design process to make the research outcomes and resources more useful and culturally relevant (Roehr et al., 2022).
Group 2	Philanthropy project	A student philanthropy project is a high-impact practice that provides students with an opportunity to understand social problems in the local community through hands-on experience of learning more about the community's needs and how local non-profit organizations offer support (Olberding, 2009). Philanthropy projects contribute to philanthropic tendencies, fostering a greater willingness to donate to charities and increase community engagement (Benz et al., 2020).	By learning from local non-profits working to sustain heritage culture and language, students became more socioculturally conscious, learning about generational trauma and the impacts of loss of cultural identity (Kasouaher et al., 2021).
Group 3	Data analysis	Because students had previous experience in analyzing data, they further developed these skills while critically thinking about the implications of the results.	Interpretation of the data was an intentional process, considering how values (maintaining harmony, emotional restraint) can differ between cultures, potentially impacting the meaning of the results.
Group 4	Create website content	While one group built the website, another group wrote the content to be used. Students translated scientific jargon into understandable language to communicate the preliminary results of the study and resources.	To exemplify the transparency of the study, students considered how the information was presented, using culturally appropriate language and tone. Rather than only sharing the results, students aimed to add resources, normalize specific cultural experiences, and empower families.
All students	Dissemination of project(s)	Students presented posters at regional and university conferences, modeling authentic methods for disseminating research.	Throughout the poster presentations, students framed the study within social and cultural contexts and used inclusive, respectful language.

one or more languages other than English. Students discussed how the consequences of the removal of this program transcend beyond the high school students' transcripts and how language opens the door to learning about culture and others' experiences. Closing the door to languages other than English in the classroom limits cultural understanding. For the heritage language speakers, especially children who hear this message, it encourages them to further move away from their heritage language.

13.8 CONCLUSION

This case study demonstrates how CRR can be integrated into an advanced research methods course, offering a model that can be adapted for both introductory and advanced classroom settings. Students developed transferable skills relevant in academic and workforce settings. While working on teamwork, collaboration, and critical thinking, students' newly acquired knowledge of the challenges faced by an underrepresented community granted them an opportunity to advocate and support approaches through the creation of a sustainable website and grant donation. CRR laid the framework for this yearlong project, enabled introductory research methods courses to incorporate the tenets of CRR – collaboration, support, and engagement of the community members of interest – at each step of the research process to foster students' understanding of diverse groups, and promoted stronger communities through the application of psychological research methods.

REFERENCES

American Psychological Association (APA). (2023). *APA Guidelines for the Undergraduate Psychology Major: Version 3.0.* https://www.apa.org/about/policy/undergraduate-psychology-major

Benjamin, D. J., Brown, S. A., Brown, T. C., DellaVigna, S., Diamond, P. A., & Noah, A. (2020). Predicting mid-life capital formation with pre-school delay of gratification and life-course measures of self-regulation. *Journal of Economic Behavior & Organization, 179*, 761–780. https://doi.org/10.1016/j.jebo.2019.08.016

Benz, T. A., Piskulich, J. P., Kim, S., Barry, M., & Havstad, J. C. (2020). Student philanthropy and community engagement: A program evaluation. *Innovative Higher Education, 45*, 17–33. https://doi.org/10.1007/s10755-019-09484-8

Berryman, M., SooHoo, S., & Nevin, A. (2013). *Culturally Responsive Methodologies.* Emerald Publishing Limited.

Clark, K. B., & Clark, M. P. (1947). Racial identification and preference in Negro children. In E. L. Hartley (Ed.), *Readings in Social Psychology,* 169–178. Holt, Rinehart & Winston.

Etherington, K. (2007). Ethical research in reflexive relationships. *Qualitative Inquiry, 13*(5), 599–616. https://doi.org/10.1177/1077800407301175

Gilbert, C., & Pasque, P. A. (2023). Defining culturally responsive research: Learnings and tensions in minoritized researcher perspectives. *Journal of Diversity in Higher Education*, 18(4), 453–467. https://doi.org/10.1037/dhe0000522

Kasouaher, M., Shore, N., Culhane-Pera, K., Pergament, S., Batres, R., Castro Reyes, P., M., & Richmond, A. (2021). Strategies to enhance culturally responsive research: Community research recommendation tool. *Progress in Community Health Partnerships: Research, Education, and Action*, 15(3), 413–418. https://doi.org/10.1353/cpr.2021.0042

Ladson-Billings, G. (1995). Toward a theory of culturally relevant pedagogy. *American Educational Research Journal*, 32(3), 465–491. https://doi.org/10.3102/00028312032003465

Lahman, M. (2022, August 17). Culturally responsive research ethics. *SAGE Research Methods Community*. https://researchmethodscommunity.sagepub.com/blog/culturally-responsive-research-ethics

Mertens, D. M. (2017). Transformative research: Personal and societal. International Journal for Transformative Research, 4(1), 18-24. https://doi.org/10.1515/ijtr-2017-0001

Mischel, W., Ebbesen, E. B., & Zeiss, A. R. (1972). Cognitive and attentional mechanisms in delay of gratification. *Journal of Personality and Social Psychology*, 21(2), 204–218. https://doi.org/10.1037/h0032198

Naufel, K. Z., Appleby, D. C., Young, J., Van Kirk, J. F., Spencer, S. M., Rudmann, J., & Richmond, A. S. (2018). *The Skillful Psychology Student: Prepared for Success in the 21st Century Workplace*. American Psychological Association. https://www.apa.org/careers/resources/guides/transferable-skills.pdf

Olberding, J. C. (2009). Indirect giving to nonprofit organizations: An emerging model of student philanthropy. *Journal of Public Affairs Education*, 15(4), 463–492.

Roberts, S. O., Bareket-Shavit, C., Dollins, F. A., Goldie, P. D., & Mortenson, E. (2020). Racial inequality in psychological research: Trends of the past and recommendations for the future. *Perspectives on Psychological Science*, 15(6), 1295–1309. https://doi.org/10.1177/1745691620927709

Roehr, P., Irrgang, M., Watari, H., & Kelsey, C. (2022). Considering the whole person: A guide to culturally responsive psychosocial research. *Methods in Psychology, 6*, Article 100089. https://doi.org/10.1016/j.metip.2021.100089

Villegas, A. M., & Lucas, T. (2007). The culturally responsive teacher. *Educational Leadership*, 64(6), 28–33. https://pdo.ascd.org/lmscourses/PD13OC002/media/Module6_CulturallyResponsiveTeacher.pdf

Watts, T. W., Duncan, G. J., & Quan, H. (2018). Revisiting the Marshmallow Test: A conceptual replication investigating links between early delay of gratification and later outcomes. *Psychological Science*, 29(7), 1159–1177. https://doi.org/10.1177/0956797618761661

PART IV

Teaching about statistics and research tools in psychological research methods

14. 'It is impossible to run a full experiment in one term!' Using secondary datasets to create effective short-term research projects

Jacqueline A. Goldman

Providing students with hands-on research experience is a critical component of higher education, especially in fields such as psychology, education, and social sciences. Further, having research skills is part of the *APA Guidelines for the Undergraduate Psychology Major: Version 3.0* and the APA Introductory Psychology Initiative (IPI) student learning outcomes (APA, 2021, 2023). However, the traditional approach of conducting primary research presents significant challenges. Students often face constraints related to time, ethical approval, participant recruitment, and data collection (Johnston, 2017). Given these limitations, secondary data analysis emerges as an effective alternative, allowing students to engage in meaningful research without the logistical barriers of primary data collection (Cheng & Phillips, 2014). This chapter explores the advantages of using secondary data, ethical considerations, limitations, and best practices for analysis. Additionally, this chapter provides pedagogical strategies for integrating secondary data analysis into research methods courses.

Before psychology majors enroll in dedicated research methods courses, foundational exposure to research concepts often occurs in introductory and specialized classes. These early courses familiarize students with the scientific method, encompassing hypothesis formulation, data collection, analysis, and interpretation, thereby fostering critical thinking skills essential for evaluating psychological information. For instance, introductory psychology textbooks emphasize the importance of empirical evidence and outline research methods including descriptive and experimental approaches (Gurung & Christopher, 2020). Such early integration of research principles across the curriculum ensures that students build a robust foundation, preparing them for more advanced methodological training in subsequent courses.

14.1 WHY A SECONDARY DATASET?

The university I work at runs on a quarter system; that means 10 weeks total from going over the syllabus to when we are handing out final exams (11 weeks if we're lucky!). Within that short time, our research methods students (an upper division writing-intensive course) are expected to go through all the steps of creating a study; collecting, analyzing, and interpreting data; and writing a full psychological study. One of those steps by itself can take weeks, and within this timeframe students have a plethora of other responsibilities that are pressing on their time and resources. Within our field of practice, we give journal reviewers, who are experts in their field and have years of practice, 4–6 weeks to give feedback on already written manuscripts. Expecting undergraduate students to conduct a full research project in a similar time allotment does not allow for work that lends itself to quality or an adequate reflection of true practice in the field. Speeding up the research process can mean sacrificing key steps that should be given adequate time for focus and revision. Furthermore, for many students, the terminology of research methods is challenging in itself (see Cross, Chapter 7, this volume). One way we can give students back substantial time and increase the quality of projects is through using a secondary dataset.

Collecting original data requires substantial time, sometimes financial resources, and ethical considerations, all of which can be challenging for students working within the constraints of a semester-long course. Even instructors I know that do collect data often constrain themselves to descriptive or correlational studies or suffer from small sample sizes and are consequently underpowered. Using secondary data, which has already been collected and processed by other researchers or organizations, allows students to focus on developing analytical and critical thinking skills rather than navigating complex institutional review board (IRB) approval processes and recruitment challenges (Rimando et al., 2015). Secondary data often provides access to large, representative samples that students might otherwise be unable to obtain, thereby improving the reliability and generalizability of their findings (Cheng & Phillips, 2014).

The use of secondary data supports students in honing their statistical analysis and interpretation skills instead of spending too much time focusing on data collection and insufficient sample sizes. Because these datasets are often derived from well-designed studies with rigorous methodologies, students can engage with high-quality data (pre-registered datasets with reliable and valid scales) while learning to apply statistical analytical techniques (Cheng & Phillips, 2014). This approach also helps students develop a deeper understanding of the research process by exposing them to real-world data limitations, such as missing values or measurement inconsistencies, which they must learn to address (Woods et al., 2021). Leveraging secondary data in a research methods course provides an efficient, ethical, and educationally valuable alternative to primary data collection, enabling students to engage meaningfully with the research process without being hindered by logistical constraints.

14.1.1 Cost-Effectiveness and Time Efficiency

One of the most compelling reasons for incorporating secondary data analysis into student research is its significant cost-effectiveness and time efficiency. Unlike primary data collection, which requires extensive planning, time to factor in obtaining IRB approval, and time spent collecting data, secondary data is readily available through various academic, government, and industry sources (Johnston, 2017). This accessibility eliminates the burdens associated with designing surveys, conducting interviews, or performing experiments, making research more feasible for students, especially those with limited resources. Beyond time savings, secondary datasets allow instructors to provide more scaffolding on the course content and methodology. When students are not focused only on designing survey instruments or managing experimental logistics, they can instead devote more effort to developing proficiency in statistical methods, data visualization, and interpretation techniques and allow faculty to focus on teaching these core skills as well (Smith, 2008).

14.1.2 Access to Large and Longitudinal Datasets

A unique component of secondary data is its ability to provide access to large-scale and longitudinal datasets, which are often beyond the reach of individual students to collect independently. The scope and scale of such data, encompassing diverse populations over extended periods, make it possible for students to explore complex and multifaceted research questions that would be impractical, if not impossible, to investigate through primary data collection (Vartanian, 2011). Instead of students running basic analyses on minimal sample sizes with low statistical power, students can analyze interesting interactions and predictions of variables or look at changes over time. Only about 4% of undergraduate psychology students will go on to a research-focused PhD program (APAn, 2017) where they will need the skills to develop and conduct their own research project from start to finish, but all students will benefit from knowing how to clean, analyze, and interpret real-world data.

14.1.3 Real-World Data and Practical Research Experience

Using secondary data provides students with the opportunity to engage directly with real-world datasets, offering an experience that closely mirrors the kind of research conducted in both academic and professional settings. Unlike the more controlled environment of primary data collection, secondary data often comes with inherent challenges, such as missing values, inconsistencies, and biases. This exposure to 'messy' and complex datasets is an essential skill for students aspiring to careers in data analysis, policy research, social science, and many other fields that rely on large-scale data (Bishop & Kuula-Luumi, 2017). In professional settings, analysts and researchers frequently work with incomplete, unstructured, or imperfect data, and being able to navigate these challenges effectively is a key component of their skill set.

By engaging with secondary data, students not only practice data cleaning and preparation techniques, such as handling missing data or resolving discrepancies, but they also gain practical experience in working with large datasets that span various variables, sources, and time periods. This process involves sorting through vast amounts of data, identifying patterns, and making informed decisions about how to deal with outliers, measurement errors, and conflicting information. Such hands-on experience is crucial in fostering students' abilities to think critically and develop the problem-solving skills necessary to draw accurate conclusions from data—skills that are highly valued in many sectors, including healthcare, economics, policy, and business.

When students use secondary data, they must evaluate the credibility of the data collection methods and sources, assessing whether the data was collected ethically and whether it accurately represents the populations or phenomena being studied. For example, when working with survey data, students may need to consider factors like sampling bias, question design, or the social context in which the data was collected. These evaluations encourage a more sophisticated understanding of research design and methodology, as students learn that even well-established datasets can have inherent flaws that need to be considered when interpreting results (Tripathy, 2013). In my courses, we go through landmark ethical dilemmas that have come out of our field, discuss why they are unethical, and then brainstorm how we can prevent them in the future (many students mentioning pre-registration as a helpful method to prevent bad data practices).

14.2 LIMITATIONS OF SECONDARY DATA

Despite its numerous advantages, secondary data analysis comes with certain limitations that students and instructors must be mindful of when designing and conducting their research. While secondary data provides access to large, rich datasets, it does not offer the same level of control over the data collection process as primary research does. One of the primary concerns associated with secondary data analysis is the lack of control over data collection methods. Since students did not design or implement the original study, they must accept the methods used by the original researchers, which may not always align with their own research objectives. For example, the variables of interest to a student may not have been measured or operationally defined in the way that best suits their research questions, or the data may be limited in scope due to the focus of the original study. This misalignment can pose challenges for researchers trying to answer specific questions or test hypotheses that were not part of the initial research design (Dunn et al., 2015). To encourage students to embrace secondary data analysis, it is helpful to highlight the unique opportunities it offers. By utilizing existing datasets, students can focus more on developing their analytical and interpretive skills, engaging with complex data without the time and resource constraints of primary data collection. This approach allows them to explore large-scale or longitudinal data that would otherwise be inaccessible, providing a broader context for their research questions. Emphasizing these advantages can help students appreciate the value of secondary data in conducting meaningful and efficient research.

One component to be wary of when choosing your dataset is that secondary data has the potential for outdated information, particularly in the case of datasets that are several years or even decades old. Many secondary datasets, especially those from long-term studies or government surveys, may not reflect current trends or societal changes. For example, a dataset collected in the early 2000s might not capture the impact of recent technological advancements, changes in political or economic contexts, shifts in social attitudes such as no longer defining gender as a binary, or how early datasets may not allow for current ways of identifying race or gender which are defined on a spectrum. For example, a student studying the effects of social media on adolescent mental health may find it challenging to work with datasets that were collected before social media platforms like Instagram and TikTok became widespread, as these platforms may have unique impacts that older datasets do not capture. As a result, students must critically assess the relevance and timeliness of the secondary data they choose to use. If the data does not reflect the current environment or address the issues that are most pressing today, the findings could be less meaningful or applicable to contemporary problems and will lack generalizability (Vartanian, 2011). Similarly, a dataset focused on labor market trends from the early 2000s may fail to reflect the effects of recent economic disruptions, such as the COVID-19 pandemic or the rise of the gig economy.

Using secondary data offers efficiency and access to large datasets, but it also entails certain limitations that are worth mentioning. One significant drawback is the lack of hands-on experience in data collection, which can impede students' understanding of the complexities involved in gathering data firsthand. This includes challenges such as designing appropriate methodologies, ensuring data quality, and addressing ethical considerations. Without this experience, students may miss out on developing critical skills necessary for conducting comprehensive research. Additionally, secondary data may not align perfectly with the specific research questions or contexts students are exploring. Since the data was collected for different purposes, there might be gaps or inconsistencies that limit its applicability. This can restrict students' ability to draw accurate conclusions or fully understand the nuances of their research topics. Although these are detriments in using a secondary dataset, the benefits in having access to more complex datasets that can offer more interesting and complicated analyses may outweigh these limitations.

The lack of involvement in the data collection process can also make it more difficult for students to understand the nuances of how the data was gathered. Without the ability to directly interact with participants or observe the collection process, students might miss important contextual details or subtle biases inherent in the data collection methods. This lack of familiarity with the original study design can make it harder to fully interpret or critique the data, especially when dealing with complex, multi-layered datasets. While secondary data analysis presents certain challenges such as limited control over data collection methods and potential misalignment with specific research objectives, it also offers significant advantages.

By utilizing existing datasets, students can engage with complex, real-world data, allowing them to focus on developing analytical and interpretive skills without the time and resource constraints of primary data collection. This approach not only provides access to large-scale or longitudinal data that would otherwise be inaccessible but also enables students to explore broader contexts for their research questions. Emphasizing these benefits can help students appreciate the value of secondary data in conducting meaningful and efficient research. Building on this understanding, secondary data analysis can be effectively applied in educational research to analyze trends and psychological phenomena with real data, making the impact of the practice more compelling for students.

14.3 PRACTICAL APPLICATIONS IN EDUCATIONAL AND MENTAL HEALTH RESEARCH

14.3.1 Analyzing Trends and Psychological Phenomena Using Secondary Data

Students in education and psychology courses can leverage secondary data to examine educational trends, disparities, and policy impacts. For example, data from the National Center for Education Statistics provides insights into student achievement, school funding, and teacher effectiveness. By analyzing such data, students can explore questions related to educational inequality, the effects of socioeconomic status on academic performance, or the impact of standardized testing policies (Goyette, 2008).

If students wish to look more specifically at psychological and social phenomena, the General Social Survey (GSS) would be a good source, as it provides extensive data on a wide array of topics, including public opinion, social attitudes, and demographic trends. This dataset is invaluable for students interested in exploring social issues such as political beliefs, mental health trends, social identity, and public attitudes toward various societal issues. The GSS, conducted by the National Opinion Research Center, has been a crucial resource for understanding societal changes over time and can help students investigate how factors like education, age, and geographic location influence social and political views (Smith et al., 2019). For instance, students could use the GSS to study the evolution of political polarization in the United States over several decades or examine how shifts in public opinion align with major cultural or political events.

In addition to political and social attitudes, the GSS provides valuable data on mental health trends, allowing students to analyze how mental health perceptions and diagnoses have changed across different demographic groups over time. Data from the GSS can help students track the prevalence of conditions such as depression or anxiety and explore potential contributing factors such as socioeconomic status, access to healthcare, or influences of the pandemic (Smith et al., 2019). Similarly, the Healthy Minds Study (HMS) dataset can be used by students to examine trends in college student mental health by formulating research questions related to psychological well-being, access to mental health services, and demographic differences in mental health outcomes. The HMS has collected data from hundreds of colleges and universities across the United States, making it one of the most robust sources of information on mental health trends among young adults in higher education (Healthy Minds Network, 2023). The dataset is particularly notable for its breadth and depth, covering a wide range of mental health indicators, such as depression, anxiety, suicidal ideation, substance use, and overall well-being. Additionally, HMS includes information on students' attitudes toward mental health services, their help-seeking behaviors, and structural barriers to accessing care, which allows researchers to examine not just mental health outcomes but also systemic and personal factors influencing mental healthcare utilization.

Both the GSS and HMS provide students with the opportunity to explore psychosocial phenomena within a broader societal context, offering insights that go beyond individual behavior and delve into how social structures, cultural norms, and public policy shape psychological and social outcomes. These datasets also allow students to engage with large-scale, longitudinal data that would be difficult to gather through primary data collection, helping to build critical research skills such as data analysis, interpretation, and the ability to recognize patterns across diverse populations. There are a plethora of other secondary datasets widely available for student use that provide students a unique opportunity to engage with interesting variables and diverse subject pools that would never be feasible for students to collect on their own in a semester or even during a course sequence. For instance, in my research methods course, we use the HMS dataset from 2022. Since it is a robust dataset, I cut down the variables accessible to students from 200+ to just 75. This gives students autonomy in choosing what variables they want to see interact, but does not overwhelm them with the burden of choice. This study recruits mostly from the United States, but offers a much more diverse dataset in terms of gender, race, and generation status with over 90,000 participants.

14.4 PEDAGOGICAL STRATEGIES FOR INCORPORATING SECONDARY DATA PROJECTS INTO RESEARCH METHODS COURSES

There is no denying the benefits of using a secondary dataset for a research methods course when it comes to the opportunities for unique analyses, diverse subject pools, longitudinal data, and complex research questions (Johnston, 2017; Smith, 2008). For some, the drawback of a secondary dataset is the complication of inserting the dataset into the course structure and providing appropriate pedagogy to get the most out of the project while also allowing students the autonomy to choose projects and designs that still fit their interests.

Instructors can begin by providing students with pre-approved datasets that align with the course's learning objectives. The key is to select datasets that are both accessible to students and sufficiently rich to allow for meaningful analysis. Many of the publicly available datasets, like the previously mentioned GSS and HMS, come with highly structured codebooks and copies of the questionnaires. Unfortunately, sometimes too much choice can be overwhelming for students. For example, the HMS dataset has at least 50 variables within the standard modules, which do not include the elective modules. Giving students full access to the entire dataset with seemingly unlimited choice can create decision fatigue and frustrate them (Iyengar & Lepper, 2000). To help navigate this issue, some pre-work on datasets is highly encouraged. Just because you are given access to the full dataset does not mean your students also need access to ALL the data. Choosing 20–30 variables that may be of interest to your students will empower students to have autonomy in their research questions but also limit decision fatigue as well as streamline some of the process of weeding out research questions that are too overwhelming or complex.

Once the dataset has been cleaned and truncated, instructors can guide students through the research process, helping them to formulate specific research questions that are both manageable and relevant to the dataset. For example, students might begin by asking broad questions about social behaviors, such as 'How do socioeconomic factors influence smoking rates across different states?' or more focused questions, like 'What is the relationship between age and physical activity levels in urban populations?' This step is essential because it helps students develop the skill of narrowing down broad topics into clear, actionable research questions that can be answered through secondary data analysis. Given that their research questions will be guided by data that is already available, the question of statistical power and relevance is easily answered.

Instructors can also help students break down the research process into smaller, manageable steps, including:

- Data exploration: Students should first familiarize themselves with the dataset, understanding its variables, structure, and limitations. This step might involve creating summary statistics, visualizing key trends, and identifying any issues with missing data or measurement error.
- Data cleaning and preparation: Students will need to clean the data by addressing issues such as missing values, outliers, or inconsistencies in variable definitions. This step provides an opportunity to teach students valuable data manipulation skills, such as recoding variables, handling missing data, and checking for outliers. This can also include scoring the dataset, as some latent variables may need to be calculated. If this step does not seem feasible in a shortened term (did I already mention my term is only 10 weeks long?) this step can be done ahead of time by the instructor.
- Data analysis: After preparing the dataset, students can proceed with statistical analyses that are appropriate for their research questions. This could involve descriptive statistics, regression analysis, or hypothesis testing, depending on the nature of the research question. Instructors can guide students in selecting the most suitable analytical techniques and interpreting their results accurately.
- Interpretation and presentation of findings: The final stage of the assignment involves interpreting the results considering the original research question and preparing a clear, well-structured report or presentation. Instructors can teach students how to present their findings in a way that is both accessible and rigorous, emphasizing the importance of communicating results effectively to both academic and non-academic audiences. This might include creating visualizations, writing a concise summary of the findings, and discussing the implications of the results. Box 14.1 is an example of the discussion section assignment I provide in my research

methods course after we have gone over specific examples of data interpretation and connection to literature in class.

BOX 14.1 EXAMPLE OF A DISCUSSION ASSIGNMENT

Learning Outcomes

- Summarize results and explain how they fit with current research on the topic.
- Examine the limitations and future directions of a research project.

Instructions

The discussion section of any research paper provides the interpretation of your results considering what is already known about the topic of your work. The discussion always ties back to the introduction section in that you will likely refer to the questions, hypotheses, and literature you already discussed. However, it should not merely be a restatement of those ideas. Instead, the discussion section tells us how your study has moved forward from the place where you left off. Fundamental questions to answer within your discussion section are:

- Do your results provide answers to your testable hypotheses? If so, how do you interpret your findings?
- Do your findings agree with what others have shown? If not, do they suggest an alternative explanation or perhaps an unforeseen design flaw in your study (or others' studies)?
- Given your conclusions, what is our new understanding of the problem you investigated and outlined in the introduction?
- If warranted, what would be the next steps in 'your' study? For example, what other experimental questions or methods should be studied next (based on what we now know)?

Throughout this process, instructors can provide continuous support through feedback and reflection, helping students refine their analysis, improve their interpretation of the results, and ensure that their conclusions are grounded in the data. By guiding students through these steps, instructors also help them develop essential research skills, including critical thinking, statistical reasoning, and the ability to assess the quality and limitations of data.

As students confront challenges like incomplete datasets and measurement errors, they learn to think critically about how data is collected and interpreted in various fields of research. This helps them build confidence in their ability to navigate the complexities of secondary data analysis and apply these skills to future academic and professional endeavors. Remember, research is messy. There will be mistakes and some publicly available datasets may not be as rigorous or use the theoretical frameworks or operational definitions that students are used to. That is indeed part of the research process, and getting students to experience the mess in a more scaffolded and resourced format will be overall more helpful for their enjoyment and long-term engagement in quantitative research methods.

14.5 CONCLUSION

The utilization of secondary data in student research projects presents a powerful opportunity for hands-on learning while addressing many of the logistical challenges associated with primary data collection. Unlike primary research, which often involves time-consuming and resource-intensive processes such as recruiting participants, conducting surveys, or running experiments, secondary data analysis allows students to bypass these challenges and immediately engage with real-world data. This not only saves time and financial resources but also provides students with the chance to focus on challenging and timeconsuming components, such as data analysis, interpretation, and critical evaluation and dissemination of the findings. Further, with this experience students can participate firsthand in replication work and the Collaborative Replication and Education Project if they are looking to create projects that would give them experiences to add to their CVs (Wagge 2019).

By leveraging existing datasets, students can delve into complex research questions without the need for starting data collection from scratch. For example, they may analyze long-term trends in social behaviors using national surveys or explore health outcomes using data from public health databases. These datasets, often collected by governmental agencies, research institutions, or non-profit organizations, are typically rich in detail and span large samples, offering students the opportunity to examine issues at a scale that would be difficult or impossible to achieve with primary data collection. This exposure to high-quality secondary data allows students to engage in rigorous, real-world research that mirrors the work of professional researchers and policy analysts.

In addition to providing exposure to large-scale datasets, secondary data analysis enhances students' analytical skills by requiring them to work with pre-existing data that may have imperfections, such as missing values, measurement errors, or changes in data collection methods. By working through these challenges, students gain valuable experience in data cleaning, data manipulation, and statistical analysis – skills that are highly sought after in both academic and professional settings. Through these tasks, students learn how to handle data efficiently, select appropriate analysis techniques, and draw valid conclusions based on their findings. These experiences are not only beneficial for their immediate academic goals but also prepare them for future research roles in academia, industry, or government.

Educators play a crucial role in facilitating this process. Instructors not only provide students with guidance on how to use secondary data effectively but also ensure that they understand the ethical implications of working with pre-existing data. This includes teaching students how to properly cite data sources, handle sensitive information with care, and adhere to ethical research standards such as maintaining confidentiality and avoiding biases in data interpretation. By supporting students through the research process and providing constructive feedback, educators help foster a deeper understanding of data analysis and reinforce ethical standards in research.

As the availability of secondary data continues to grow, its integration into both undergraduate and graduate research will remain an invaluable pedagogical tool. The increasing accessibility of datasets from a variety of disciplines – such as health, education, economics, sociology, and psychology – provides students with a wealth of material to explore complex social phenomena, test hypotheses, and engage in interdisciplinary research. Furthermore, many of these datasets are accompanied by documentation that helps students understand how the data was collected, the measures used, and the limitations of the dataset. This transparency is essential for fostering research literacy and helping students develop the analytical skills they need to navigate complex datasets effectively.

In an era where big data and data science are becoming integral to many professional fields, engaging with secondary data equips students with the tools to excel in these domains. The ability to analyze large datasets and extract meaningful insights is increasingly important across industries, from public health and economics to marketing and social policy. By incorporating secondary data analysis into academic curricula, educators ensure that students are prepared to meet the demands of the data-driven job market and engage in meaningful, evidence-based research.

REFERENCES

American Psychological Association. (2017, October). Datapoint: The state of psychotherapy training. *Monitor on Psychology.* https://www.apa.org/monitor/2017/10/datapoint

American Psychological Association. (2021). *APA Introductory Psychology Initiative (IPI) Student Learning Outcomes for Introductory Psychology.* https://www.apa.org/about/policy/introductory-psychology-initiative-student-outcomes.pdf

American Psychological Association. (2023). *APA Guidelines for the Undergraduate Psychology Major: Version 3.0.* https://www.apa.org/about/policy/undergraduate-psychology-major.pdf

Bishop, L., & Kuula-Luumi, A. (2017). Revisiting qualitative data reuse: A decade on. *Sage Open*, *7*(1), 1–15. https://doi.org/10.1177/2158244016685136

Cheng, H. G., & Phillips, M. R. (2014). Secondary analysis of existing data: Opportunities and implementation. *Shanghai Archives of Psychiatry*, *26*(6), 371–375. https://doi.org/10.11919/j.issn.1002-0829.214171

Dunn, K., Arslanian-Engoren, C., DeKoekkoek, T., Jadack, R., & Scott, L. D. (2015). Secondary data analysis as an efficient and effective approach to nursing research. *Western Journal of Nursing Research*, *37*(10), 1295–1307. https://doi.org/10.1177/0193945915570042

Goyette, K. A. (2008). College for some to college for all: Social background, occupational expectations, and educational expectations over time. *Social Science Research*, *37*(2), 461–484. https://doi.org/10.1016/j.ssresearch.2008.02.002

Gurung, R. A. R., & Christopher, A. (2020). Teaching the foundations of psychological science. In J. Zumbach, D. Bernstein, S. Narciss, & G. Marsico (Eds.), *International Handbook of Psychology Learning and Teaching*. Springer International Handbooks of Education. Springer. https://doi.org/10.1007/978-3-030-26248-8_20-1

Healthy Minds Network. (2023). Healthy Minds Study among colleges and universities, year 2023. Healthy Minds Network, University of Michigan, University of California Los Angeles, Boston University, and Wayne State University. https://healthymindsnetwork.org/research/data-for-researchers.

Iyengar, S. S., & Lepper, M. R. (2000). When choice is demotivating: Can one desire too much of a good thing? *Journal of Personality and Social Psychology*, *79*(6), 995.

Johnston, M. P. (2017). Secondary data analysis: A method of which the time has come. *Qualitative and Quantitative Methods in Libraries*, *3*(3), 619–626. https://www.qqml-journal.net/index.php/qqml/article/view/169

Rimando, M., Brace, A., Namageyo-Funa, A., Parr, T. L., Sealy, D.-A., Davis, T. L., Martinez, L.M., & Christiana, R. W. (2015). Data collection challenges and recommendations for early career researchers. *The Qualitative Report*, *20*(12), 2025–2036. https://nsuworks.nova.edu/tqr/vol20/iss12/8

Smith, E. (2008). *Using Secondary Data in Educational and Social Research*. McGraw-Hill Education.

Smith, T. W., Davern, M., Freese, J., & Morgan, S. L. (2019). *General Social Surveys, 1972–2022: Cumulative Codebook*. National Opinion Research Center.

Tripathy, J. P. (2013). Secondary data analysis: Ethical issues and challenges. *Iranian Journal of Public Health*, *42*(12), 1478–1479. https://www.ncbi.nlm.nih.gov/pmc/articles/PMC4441947/

Vartanian, T. P. (2011). *Secondary Data Analysis*. Oxford University Press.

Wagge, J. R. (2019). Publishing research with undergraduate students via Replication Work: The Collaborative Replications and Education Project. *Frontiers in Psychology*, *10*. https://doi.org/10.3389/fpsyg.2019.00247

Woods, A. D., Davis-Kean, P., Halvorson, M. A., King, K. M., Logan, J. R., Xu, M., Bainter, S., Brown, D., Clay, J. M., Cruz, R. A., Elsherif, M. M., Gerasimova, D., Joyal-Desmarais, K., Moreau, D., Nissen, J., Schmidt, K., Uzdavines, A., Van Dusen, B., & Vasilev, M. R. (2021). Missing data and multiple imputation decision tree. *PsyArXiv*. https://doi.org/10.31234/osf.io/mdw5r

15. Measure once: Covering measurement in a research methods course

Rosalyn Stoa

> (Measurement) is the logical basis of quantitative science with all its mathematical beauty, conceptual scope, empirical power, and practical utility
> Michell (1997, p. 358)

Measurement is the backbone of good research. Without quality scales and assessments, nothing in research can be considered valid or reliable. Unfortunately, many psychology undergraduate (and, in many cases, graduate) curricula do not offer or require a course in measurement (McKelvie, 2000; Meier, 1993; Friedrich et al., 2018). Despite repeated calls for coursework in psychological testing and measurement (Aiken et al., 2008; Lambert, 1991; McGovern et al., 1991), most students will have very little exposure to psychometric concepts. Even when covered, measurement concepts are challenging for undergraduates in a research methods course (Stoa et al., 2022). If a student's school is not one of the 5–9% of undergraduate psychology programs that require students to take a psychometrics and testing course (Friedrich et al., 2018; Norcross et al., 2016), where will they learn the basics of measurement?

I argue that the *very basics* of scale development deserve more attention in a research methods course. Very few undergraduate psychology curriculums offer a measurement course (Friedrich et al., 2018), and less than half of all psychology graduate students will take a measurement course (Aiken et al., 2008). This results in poorly understood measurement of constructs (Henson et al., 2010; White & Stovner, 2024), substandard reporting of psychometrics (Henson et al., 2010; Hole, 2015; Hussey & Hughes, 2020), and ultimately leads to the development of conceptually inadequate, invalid, and unreliable measures. The lack of instruction related to measurement exacerbates the replication crisis in psychology and emboldens ignorance when using scales in applied settings (Hussey & Hughes, 2020; Lilienfeld & Strother, 2020; Neal et al., 2020). In this chapter, I acknowledge the shortcomings of undergraduate- and graduate-level measurement training with the hope of making measurement principles more accessible to all.

Often, measurement and psychometrics are treated as secondary topics in research methods, with perhaps a lecture on reliability, where students are expected to recognize statistics like Cronbach's Alpha or understand the value of test-retest reliability. We assume that if they intend to continue in research, they will learn more about psychometrics at the graduate level. Recall, however, that *your research methods class may be the only experience they ever have with research,* and it's highly likely that your students will end up in a business-related job (Thomas, 2018; CWS, 2019a) where *they may eventually need to make and evaluate a survey.*

What students learn about scale development and measurement in a research methods class may be one of the *most* valuable things they can take from that class. Whether your students continue into graduate training or pursue an applied role after graduation, understanding the basics of scale development can enhance a student's marketability (Finney & Pastor, 2012; Leventhal & Thomson, 2021). Indeed, students in my research methods class tend to report the lectures on measurement and scale development as very practically relevant, saying:

> 'The first big takeaway I would say was the selecting and creating valid measures material. I can quite confidently say that, in an applied setting, the way I would now search for, decide on, create, or adapt a measure to gain some clarity or insight into a construct is vastly different than what I would have done prior to this course. It's a perfect example of something that seems obvious to do now, but I am not sure I would have given the attention to [it] prior to having to practice and justify doing it in this class.'
>
> '[An] important takeaway for me has been sharpening the way in which I create measures. When creating surveys in the past, I had not previously inspected existing research to understand what scales exist and have been validated. This seems so obvious now, as it's important to make sure the way I'm measuring constructs is in fact valid and reliable. In research for various class assignments, I have even noticed overlap between existing scales and surveys that my company publishes for "employee listening efforts." Connecting these dots has been valuable for me, and when I am creating future scales, I will first start by exploring what already exists in published research, and how I can perhaps utilize or adapt that.'
>
> 'My first takeaway was the distinction between selecting a valid measure versus creating one. Recognizing the characteristics of valid measure and being able to select one that aligns with specific research needs is a critical skill in many psychology roles. Equally important is the ability to create a valid measure when necessary. This process requires an understanding of validity principles, ensuring the tools developed meet the standards of research and application.'

Introducing measurement and scale development into a research methods class does not need to be an overwhelming process. Simply conveying key components to identify and craft effective items can be enough to inspire students to engage with these concepts more deeply than they otherwise might.

Drawing from my experience teaching undergraduate measurement (in-person) and master's-level research methods (online), I will discuss the structure and content of the classes devoted to measurement and various strategies to help students develop a nuanced understanding of measurement principles in a research methods course.

15.1 CLASS STRUCTURE

My master's-level research method class spends two weeks on measurement. In these two weeks, they have two lectures, two chapters, two discussions, two assignments, and a handful of journal articles. The weeks are divided into (1) selecting valid measures and (2) creating valid measures.

15.1.1 Teaching Selecting Valid Measures

There are two learning objectives for the week of selecting valid measures:

1. Interpret reliability and validity evidence to evaluate published measures of psychological constructs.
2. Choose appropriate measures to fit a particular research goal and context.

This week is designed to teach students how to identify what makes a good scale and find validated scales in the literature. In the lecture, we discuss the basics of classical test theory. I emphasize that *all measurement has error,* and we can reduce that error by using valid (i.e., accurate) and reliable (i.e., consistent) scales. This tends to create a 'huh, I suppose that makes sense' reaction for many of them. Before this week, I recommend covering the basics of validity as it relates to research (i.e., construct, statistical, internal validity, and external validity). Ensure these are reviewed before introducing the validity of measurement as many students find validity conceptually challenging (Stoa et al., 2022). Validity in measurement can be introduced as overlapping with previously learned views of validity as applicable; approaches to validity in measurement support the validity of the research overall.

15.1.1.1 Class content
In this week, I introduce reliability as 'the degree to which variance in test scores is due to real variance (differences) among people and not due to error' (Rindskopf, 2001). This is a more complicated definition than students tend to expect, and I give them a moment to process this definition. I simplify this technical definition to 'the stability of scores' and 'given nothing else changes, will you get the same results if you repeat the measurement?' I emphasize that

the higher the error, the lower the reliability. For example, suppose a survey about mood was administered to different people under different conditions (e.g., on different days, in different environments, or with poorly worded questions). Test scores may fluctuate widely due to those external factors, leading to high error and low reliability. However, suppose the mood survey was administered under the same conditions for all people. In that case, any differences in scores are likely reflective of true individual differences, resulting in lower error and higher reliability. This is a great time to introduce classical test theory (i.e., observed score = true score + error; see DeVellis, 2006, 2017 for more) and discuss the flaws and biases inherent to research and measurement that introduce error. In this time, I use the bullseye example to demonstrate how something can be reliable but not valid or valid but not reliable (Figure 15.1). In this diagram, hits on a target demonstrate how something can be valid but not reliable (hits near the bullseye, but not consistent), reliable but not valid (hits near each other, but not the bullseye), neither valid nor reliable (hits neither near the bullseye nor near each other), and valid and reliable (bullseye!).

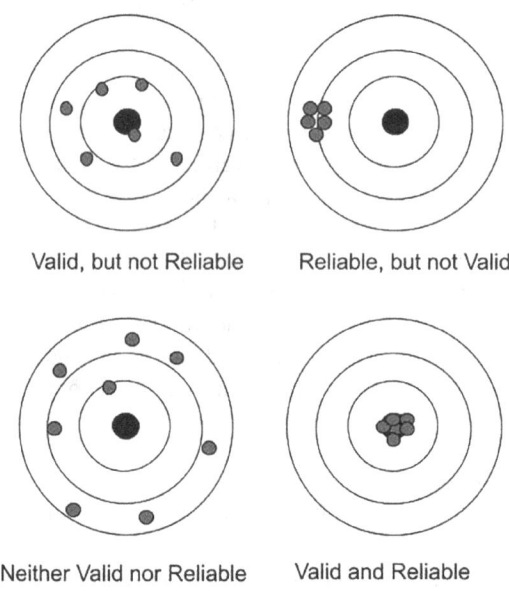

Source: Author's own work.

Figure 15.1   *Bullseye example*

After discussing the general definition of reliability, I introduce the types of reliability, including test-retest, parallel/alternate forms, internal consistency (Cronbach's Alpha), and scorer reliability.

When teaching validity in measurement, I introduce the traditional approach (content, criterion, and construct; Landy, 1986) and map it onto the new approach (appropriate content, response processes, internal structure, relationships with other variables, and consequences of testing; see Figure 15.2; American Educational Research Association et al., 2014; SIOP, 2018 for more information). Under the new approach, validation is seen as a process that justifies claims made about a scale (Kane, 2006; Shaw & Crisp, 2011). This means that the new approach of gathering validity evidence involves the specified use of the test for a particular purpose, the proposed interpretations and actions based on test scores, and the idea that validity is a continuing process that depends on test use, interpretation, and population.

In both my measurement and research methods classes, it is more important to me that students know and understand the new approach to validity rather than the traditional approach. Why? I want them to think about how our tests affect the conclusions we draw. I don't care to have them spend their limited time struggling to remember the difference between confusing 'traditional' validity terminology. Again, *most of our students will not become academics* (CWS, 2019b). Therefore, it is much more useful to teach validity as a way of thinking about *what might influence the conclusions drawn from this scale or research*. Students in my class tend to find the new approach easier to remember, as it tends to be more applicable to tests they have taken or may create. It changes their way of thinking about item creation and encourages them to question testing in a new way. Students begin to take on the test developer's perspective and wonder, 'Is this really getting at the content I want to examine? Are test takers reading the questions the same way I am? How can I test statistically for validity? How is it related or unrelated to other variables? What are the consequences of someone taking this test?' However, there is a need to test this empirically, although learning strategies would suggest that the more that a student can elaborate on the content and relate it to their own life, the better they encode the material (Dunlosky et al., 2013).

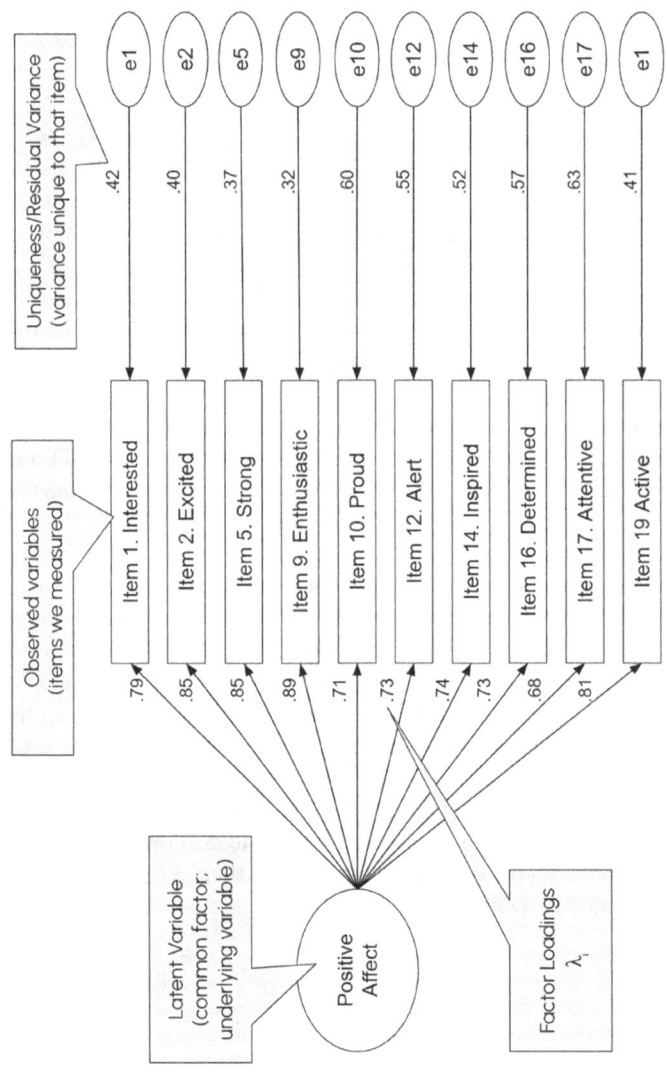

Source: Author's own work.

Figure 15.2 Trinitarian view of validity mapped onto new approaches

15.1.1.2 Class assignment

Students are tasked with identifying a construct they want to measure and finding an existing scale that purports to measure that construct. Students evaluate the scale by addressing the following questions:

- Has this scale been used in other studies?
- Does the scale demonstrate consistent reliability and validity across studies? How do you know?
- Have any other studies critiqued the scale, and if so, what were the concerns?
- Are there other scales that are widely used to measure this construct, and if so, how does your chosen scale compare?

Finally, students must analyze at least three studies that have used or discussed the scale and determine whether this is an appropriate scale for their own research project. This assignment helps students explore a construct of interest while reminding students that many validated scales already exist, eliminating the need to create one from scratch. It also encourages them to critically engage with the literature by applying their understanding of reliability and validity.

15.1.2 Teaching How to Create Valid Measures

The second week on measurement dives into scale development. I encourage including this topic because many students will create a survey at some point in their careers. The two key learning objectives for this week are:

1. Gain a foundational understanding of item generation and scale validation.
2. Learn how to analyze and evaluate scale items.

A recommended reading for this week is Heggestad et al. (2019), which explores validity concerns and challenges with scale adaptation in organizational sciences. Both students and researchers often modify existing scales; this paper helps one make informed and effective adjustments. It is a valuable addition to any research methods or measurement course as it covers important topics while remaining accessible and free of heavy jargon.

For a more advanced perspective, I recommend Allen et al. (2022), which calls for greater attention to the development and evaluation of single-item measures. This paper presents arguments for and against their use and discusses reliability and validity assessment methods. While this reading may be a bit complex for undergraduates still grasping basic reliability concepts, it is well-suited for honors, measurement-focused, or graduate-level courses.

15.1.2.1 Class content

In lecture, we discuss reasons for developing a new scale. Perhaps existing scales are insufficient, or a well-fitting scale for a specific construct does not exist. In other cases, access to the original scale may be restricted. We also cover the key characteristics of well-designed items (e.g., clarity, brevity, word choice, double-barreled, similar item stems; for more, see DeVellis, 2017), and I guide students through an exercise in which they evaluate items based on the characteristics we discussed (See the section 'Think-Pair-Share Item Improvement').

I provide a quick lesson on scale validation to help students grasp the rigor of item generation and evaluation. This introduction offers a framework for scale development and clarifies where various types of validity fit into the process. The lesson briefly covers:

1. **Item Creation** (appropriate content, response processes) – Reviewing previous literature, discussing items with subject matter experts, and pilot testing items.
2. **Data Collection** (response processes) – Ensuring items function as intended.
3. **Test Dimensionality** (internal structure) – Conducting exploratory or confirmatory factor analysis to evaluate how well items measure the intended construct.
4. **Test Reliability** – Assessing reliability through test-retest, split-half reliability, parallel forms, and internal consistency
5. **Test Validities** (relationships with other variables) – Examining how the construct correlates with related measures
6. **Item Difficulty and Discrimination** – Determining how well items differentiate between individuals high and low on the construct.

I emphasize factor analysis to illustrate the relationships between items, the underlying construct, and measurement error (see Figure 15.3). While dimensionality is often more relevant for advanced classes, I have found that once students understand how to write effective items, they are more receptive to learning how items are statistically interrelated.

Finally, students are introduced to the model fit indices they should look for when reading research papers. This class does not cover details on improving model fit, as these topics will be addressed in their measurement class. However, if a program does not require such a course, providing additional

Covering measurement in a research methods course 207

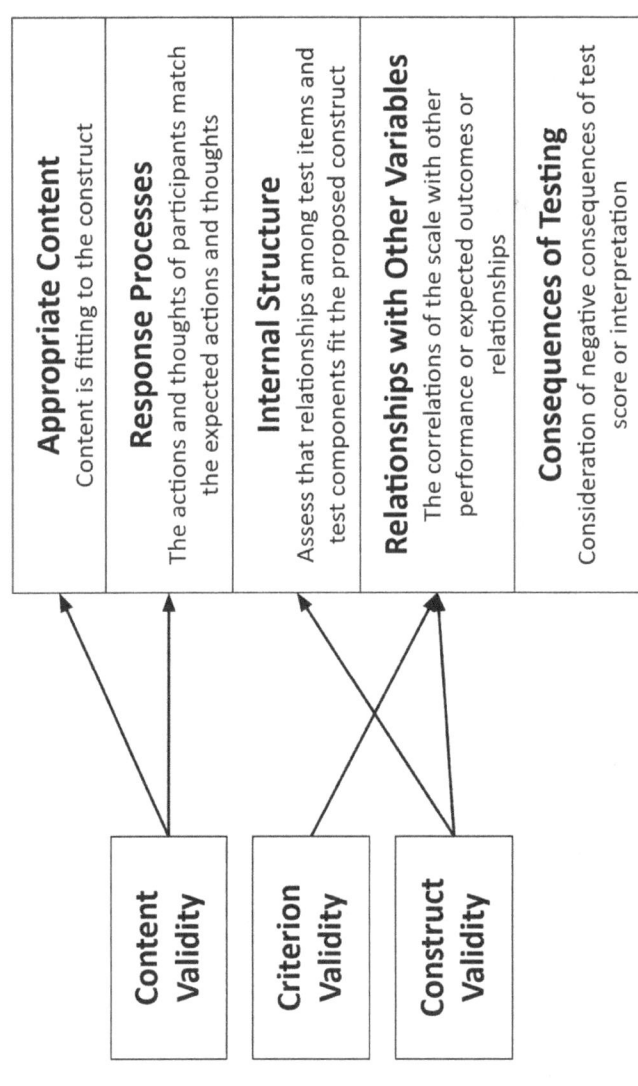

Source: Author's own work.

Figure 15.3   Teaching dimensionality

context on how these indices can be improved is recommended. I focus their attention on finding four to five key statistics (see Byrne, 1994; Hu & Bentler, 1999; Marsh et al., 2004 for more detail):

- **Chi-Square (χ^2)** – Non-significant values suggest a good fit, but with larger samples, this is often unrealistic, so it is not heavily relied upon.
- **Comparative Fit Index (CFI)** – A value > 0.90 is considered acceptable.
- **Tucker-Lewis Index (TLI)** – A value > 0.90 is considered acceptable.
- **Root Mean Square Error of Approximation (RMSEA)** – A value < 0.10 indicates acceptable fit.
- **Standardized Root Mean Square Residual (SRMR)** – A value < 0.10 indicates acceptable fit.
- **Factor Loadings** – Loadings ≥ 0.40 suggest strong item-construct relationships.

Once students have a basic understanding of how to evaluate their own items, I recommend reviewing Cronbach's Alpha and discussing how individual items influence this value and what values should be aimed for, as well as other forms of reliability (e.g., test-retest, split-half reliability, parallel forms). This class can be used as a form of distributed practice, elaborative interrogation, and self-explanation (Dunlosky et al., 2013; Gurung & Dunlosky, 2023) by integrating topics learned in this class period with previously learned topics such as validity, reliability, sampling, and ethics. For example, I ask students to reflect on this question:

> Consider that you created a rating scale to measure the satisfaction of workers at a manufacturing plant. You create a 10-item scale with items such as 'I am content with my working conditions.' The items use a 1–7 Likert-type scale, where 1 represents 'strongly disagree' and 7 represents 'strongly agree.' Describe the kinds of conclusions we can and cannot draw based on the responses to these items.

This often sparks conversations around how items are worded, how students might assess validity and reliability, and whether group differences affect how someone responds. These conversations prompt students to engage more deeply with the material and each other (Mudelsee & Jurkowski, 2021).

15.1.2.2 Class assignment

Students are tasked with asking ChatGPT to generate items for the construct of interest from the previous week and experimenting with a few different prompts. They must report at least one set of the items and discuss how varying prompts influenced the suggestions provided by ChatGPT. As a part of this assignment, students reflect on whether ChatGPT followed good item-writing practices. They are also asked to consider the advantages and risks of using AI to create survey items. They determine whether they would use ChatGPT for item generation in their professional work and must provide at least three peer-reviewed journal citations that support their decision.

This assignment may spark some debate, but the reality is that ChatGPT is here to stay. Our goal should be to equip students with the skills to use AI ethically and critically, recognizing its potential as a powerful and useful tool. Some research even suggests that AI may generate better personality assessments than an individual could (Fan et al., 2023; Hernandez & Nie, 2022). When reflecting on this assignment, students identify the biased and bad items that ChatGPT makes. However, they also recognize how to write effective prompts, recognize quality items, and revise problematic items. The requirement to include scholarly references also encourages students to explore AI-related literature, such as its ethical considerations, validity, and applications in assessment.

Finally, this week's discussion requires students to revisit the scale they posted the previous week. They will create or rewrite 3–4 new items for that scale and should adhere to best practices in item writing. Students must respond to at least two peers and are reminded to be open to feedback as item writing is an iterative process.

15.2 MEASUREMENT IN-CLASS ACTIVITIES

The following are a few in-class activities that students enjoy and find valuable. These activities utilize best practices in teaching and learning (Angelo & Zakrajsek, 2024; Dunlosky et al., 2013; Richmond et al., 2022) to increase students' engagement with the material and apply what they have learned to their own lives.

15.2.1 Think-Pair-Share Item Improvement

Students reflect on the following items relating to extraversion and are asked to (1) identify strong and weak items and (2) rewrite the weak items to improve clarity, relevance, and psychometric quality using best practices in item writing (Table 15.1). You can start this discussion by defining extraversion or coming up with another interesting construct with items for students to dissect. This activity can take between five and ten minutes.

Table 15.1   Think-pair-share: Item improvement

Item	Potential problem	Suggested revision
I enjoy ragers.	Jargon, appropriate content	I feel energized when I am around others.
I dislike making new friends.	Different item stem, reverse coding can sometimes cause issues, social desirability bias	I prefer to maintain my existing friendships rather than making new ones.
I am skilled in handling social situations.	N/A – example of good item	-
I am told I am very funny by a lot of people.	Different item stem, appropriate content	I enjoy keeping the conversation lively.
I feel comfortable around people.	N/A – example of good item	-
I consider myself to be a convivial, fun-loving person who likes to be the center of attention.	Double barreled, advanced language, appropriate content	I thrive in social situations.

Note: Assume a response scale of 1 = 'strongly disagree' and 5 = 'strongly agree'.

15.2.2   Item Writing

To illustrate the challenges of writing good survey items, begin the class on item writing by giving students 3–5 minutes to generate 3–5 items for a construct of their choice. On the back of the paper, they should write the name of the construct at the top, along with their definition of that construct. They keep this paper until the end of the lecture.

During the lecture, cover best practices in item writing and revisit key validity concepts. If you have time, use the 'Think-Pair-Share: Item Improvement' activity to critique poorly written items and discuss how to improve them.

At the end of the lecture, students swap their short scales with a classmate and take 10–15 minutes to respond to each other's items, thinking out loud as they do. If time permits, encourage them to collaborate on improving items.

In the activity debrief, prompt students to identify which forms of validity were at play in this activity. Ideally, they should recognize that writing appropriate content is difficult, vague or biased wording can impact validity, response processes may not align with the intended meaning (leading to misinterpretation), and consequences of testing emerge when one considers how their peers may score. This exercise not only reinforces how challenging good item writing can be—it deepens students' understanding of validity in measurement through direct experience.

15.2.3 Bad Tests

This is always a fun class discussion. Before diving into what makes a bad test, use a Think-Pair-Share activity where students talk with a partner about a bad test they have taken. There is no need to tie it to class content yet; just allow them to laugh and vent. After regrouping, invite volunteers to share their experiences, which will hopefully lead to lively and engaging conversation. Everyone has a bad test story – whether it's a nightmare driving test, awkward job assessment, or unfair academic exam – and the range of examples never disappoints.

In my measurement class, I schedule this discussion a few weeks in, after we've built psychological safety and covered essential concepts like validity, reliability, and measurement error. By this point, students often connect their stories to course concepts naturally, but if not, I guide them to think about how these concepts relate to their lives.

This discussion could take a different angle in a research methods class: explore what happens when people do not have proper training in measurement and how poor test design impacts decision-making. Regardless of the context, this activity engages students while reinforcing the importance of well-designed measures.

15.2.4 Write an Item for My Exam

After I teach about best practices in item writing, I give students a responsive writing prompt: 'Write an example of an item you might see on the exam, following principles of good item writing taught in class. Indicate what you believe should be the correct answer.' Students love to joke that this is just a sneaky way for me to avoid writing my own exam questions (since their exams are multiple choice). To be fair, when I come across a particularly well-written item, I add it to my item bank!

I love this activity for two reasons. First, it gives students hands-on practice applying good item-writing principles, reinforcing what they have learned. I usually assign this a few days after our item-writing lesson to encourage retrieval practice. Second, it gives me insight into which concepts are sticking; students tend to write questions on a surprisingly wide range of topics, not just the ones we covered that day.

15.2.5 Memes

Memes can be a valuable (and entertaining) way to communicate information in the classroom (Kath et al., 2022; Tidy et al., 2024). I regularly incorporate memes into my slides (often sourced from @iopsychmemes on Instagram or LinkedIn). About halfway through the semester, I offer extra credit to students who make memes about class material, encouraging them to reflect on course material and engage with the content.

When students make memes about class content, they must synthesize material from the course and popular media in a 'Relate-Create-Donate' manner (Anderson & Krathwohl, 2001; Shneiderman, 1998). This framework suggests that relating to and personalizing the material, creating something new, and sharing their creations can help students better identify and internalize class material (Sidekerskienė & Damaševičius, 2024). It's a great way to connect with students on a personal level and, if you are lucky, they will make a couple about you as well. All in good fun!

15.2.6 Critique a Scale

Another way to reinforce validity is through a scale critique assignment. Students are paired up or form small groups to select a scale validation, measurement, or psychometric paper from a list of pre-approved journals. The task is to critically evaluate the author's evidence for:

- Appropriate content
- Response processes
- Internal structure
- Relationships with other variables
- Consequences of testing

This assignment often sparks thought-provoking discussions around what constitutes strong validity evidence and how published, peer-reviewed studies may still overlook key aspects of validity. Students are encouraged to consider what they might have done differently as researchers to strengthen the evidence for validity.

A frequent theme that emerges is the consequences of testing, particularly concerning historically marginalized groups. The conversation often reveals how measurement decisions can have real-world ethical and practical implications. It's always interesting to see students begin to recognize the broader impacts of test development on certain groups.

15.3 CONCLUSION

Measurement is crucial to research methods and can be integrated into various lectures across the semester. In an ideal world, measurement would be its own semester-long course. However, students can learn the basics of measurement quite quickly in a research methods course – enough to be able to find and evaluate published scales and create and examine their own items.

Teaching measurement (and research methods) does not have to be dry – it can be engaging and interactive! The activities listed here are rooted in learning strategies, but empirical testing is needed to evaluate their true effectiveness and the value of integrating measurement principles into research methods. By incorporating active assignments that break up the lecture format and foster conversation and dialogue, students can potentially recognize the challenges of good measurement and incorporate best practices in scale development throughout their academic career and beyond.

REFERENCES

Aiken, L. S., West, S. G., & Millsap, R. E. (2008). Doctoral training in statistics, measurement, and methodology in psychology: Replication and extension of Aiken, West, Sechrest, and Reno's (1990) survey of PhD programs in North America. *American Psychologist*, 62(1). https://doi.org/10.1037/0003-066X.63.1.32

Allen, M. S., Iliescu, D., & Greiff, S. (2022). Single item measures in psychological science: A call to action [Editorial]. *European Journal of Psychological Assessment*, 38(1), 1–5. https://doi.org/10.1027/1015-5759/a000699

American Educational Research Association, American Psychological Association, & National Council on Measurement in Education (Eds.). (2014). *Standards for Educational and Psychological Testing*. American Educational Research Association.

Anderson, L. W., & Krathwohl, D. R. (2001). *A Taxonomy for Learning, Teaching and Assessing: A Revision of Bloom's Taxonomy of Educational Objectives: Complete Edition*. Longman.

Angelo, T. A., & Zakrajsek, T. D. (2024). *Classroom Assessment Techniques: Formative Feedback Tools for College and University Teachers*. Jossey-Bass.

Byrne, B. M. (1994). *Structural Equation Modeling with EQS and EQS/Windows*. Sage Publications.

Center for Workforce Studies (CWS; 2019a). *CWS Data Tool: Careers in Psychology* [Tableau Dashboard]. https://www.apa.org/workforce/data-tools/careers-psychology

Center for Workforce Studies (CWS; 2019b). *Center for Workforce Studies Data Tool: Degree Pathways in Psychology* [Tableau Dashboard]. https://www.apa.org/workforce/data-tools/degrees-pathways

DeVellis, R. F. (2006). Classical test theory. *Medical Care*, 44(11), S50–S59. https://doi.org/10.1097/01.mlr.0000245426.10853.30

DeVellis, R. F. (2017). *Scale Development: Theory and Applications*. Sage Publications.

Dunlosky, J., Rawson, K. A., Marsh, E. J., Nathan, M. J., & Willingham, D. T. (2013). Improving students' learning with effective learning techniques: Promising directions from cognitive and educational psychology. *Psychological Science in the Public Interest, 14*(1). https://doi.org/10.1177/1529100612453266

Fan, J., Sun, T., Liu, J., Zhao, T., Zhang, B., Chen, Z., Glorioso, M., & Hack, E. (2023). How well can an AI chatbot infer personality? Examining psychometric properties of machine-inferred personality scores. *Journal of Applied Psychology, 108*(8), 1277–1299. https://doi.org/10.1037/apl0001082

Finney, S. J., & Pastor, D. A. (2012). Attracting students to the field of measurement. *Educational Measurement Issues and Practice, 32*(2). https://doi.org/10.1111/j.1745-3992.2012.00228.x

Friedrich, J., Childress, J., & Cheng, D. (2018). Replicating a national survey on statistical training in undergraduate psychology programs: Are there "new statistics" in the new millennium? *Teaching of Psychology, 45*(4), 312–323. https://doi.org/10.1177/0098628318796414

Gurung, R. A. R., & Dunlosky, J. (2023). *Study like a Champ: The Psychology-Based Guide to "Grade A" Study Habits.* APA LifeTools. https://doi.org/10.1037/0000327-000

Heggestad, E. D., Scheaf, D. J., Banks, G. C., Monroe Hausfeld, M., Tonidandel, S., & Williams, E. B. (2019). Scale adaptation in organizational science research: A review and best-practice recommendations. *Journal of Management, 45*(6), 2596–2627. https://doi.org/10.1177/0149206319850280

Henson, R. K., Hull, D. M., & Williams, C. S. (2010). Methodology in our education research culture: Toward a stronger collective quantitative proficiency. *Educational Researcher, 39*(3), 229–240. https://doi.org/10.3102/0013189X10365102

Hernandez, I., & Nie, W. (2022). The AI-IP: Minimizing the guesswork of personality scale item development through artificial intelligence. *Personnel Psychology, 76*(4). https://doi.org/10.1111/peps.12543

Hole, K. (2015). An investigation of the quality of student-developed surveys and ratings scales and psychometric reporting practices in doctoral dissertations. [Doctoral dissertation, Kansas University]. KU Scholar Works. https://kuscholarworks.ku.edu/entities/publication/fd47c439-570d-4869-9095-9d0d81a6e3e9

Hu, L-t., & Bentler, P. M. (1999). Cutoff criteria for fit indexes in covariance structure analysis: Conventional criteria versus new alternatives. *Structural Equation Modeling: A Multidisciplinary Journal, 6*(1). https://doi.org/10.1080/10705519909540118

Hussey, I., & Hughes, S. (2020). Hidden invalidity among 15 commonly used measures in social and personality psychology. *Advances in Methods and Practices in Psychological Science, 3*(2). https://doi.org/10.1177/2515245919882903

Kane, M. T. (2006). Validation. In R. L. Brennan (Ed.), *Educational Measurement.* (4th Ed.), 17–64. American Council on Education/Praeger.

Kath, L. M., Schmidt, G. B., Islam, S., Jimenez, W. P., & Hartnett, J. L. (2022). Getting psyched about memes in the psychology classroom. *Teaching of Psychology, 51*(3). https://doi.org/10.1177/00986283221085908

Lambert, N. M. (1991). The crisis in measurement literacy in psychology and education. *Educational Psychologist, 26*(1), 23–35. https://doi.org/10.1207/s15326985ep2601_2

Landy, F. J. (1986). Stamp collecting versus science: Validation as hypothesis testing. *American Psychologist, 41*(11), 1183–1192. https://doi.org/10.1037/0003-066X.41.11.1183

Leventhal, B. C. & Thomson, K. N. (2021). Surveying the measurement profession to assist recruiting in the United States. *Educational Measurement Issues and Practice, 40*(3). https://doi.org/10.1111/emip.12431

Lilienfeld, S. O., & Strother, A. N. (2020). Psychological measurement and the replication crisis: Four sacred cows. *Canadian Psychology, 61*(4). https://doi.org/10.1037/cap0000236

Marsh, H., Hau, K-T., & Wen, Z. (2004). In search of golden rules: Comment on hypothesis-testing approaches to setting cutoff values for fit indices and dangers in overgeneralizing Hu and Bentler's (1999) findings. *Structural Equation Modeling*, *11*(3). https://doi.org/10.1207/s15328007sem1103_2

McGovern T. V., Furumoto L., Halpern D., Kimble G. A., & McKeachie W. J. (1991). Liberal education, study in depth, and the arts and sciences major: Psychology. *American Psychologist*, *46*. https://doi.org/10.1037/0003-066X.46.6.598

McKelvie, S. J. (2000). Psychological testing in the undergraduate curriculum. *Canadian Psychology*, *41*(3), 141–148. https://doi.org/10.1037/h0086863

Meier, S. T. (1993). Revitalizing the measurement curriculum: Four approaches for emphasis in graduate education. *American Psychologist*, *48*(8), 886–891. https://doi.org/10.1037/0003-066X.48.8.886

Michell, J. (1997). Quantitative science and the definition of measurement in psychology. *British Journal of Psychology*, *88*. 335–383.

Mudelsee, L., & Jurkowski, S. (2021). Think and pair before share: Effects of collaboration on students' in-class participation. *Learning and Individual Differences*, *88*. https://doi.org/10.1016/j.lindif.2021.102015

Neal, T. M. S., Slobogin, C., Saks, M. J., Faigman, D. L., & Geisinger, K. F. (2020). Psychological assessments in legal contexts: Are courts keeping "Junk Science" out of the courtroom? *Psychological Science in the Public Interest*, *20*(3), 135–164. https://doi.org/10.1177/1529100619888860

Norcross J. C., Hailstorks R., Aiken L. S., Pfund R. A., Stamm K. E., & Christidis P. (2016). Undergraduate study in psychology: Curriculum and assessment. *American Psychologist*, *71*. https://doi.org/10.1037/a0040095

Richmond, A. S., Boysen, G. A., & Gurung, R. A. R. (2022). *An Evidence-Based Guide to College and University Teaching: Developing the Model Teacher.* Routledge.

Rindskopf, D. (2001). Reliability: Measurement. In N. J. Smelser & P. B. Baltes (Eds.), *International Encyclopedia of the Social & Behavioral Sciences*, 13023–13028. Pergamon. https://doi.org/10.1016/B0-08-043076-7/00722-1

Shaw, S., & Crisp, V. (2011). Tracing the evolution of validity in educational measurement: Past issues and contemporary challenges. *Research Matters*, *11*. https://doi.org/10.17863/CAM.100522

Shneiderman, B. (1998). Relate-create-donate: A teaching/learning philosophy for the cyber-generation. *Computers & Education*, *31*(1). https://doi.org/10.1016/S0360-1315(98)00014-1

Sidekerskienė, T., & Damaševičius, R. (2024). Pedagogical memes: A creative and effective tool for teaching STEM subjects. *International Journal of Mathematical Education in Science and Technology*, *56*(7). https://doi.org/10.1080/0020739X.2024.2328818

Society for Industrial Organizational Psychology (SIOP; 2018). *Principles for the Validation and Use of Personnel Selection Procedures.* https://www.apa.org/ed/accreditation/personnel-selection-procedures.pdf

Stoa, R., Chu, T. L. (A.), & Gurung, R. A. R. (2022). Potential potholes: Predicting challenges and learning outcomes in research methods in psychology courses. *Teaching of Psychology*, *49*(1), 21–29. https://doi.org/10.1177/0098628320979881

Thomas, J. H. (2018). Careers for psychology majors: What every student should know. *Eye on Psi Chi*, *22*(2). https://doi.org/10.24839/2164-9812.Eye22.2.20

Tidy, H., Bolton-King, R. S., Croxton, R., Mullen, C., Nichols-Drew, L., Carlysle-Davies, F., Moran, K. S., & Irving-Walton, J. (2024). Enhancing the student learning experience through memes. *Science & Justice*, *64*(3). https://doi.org/10.1016/j.scijus.2024.03.004

White, M., & Stovner, R. (2024). Breakdowns in scientific practices: How and why some accepted scientific claims may have little actual support. *Collabra: Psychology*, *10*(1). https://doi.org/10.1525/collabra.121436

16. Talking about numbers: Essential statistics for research methods

Andrew Olstad, Jacqueline A. Goldman and Regan A. R. Gurung

The British statistician George Box is thought to have said 'All models are wrong, but some are useful.' Statistics are a common part of any research endeavor and feature in every quantitative and many qualitative research studies. Consequently, the question of how and when to discuss statistics in the context of a research methods course is critical. Students, especially those majoring in psychology, often view both research methods and statistics classes with dread (Gurung & Christopher, 2022; Salkind & Shaw, 2019), and not surprisingly statistical concepts are often listed as some of the most difficult to comprehend (Cross, Chapter 7, this volume). Furthermore, studies of challenges to understanding in research method courses reveal there are many statistical concepts that are 'potholes' for student learning (Stoa et al., 2022). What then are the best ways to teach about statistical concepts in the context of a research methods class? A good starting place is to first identify the most important statistical concepts and share why they are important.

The practice of statistics is a tool to assist orderly thinking about organized data, especially large sets of data that can be interpreted numerically. This chapter provides a brief overview of the statistical mindset and a limited introduction to some basic statistical tools and concepts. Albeit short, this chapter's presence in a book on teaching research methods underscores the reality that design knowledge and statistical knowledge go hand in hand (Field, 2024). Readers interested in a much deeper dive into a particular practical context would be well served by one of the many excellent books on the subject (see e.g., Navarro, 2013). In this chapter, we will give you a solid framework for what statistical concepts are needed for students to be successful in your research methods courses.

16.1 THE STATISTICAL MINDSET

The statistical mindset is a balance between a lively curiosity and healthy skepticism. While statisticians use mathematics, the discipline is fundamentally curious about what is in the world: what we can know, what we can measure, and what we can learn about. Of course, students who are required to take a research methods or a statistics class may not yet have developed a curiosity about measurement, even though most instructors agree that describing and understanding the world are key functions of psychological science. Some savvy students are aware that statistics can be misleading and limited. This knowledge of the extent to which they can be misled by numbers is a good motivating factor to lure their attention to key statistics. It is an unfortunate truth that expertise in statistics does not prevent one from lying to others, and is not even a guarantee against being lied to (although those with a statistical mindset have an edge in detecting certain kinds of falsehoods). However, the greater good of statistical practice is that it may help you avoid lying to yourself. The need to move slowly and rigorously to demonstrate one's findings can prevent one's opinions from solidifying into belief without justification.

When approaching a research problem or any question with a statistical facet, the best advice is to take the time necessary to understand the problem, to think carefully about the relationship between the ideas one would like to measure and the outcomes recorded, and to consider multiple different representations of the data gained. Statisticians called in on projects often complain that they could have been much more helpful to researchers earlier in the projects they partner in, and yet paradoxically it seems statistics might be of little use before the data has been collected. One highly successful habit is to take a look, well before you begin your data collection, at what your data might be 'shaped like.' If you envision your data in your final results as a spreadsheet, what does each row represent? What are the column titles? Are the cells filled with decimal numbers, binary 1/0 or yes/no options, words, or something else?

In the case of a replication study, this is actually quite easy. If students have access to original data from the study being replicated, they can use that, but even if the original data is not available, it is entirely reasonable to create mock-ups of data to check one's assumptions. Each different statistical or data tool is adapted to certain types of data: for instance, linear regression is suited to quantitative (numerical) outcomes, while logistic regression is useful for binary (yes/no) outcomes. While some software packages automate this process, it's also an option to just create a spreadsheet with the relevant columns (variables) and several rows with fictitious example data. This can help answer concrete questions like: What sorts of variables are being used or compared? What relationships are being explored? What questions are being asked?

Before you begin collecting data, you should know what tools you will use. If you're planning to compare differences across groups, what are those groups and how will you measure their data values? If you're planning a regression, what are your predictor and outcome variables?

In general, in a research methods course, it's important to help students move beyond mere memorization of formulas and toward an applied understanding of how statistical tools are used to explore relationships between psychological variables. They may not be open at first to developing a statistician's mindset, but by putting the numbers in context and spending time talking about what the numbers mean, one can increase motivation and engagement for learning about designs. The topics of correlation and regression, often discussed in research methods, are central to the process of cultivating more quantitatively literate students. Both correlations and regressions form the bridge between descriptive statistics and prediction-based inferential models. Students should come away from these lessons not only knowing how to perform these analyses, but also when to use them and how to interpret the output meaningfully.

16.2 THE VISUAL TRICK

> The simple graph has brought more information to the data analyst's mind than any other device. It specializes in providing indications of unexpected phenomena.
> John Tukey

Graphing data is generally essential at the start of any sort of data analysis. In a research methods course that discusses how the main types of research design are descriptive, correlational, and experimental, introducing the utility of graphs and figures early on provides many engaging ways to get students enthused about numbers. For example, descriptive data can be illustrated in a wide variety of ways. Consider the thorough investigation of this topic by Edward Tufte in *The Visual Display of Quantitative Information* (2001).

The heart of the argument revolves around a certain sort of humility: clear graphs can highlight patterns and foster deep understandings. While complicated mathematical models come in and out of vogue, and may be very useful tools when used well, a graphical exploration will almost always precede them – and a graphical explanation will have to follow if you wish to explain your results beyond a narrow circle of specialists.

Beyond illustrating data creatively in descriptive studies, graphs are important tools in correlational studies and experiments as well. In the former, graphs display the nature of associations between variables and allow a test of many aspects of statistical validity. Scatterplots, for example, can help researchers check for outliers and observe if relationships between variables are linear or curvilinear. Box and whisker plots, violin plots, and pirate plots (made using R) allow displays of spread and precision. Such graphs provide significantly more information than just sets of means (see Chapter 1). While both the numerical summary and the graph represent the same data and give similar amounts of information, the box plot is much more accessible to most readers.

16.3 CRITICAL STATISTICAL CONCEPTS

Five big ideas – p-values, effect sizes, power, comparing differences, and modeling – can help you harness the power of your data to tell a compelling statistical story. P-values establish whether we have evidence of some effect, but are limited. Effect sizes – from simple averages and differences to more esoteric measures – start to make the case for how much these credible effects will really matter. We incorporate both of those into our comparisons and our models.

16.3.1 P-values

Traditional ('frequentist') statistical approaches generally hinge on the idea of a p-value, the probability of finding a data pattern at least as extreme as the evidence in question, given some statistical assumption. In the graph shown in Figure 16.1, there seems to be a linear relationship between students' practice quiz scores and their actual quiz scores. But maybe this is just a fluke! A p-value gives a chance to quantify this possibility. The p-value here is about 0.001, quite a small value. It tells us that *if* there's really no relationship between students' pre- and post-test scores, we would only see such a strong

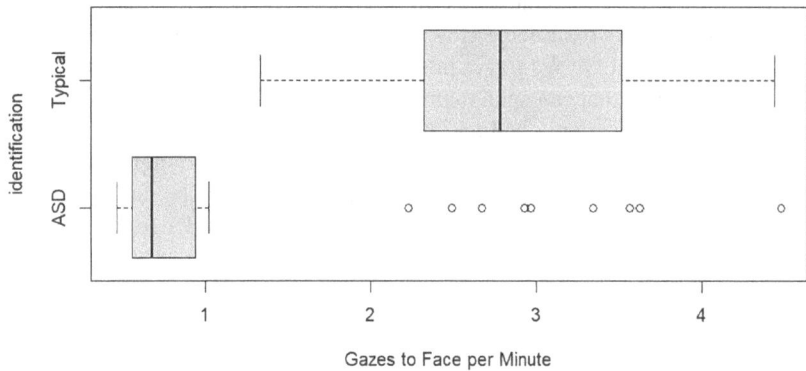

Source: Authors' own work.

Figure 16.1   *A p-value for a simple linear regression*

relationship in the data we happened to collect about one time in one thousand. There's a lot to be careful about, which we'll see below: even experts misinterpret p-values regularly.

While p-values are the most common way of describing the strength of evidence, they are misunderstood, misinterpreted, and misapplied with astonishing regularity. So much so, that in 2016 the American Statistical Association released a 'Statement on p-values,' focused largely on warnings about their misuse. As recounted in 'The ASA Statement on p-Values: Context, Process, and Purpose,' the objection to p-values in a nutshell is the fundamentally circular arguments used to justify their prominence:

Q: Why do so many colleges and grad schools teach $p = 0.05$?

A: Because that's still what the scientific community and journal editors use.

Q: Why do so many people still use $p = 0.05$?

A: Because that's what they were taught in college or grad school.

As a practical matter, researchers need to be able to point to 'significant' p-values for publication in many (certainly not all) journals. However, it is essential that this facet of statistical analysis be understood for what it is: one aspect of a statistical analysis, and far from its entirety.

16.3.2 Effect Sizes

An effect size is any measure of the amount of some observed difference or phenomenon. These are the statistics people will usually quote in the general parlance: What is the percentage of growth we're seeing? How much effect do we expect from this treatment? How fast is something changing with relation to some other quantity? We sometimes move beyond these basics to more complicated measures that can span many cases and give us comparable figures.

Students who have only had an introductory course before taking research methods or who see their possible statistics prerequisites as simply filled with numbers often miss the importance of the effect size. Easily summarized as being the strength of the relationship between variables under study, an effect is easiest discussed in the context of a correlational coefficient (formally the Pearson correlation coefficient, r), is the effect size, quantifying the strength of the association between two variables.

Students should understand that correlation is a measure of association between two continuous variables. Introduce Pearson's r as a statistic that quantifies both the direction (positive or negative) and the strength (from -1 to $+1$) of a linear relationship. Emphasize that correlation does *not imply causation* and use real-world psychological examples – like the relationship between sleep and concentration – to highlight this point. Teaching students to interpret scatterplots, recognize linear versus curvilinear patterns, and assess practical significance (not just statistical significance) will help them build critical data literacy skills.

It takes some work for students to also note there are other measures of effect size such as Cohen's d and that most statistical programs can generate the effect for F-tests and t-tests. Providing the guidelines for levels of magnitude, such as small effects of around 0.1, moderate of around 0.3, and strong of over 0.5, proves somewhat reassuring. Students previously conditioned to just interpret correlations as strong if closer to 1 now have a better way to demarcate different levels of magnitude.

16.3.3 Power

No discussion of effect size and p-values is complete without also discussing the concept of statistical power, the ability of a study to find a sizable effect, given an adequate sample. Especially in research methods classes where students collect their own data (but in actual research as well), it is not always easy to get an adequate sample. What is an adequate sample? Students often believe it is as many participants as possible, at least 1,000, or at least 25 for every cell of an experiment.

Taking the time to explain the concept of power and consequently sharing when a study may not find a significant result because it is underpowered can be mind expanding for students. For example, when their own studies have a large enough sample but still do not find significant findings, knowing about power precludes their discussion sections claiming the major limitation was not enough participants, and their future directions section purely proclaiming 'need more participants.'

Power is calculated using three main variables. First, you need sample size, then you need an effect size, and finally you need to set the p-value. When a study is complete, you have these three pieces of information and can calculate power, which should be reported in final papers. To calculate what an adequate sample will be, one needs to set values for the other three values. Conventionally, the p-value is set to 0.05, the power is set to 0.80, and a moderate effect size of 0.20 is a good starting point. By using a program such as G*Power, a student can calculate the sample needed once they select the test they are using (see examples in OSF).

16.3.4 Same or Different? Comparing Group Means

Every experimental design involves the testing of group means. Even correlational designs where there is one categorical variable and one continuous variable will involve testing of group means. To this end, understanding how to do so and the different ways to do so are critical skills for the social scientist's toolbox. Having a good grasp of this concept can be a valuable marketing skill for students going straight into the workforce as well.

One fundamental task in research is to discover whether two groups of people/places/things/events are different from one another. This may be accomplished graphically, but if the graph is not clear or researchers want a more objective-style summary, certain hypothesis tests will lead to p-values. One can get a clear data representation from a data set about car mileages for 4-, 6-, and 8-cylinder cars (e.g., from the R ggplot2 package, Figure 16.2). It is possible to get a p-value here, but it's probably not necessary, since visual inspection is enough to show the difference. However, t-tests allow you to compare the 4- and 8-cylinder cars. The 4-cylinder cars average 26.7 mpg while the 8-cylinder cars average 15.1 mpg. The p-value testing their equality (a 'Welch's 2 Sample T Test') is 1.641e-06 or 0.000001641. This says that two randomly chosen groups of this size and data spread should almost never have such a large difference in their averages. In contrast, the p-value for the difference between the 4- and 6-cylinder engines is less overwhelming, but still conclusive at 0.0004048. But again, the graph was more useful to convince us there was actually a difference.

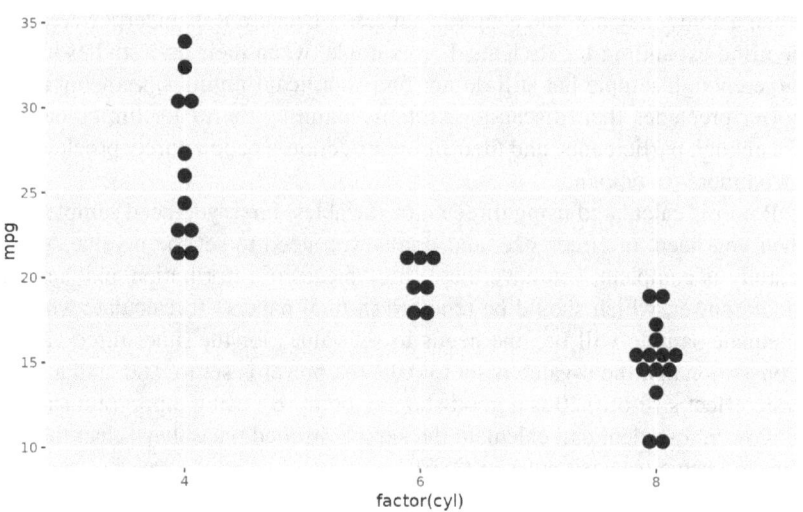

Source: Authors' own work.

Figure 16.2   *Plotting miles per gallon by engine cylinder*

This example nicely shows how illustrating data and calculating p-values while testing group means can go hand in hand. For most students in a research methods class, there are even more basic decisions to be made. What is the best test for me to use given a particular research question? Box 16.1 below provides a useful decision tree to help. The section that follows expands on the chi-square test, one of the more challenging tests for students to understand.

> **BOX 16.1 LOOKING AT YOUR RESEARCH QUESTION: ARE YOU A) COMPARING MEANS OR B) TESTING RELATIONSHIPS?**
>
> **A. Comparing Means**
>
> → How many groups do you have?
> - **One group**
> - → Do you know the population standard deviation?
>   – Yes → **Z-test**
>   – No → **One-sample t-test**
> - **Two groups**
> - → Are the groups related (e.g., pre/post, same participants)?
>   – Yes → **Paired-sample t-test**
>   – No → **Independent-samples t-test**
> - **More than two groups**
> - → **One-way ANOVA**
>
> **B. Testing Relationships**
>
> → What type of variables are you analyzing?
> - **Both variables are continuous**
> - → Are you examining association or prediction?
>   – Association → **Correlation (e.g., Pearson's r)**
>   – Prediction → **Simple linear regression**
> - **Variables are categorical**
> - → **Chi-square test of independence**

16.3.5 The Chi-Square

Chi-square tests offer a valuable entry point into non-parametric statistics, especially for psychology students who are more comfortable working with categories than with continuous variables. These tests are easy to grasp conceptually, making them ideal for building student confidence with inferential analysis. They also help students understand the importance of expected versus observed outcomes – an essential idea in statistical reasoning. Students should understand that chi-square tests assess whether there is a statistically significant association between two categorical variables. The two most common applications they need to recognize are:

- Chi-square test of independence (e.g., are therapy preferences independent of gender?)
- Chi-square goodness-of-fit test (e.g., do responses to a Likert item follow an expected distribution?)

You should emphasize that these tests work with frequency counts (not means), and are most useful when data are organized into contingency tables. Students should learn how to:

- Create and interpret contingency tables
- Understand the concept of expected frequencies
- Use the chi-square statistic to assess whether observed patterns deviate from what we would expect by chance.

It's important to introduce the assumptions of the test, such as the need for a sufficiently large sample and expected frequencies of at least five in most cells. Also, clarify that chi-square tells us if there is a relationship, but not the direction or strength – students often confuse this point with correlational analyses.

16.3.6 Modeling: Linear Regression

Linear regression builds on correlation by introducing the concept of prediction. You can teach students how one variable (predictor) can be used to estimate another (outcome) using a regression equation. Clarify the meanings of slope and intercept and how they relate to psychological theories (e.g., how increases in perceived social support predict changes in depression scores). Students should also be taught how to interpret R^2 as an indicator of how much variance in the outcome is explained by the predictor. This is a key moment to emphasize the importance of model fit and the limits of single-variable prediction.

The ANOVA test of multiple means begins to bridge us from comparison to modeling. In fact, ANOVA tests of multiple means can be thought of as a type of linear regression. In the example of cars above, the ANOVA test considered three different types of cars' gas mileage. In the world of hypothesis tests, this will be the alternative hypothesis:

Predicted MPG = mileage for 4 cylinders – extra mileage lost for 6 cylinders (for those cars) – extra mileage lost for 4 cylinders (for those cars) + some random noise

compared to the null hypothesis:

Predicted MPG = mileage for cars + some random noise

But we can do a little better! With simple linear regression, instead of thinking of this as three categories, we can think about this as a single numerical variable (cylinders) instead, and the null hypothesis becomes:

Predicted MPG = (mileage for cars) - (mileage per cylinder)* (number of cylinders) + some random noise

versus the same null hypothesis:

Predicted MPG = mileage for cars + some random noise

In this case, the p-value is also significant, but we get a somewhat simpler model because we only have to estimate one number past the starting average (the effect per cylinder rather than the two group offsets). This model predicts a linear effect, but of course not all effects are linear. The general attempt is to find the simplest mathematical model that works to describe what we want. So while there are many curves, we tend to use quadratics for any curve, and while there are many functions that go from 0 to 1 we tend to use logistic curves for any binary predictors. We try, as Einstein didn't quite urge us, to make our explanations as simple as possible but no simpler. For instructors of research methods who do not also teach statistics, the OSF link for the book (osf.io/pd7wb/) features a table of commonly used statistical tests, statistical equations students would have encountered in a prerequisite statistics course and may find handy, an explanation of the test, and an example.

16.3.7 A Note On Multiple Predictors

It is very common to build models that use many predictors (whether in linear, quadratic, or logistic models) to predict a single outcome. These multiple regression models are deceptively simple to get from any statistical package, or even Excel. However, they are often breezily described when more caution is needed. In general, a regression model tries to isolate each term and describe its effect separate from any others, *'ceteris paribus.'* When necessary, an interaction term will track how two variables' effects intermingle, as in the case of drug interactions, where two pharmaceutically interesting drugs will have combined or 'multiplicative effects' separate from what either of them might do in isolation or simple addition. Caution is warranted!

16.4 BAYESIAN ALTERNATIVES

All the topics above, with their p-values, derive from a particular branch of statistical thought sometimes called 'frequentism,' which became formalized and extremely popular from about a century ago. A much older approach, 'Bayesian statistics,' was available more than a century before that.

Bayesian statistics offer a world without the confusions of p-values, with two tradeoffs. First, as a practical matter, Bayesian framings often immediately run into computational and mathematical problems that were prohibitive until recent advances in computing power and techniques. More fundamentally, Bayesian approaches invite a more subjective approach to probability. To solve any Bayesian question, it is necessary to specify in advance a level of belief in the likelihood of certain events. These 'prior probabilities' are much of the appeal of a Bayesian approach because they can incorporate prior knowledge and belief, but at the expense of a perception of objectivity.

A real treatment of Bayesian analysis is beyond what we can offer here. However, there are more and more software tools available for tackling the 'ugly math' behind the scenes. The key idea for you to hold in mind is that any Bayesian analysis requires you to state what your prior beliefs about the subject are. This exercise can be challenging but rewarding. If you want to develop your intuitions around Bayesian reasoning, there are many useful corners of the internet. Khan Academy has a lovely explanation of Bayes' theorem using the imagined disease 'Hypothesitis,' and Socscistatistics.com has a simple calculator for the theorem, which is the start of Bayesian approaches.

16.5 IN CONCLUSION

This chapter may seem an anomaly for a book on teaching research methods. While we have been selective in the statistics we discussed and restrained in the use of statistical formulae and jargon, we do feel that discussing statistics with students in the research methods class is important. In some classes, students are either given data (see Goldman, Chapter 14, this volume), participate in open science replications (see Wagge, Chapter 9, this volume), or even collect their own data from scratch. Even if all these students took a statistics class before, they are not likely to remember all the nuances of statistics and may not have learned or applied the statistics in context. Students often tell us that statistics prerequisite courses, especially if taught outside psychology, are difficult to absorb as these courses are usually not as contextualized to psychological matters. We hope that our discussion and review of some major statistical concepts with a focus on taking the statistical mindset helps teachers of research methods in their endeavors.

REFERENCES

Field, A. (2024). *Discovering Statistics Using IBM SPSS Statistics.* Sage Publishing.

Gurung, R. A., & Christopher, A. (2022). Basic research methods and statistics. In J. Zumbach, D. A. Bernstein, S. Narciss, G. Marsico (Eds.) *International Handbook of Psychology Learning and Teaching,* 421. Springer.

Navarro, D. (2013). Learning statistics with R. Lulu. https://learningstatisticswithr.com

Salkind, N. J., & Shaw, L. A. (2019). *Statistics for People Who (Think They) Hate Statistics Using R.* Sage Publishing.

Stoa, R., Chu, T. L., & Gurung, R. A. (2022). Potential potholes: Predicting challenges and learning outcomes in research methods in psychology courses. *Teaching of Psychology, 49*(1), 21–29.

Tufte, E. (2001). *The Visual Display of Quantitative Information.* Graphics Press.

Wasserstein, R. L., & Lazar, N. A. (2016). The ASA statement on *p*-values: Context, process, and purpose. *The American Statistician, 70*(2), 129–133. https://doi.org/10.1080/00031305.2016.1154108

17. Facilitating research: NVivo lab manual for undergraduate students

Marcie Coulter-Kern and Hannah Marie

Participation in qualitative research provides students with an important but often neglected part of their research training. Developing a qualitative component to student research is an impactful experience that sets them apart from many of their undergraduate peers because of their ability to organize, code, and visualize qualitative data. Quantitative instruction is common in undergraduate programs (Gurung & Stoa, 2020; Breen et al., 2022); however, having strong qualitative training allows students to engage in high-quality mixed methods research whereby researchers collect and analyze both quantitative and qualitative data within the same study (Creswell & Clark, 2011).

The growth of mixed methods research extends beyond the social sciences to the natural sciences, humanities, and professional fields of study such as healthcare, education, and business (Shorten & Smith, 2017). In fact, participating in or conducting independent research is one of the high-impact practices that predict student success and engagement at undergraduate institutions (Lanning and Brown, 2019). The barrier for most students to conducting excellent qualitative research is often a lack of proficiency in using qualitative analysis software programs. There are many qualitative analysis tools available such as ATLAS.ti, MAXQDA, and Dedoose; however, NVivo stands out for undergraduate teaching and learning due to its user-friendly interface and because it is widely used in professional, academic, and research settings.

NVivo is a qualitative data analysis software package designed to help researchers organize, analyze, and visualize unstructured or non-numerical data, such as interviews, open-ended survey responses, and focus groups (NVivo, 2020). It is ideal for undergraduates because it can be used to introduce them to rigorous, yet accessible, qualitative research practices often yielding better critical thinking skills and more engagement in research. In a study conducted with second-year undergraduate psychology students, researchers found that using NVivo actually helped students not only manage large amounts of qualitative data, but also develop critical thinking skills and research competence (Fernandes-Jesus et al., 2024).

When undergraduate students are able to effectively use qualitative research methods such as interviews and focus groups, they may gain a more nuanced understanding of their participants' attitudes and behavior through NVivo, which then helps them develop skills in data collection and thematic analysis. In fact, these practices have been found to contribute to a more enriching educational experience for students of any background (Kilgo et al., 2015).

This chapter provides a step-by-step lab guide to conducting qualitative research using NVivo for storing, organizing, exploring, and centralizing qualitative data (NVivo, 2020). More specifically, students will learn how to analyze data from interviews, surveys, fieldnotes, web pages, and journal articles (Jackson & Bazeley, 2019).

17.1 WHAT YOU CAN EXPECT FROM THESE LABS

This chapter is organized as a series of five lessons/labs that introduce students to qualitative research and include important instruction for skills such as coding, identifying themes, drawing conclusions, employing advanced data management, and running queries to visual data. These labs introduce the basics of using NVivo in the undergraduate classroom and in student research. For ease of use for the reader and instructors, we have written this manual to be directed at the student.

In the end, students will experience the insights added to their research experience by qualitative data that cannot always be expressed through numbers. We hope that students and instructors gain a richer understanding of their data by using NVivo to better organize and understand research responses to open-ended questions and learn to listen more carefully to participant answers.

The manual in this chapter is designed for students and novice NVivo users who are new to the latest version of NVivo (14), or the previous version of NVivo (13). Students can expect to learn the core functionalities in order to apply the latest version of NVivo to their project, including:

- **Importing:** Creating a copy of data from Word documents, Excel sheets, PDF files, audio files, videos, and images.
- **Organizing:** Organizing data sources (files), creating codes/coding text, creating a code structure, using cases to organize units of analysis with classifications and attributes, and using memos and linking of files to organize systematic analysis of the data.
- **Exploring:** Exploring lexical queries, word frequency, and text search; applying code and matrix queries; illustrating with visualizations such as mind maps, comparison diagrams, and chart coding

- **Centralizing:** NVivo allows compatibility with other software (e.g., Word, Excel), enabling various forms of data and/or data sources to be brought together in one place for more efficient and effective analysis.

17.2 LAB 1: CREATING A RESEARCH DESIGN FRAMEWORK

A. Selecting a research topic
B. Creating good qualitative questions
C. Developing a design framework
D. Touring the NVivo interface/workspace

Before learning about NVivo as a tool for qualitative analysis, you must first be introduced to qualitative data. Much of the instruction that undergraduates receive involves quantitative data and statistical analysis. Qualitative data is information that is often not quantifiable or able to be accurately expressed by using numbers. It is also commonly referred to as unstructured, nonnumeric data. Most methods of collecting qualitative data include the use of open-ended questions in the form of interviews or focus groups, or the use of archival data in the form of photographs, letters, diaries, and many other sources.

For this lab you will be generating research questions and creating a design framework based on the generated question. One of the most important requirements for a good research question is that it must target ideas and concepts that can be gathered through using open-ended questions. Begin by thinking about a basic idea for a research topic that you are interested in. This can be a broad description of the project idea or a series of closely related research questions for a project. For this lab, our example of a design framework exemplifies the use of a survey to gather the data and includes both qualitative and quantitative data, making it a mixed-methods approach.

17.2.1 Component A: Selecting a Research Topic

- Write out your possible research questions. Draft qualitative questions and get feedback from colleagues and potential participants.
- Write a 200-word paragraph describing how you will design the study (i.e., who, what, where, when, and how).
- What are the important variables that you will measure (e.g., anxiety, motivation, gradeless courses, etc.)?

17.2.2 Component B: Creating Good Qualitative Questions

A good qualitative question is closely related to your design framework, focused on a single concept or phenomenon, and open ended. From your questions in component A, select the research question you would like to look into the most.

17.2.3 Component C: Developing a Design Framework

Develop a design framework by creating a table as shown below in Table 17.1. This framework will include your selected research question from component B and a method to properly organize your explanations in component A.

- The first column will include your research topic. This can be written as a research question, or a hypothesis, or both, depending on how you would like to look at your study.
- The second column should be a description of your research method that you would like to use.
- The third column describes your participants, also referred to as your units of analysis.
- The fourth column outlines your variables, including any demographics you want to measure, quantitative variables, and qualitative variables.

Table 17.1   Design framework example

Research Topic	Research Method	Participants (Units of Analysis)	Variables
• What do students want from their psychology courses?	• Online survey • Mixed methods • Quantitative (closed-ended questions) • Qualitative (open-ended questions)	Incoming psychology students • First years	Student demographics • Gender • Year • GPA • Age • Parental education • Motivation • Completed work • Student opinions • Elements of a good course • Elements of a poor course • Elements that make attending a class worthwhile

Source: Authors' own work.

17.2.4 Component D: Touring the NVivo Interface/Workspace

Take a tour of the NVivo interface/workspace (Figure 17.1). Note that the NVivo workspace was modeled after Microsoft Outlook and may look slightly different when using Apple products rather than Windows.

Ribbon View is where you can find all the tools you will need for your project. Additional tabs will become available based on what is active in the Detail View.

Navigation View is where components of your project such as data, codes, and case folders are stored.

List View is found by clicking on a folder in the navigation view.

Detail View displays the content of a file from list view.

Please note, you can change the order of the list by clicking at the top of any column.

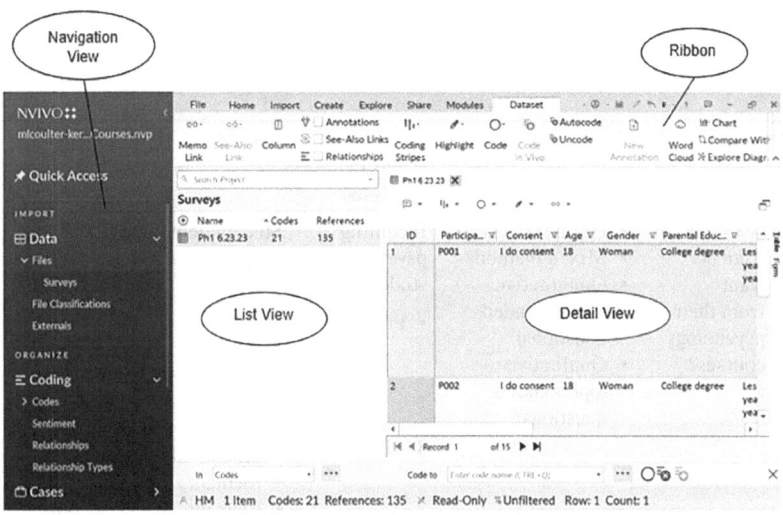

Figure 17.1   NVivo interface: Ribbon View, Navigation View, List View, Detail View

17.3   LAB 2: IMPORTING SURVEY DATA

A. The data set example
B. Clean up an Excel data set
C. Create a Project in NVivo
D. Create a folder in Files called Surveys
E. Import your data set

17.3.1   Component A: The Data Set Example

The data set called 'What Students Want' or WSW is the same data set used throughout the entirety of the NVivo lab manual. This data set was created at Manchester University with incoming psychology students as well as currently enrolled psychology students. Faculty in the Psychology Department were interested in what students would say that they wanted from their psychology courses. A survey that included demographic and open-ended questions was distributed through Qualtrics to 15 incoming first-year students and 15 returning students who were enrolled in a research methods course. Students were asked a series of closed-ended questions regarding age, gender, parental education, year, GPA, motivation, and completed work. We also asked open-ended questions: In your opinion, what makes a good psychology course, what makes a poor course, and what makes attending a class worthwhile?

The complete data set is accessible via the OSF page for this book: https://osf.io/pd7wb/.

17.3.2   Component B: Cleaning up an Excel Data Set

The data set you will be working with for this lab has been exported directly from Qualtrics. It has unnecessary columns of information that need to be deleted from the data set. The first row of the data set should be the headers (aka the variable names). Each column in the data set should have only one row of headers, and it should be the first row in the data set.

After cleaning up the Excel sheet, the column headers should include:

- Participant ID
- Consent
- Age
- Gender
- Parental education
- Year
- GPA

- Motivation
- Completed work
- Good course
- Poor course
- Worthwhile

17.3.3 Component C: Create a Project in NVivo

Open NVivo. When NVivo opens up, you will see 'Recent Files' on the left of your screen, and to the right and somewhat in the center of your screen, there is a box with a large '+' sign that you will select to create a New Project. Once you select this, you will create a project title and fill in a description for the project if you choose to, and then click next. In the next information box that appears, make sure to select 'No' for autosaving your project because otherwise it will be difficult to 'undo' any actions. We would recommend setting the save reminders to be every 15 minutes. To generate your project, select 'Create Project' on the bottom right of the information box. It may take a few moments for NVivo to process this request.

17.3.4 Component D: Create a Folder Called Surveys in Files

The next task will be to create a location in NVivo to import your survey.

Open your NVivo Project and look at the Navigation View on the far left of your screen. Right click on 'Files' and select 'New folder.' Name the folder 'Surveys' and click 'OK.' It may also be helpful to add a note to the 'Description' section to keep organized. Now when you click on the 'Files' dropdown arrow, you will see your 'Surveys' folder.

17.3.5 Component E: Import Your Data Set

Now that you have a location created, select the 'Surveys' folder under 'Files,' then select 'Import' in Ribbon View. Select the Surveys icon in the Ribbon View and select 'Excel.' Your files app will open and there you will select the cleaned-up Excel file from component A.

An information box will open and will explain what NVivo will do when you import that data. NVivo will organize the respondents from the data into 'Cases'; any closed-ended questions will be organized into a 'Case Classification,' under which 'Attributes' will be created (e.g., age, gender, etc.), and the values from the cells will be assigned. The open-ended questions will be organized into 'Codes,' and the responses will be both coded to the appropriate 'Code' and 'Case.' Click 'Next' on this information box.

In the next information box, you will make sure that only one row is indicated as the column header and then select 'Next.'

The next screen tells you where NVivo is going to store your data. Click 'Next.'

This information box will ask you to confirm which questions are open ended and closed ended by clicking and unclicking the circles shown. You can also choose not to import a given column. Click 'Next.'

In the next information box, you will uncheck 'Autocode Themes' and 'Autocode Sentiment.'

After you are done uploading the survey, here is where you will find everything:

- Excel survey: Surveys folder under Files
- Survey respondents: Cases

17.4 LAB 3: CODING THE DATA

A. Principles of coding
B. Three methods of coding
C. Managing codes

17.4.1 Process of Coding

The process of coding is an important part of getting to know the content of your data. Before identifying the themes or possibly codes within your data, read through the open-ended responses in order to get to know the data better. During this initial process of reading through the responses, read with the goal of understanding the participants' responses without trying to identify anything just yet. After the initial reading, go back through the text from the beginning, identifying common themes. These common themes will become your codes.

17.4.2 Strategies for Coding

Listed below are some strategies that will be helpful for students new to the coding process. They will help students use clear, consistent, and methodologically sound strategies to ensure that their analyses are trustworthy, meaningful, and focused.

- Frequently question the locations of codes and compare how you coded versus how someone else on your team may have coded the same data.

- Use a hierarchical system (having a parent code and adding child codes).
- Coding should be guided by your research methodology and theoretical framework.
- Keep in mind that you may change your hierarchical structure as you code and new themes emerge.

17.4.3 Component A: Principles of Coding

- Create a hierarchical system.
- Never duplicate a code; instead, remember that 'like goes with like.'
- Don't be too specific.
- You can code one piece of data to several different codes.

17.4.4 Component B: Three Methods of Coding

1. Drag and drop:
    a. Click on code folder
    b. Highlight relevant text
    c. Click and drag the text to the code to which you want to code it.
2. Right click – best for coding to several codes:
    a. Highlight the relevant text
    b. Right click on highlighted text
    c. Select 'Code Selection'
    d. Hold down the Ctrl key while selecting the codes
    e. Code to multiple items.
3. Code panel – only possible in documents:
    a. Click on the code item at the top of the file
    b. Highlight
    c. Drag the text into the panel.

If you accidentally code one piece of text multiple times to the same code, NVivo will recognize this and will not duplicate your coded text.

17.4.5 Component C: Managing Codes

To merge two individual codes together, right click on the code that you want to collapse into the other and select 'Cut' from the pop-up menu. Next, right click on the second code into which you want to merge the data and select 'Merge into Selected Code.'

To rename a code, right click on relevant code and select 'Code Properties' from the pop-up menu.

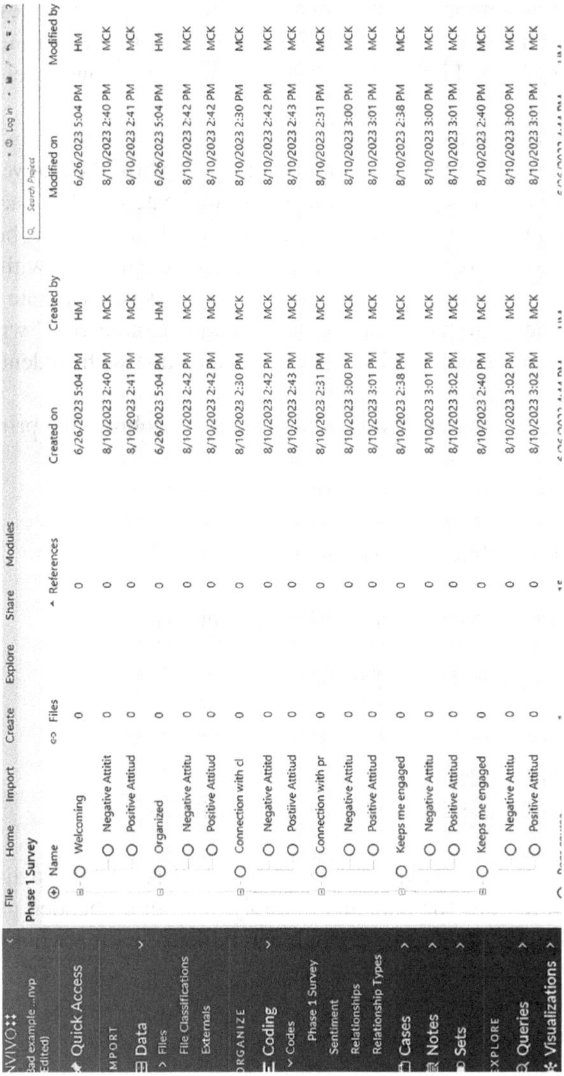

NVivo lab manual for undergraduate students   237

Source: Authors' own work.

Figure 17.2   Example of bad coding

To uncode text from within a code, highlight relevant text, right click and select 'Uncode from this Code.'

To aggregate codes (when the child code is reflected in the parent code), right click on the parent code and click on 'Aggregate Coding from Children.' This can be helpful when looking at comparisons between parent codes. Note that aggregation occurs only one level at a time. In order for data from third-level codes to be aggregated into the top-level parent code, second-level parent codes would also need to be aggregated.

Figure 17.2 is an example of bad coding because you are duplicating codes. One of the important principles of coding is 'like goes with like'; however, in this example positive and negative attitudes are duplicated within each parent code. The second reason that this is an example of bad coding is because some of the parent codes are too specific. For example, 'Connection with classmates' and 'Connection with professors' are listed here as two separate parent codes. It would be better to have just one parent code, 'Connection,' with two child codes, 'Connection with professors' and 'Connection with students' (see Figure 17.3).

Figure 17.3 is an example of good coding because it follows the principles of coding:

- Hierarchical
- No duplicate codes, 'like goes with like'
- Not too specific
- One thing can be coded to several different locations.

17.5 LAB 4: VISUALIZATIONS

A. Word Cloud
B. Project Map with Codes
C. Project Map with Case Classifications and Attributes

Visualizations can serve two main purposes. First, they can provide a different lens through which to view the data and possibly uncover embedded patterns within the data. Second, they can provide your audience with a window into the findings from your analysis.

17.5.1 Component A: Word Cloud

Generating a Word Cloud can be one of the best ways to visualize frequently used words.

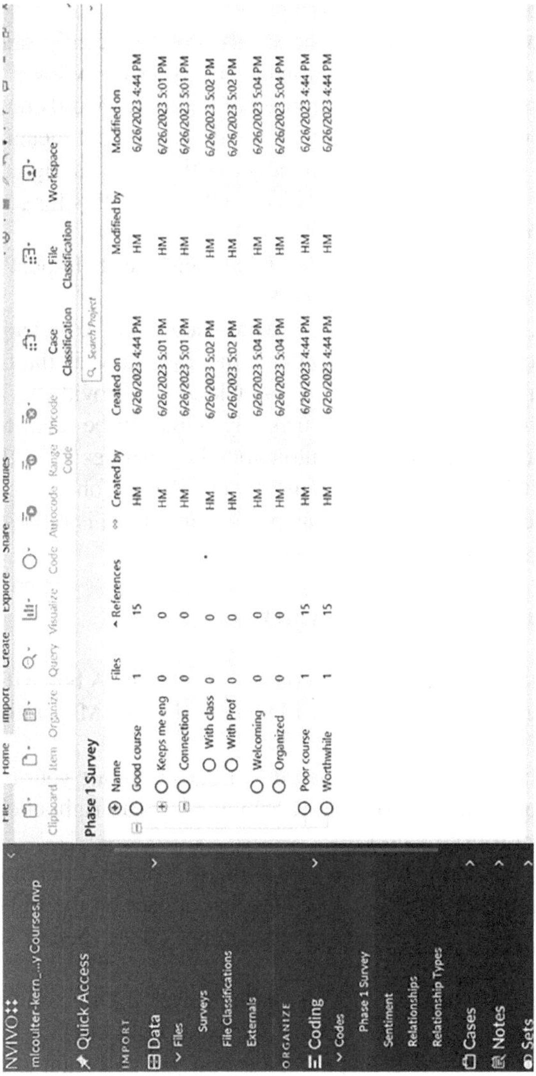

Source: Authors' own work.

Figure 17.3 *Example of good coding*

In Ribbon View, select the Explore tab > Word Frequencies > Selected Items > + sign on the left of Codes > Phase 1 Survey > check the box to the left of 'Good Course' when it appears on the right, then click 'OK.'

Change 'Display Words' to 20, and change the 'Grouping' sliding bar to be 'With Stemmed Words', then select 'Run Query.'

This will generate a 'Summary' of the words most frequently said in the data set. Select 'Word Cloud' on the right-hand side of Detail View.

This will generate a Word Cloud composed of the top 20 words in the data set. Look at the Word Cloud and identify all words that are not meaningful to the data (e.g., 'also' or 'course'). Once you identify these words, right click on each of them and select 'Add to stop word list.' After doing this for each word that you identified, re-select 'Run Query.'

For the last step, right click on the Word Cloud and select 'Export' to save the Word Cloud as an image (.png).

Note: Right click on 'Frequency List' in Word Cloud to dive in deeper

Tag Cloud: Out of all of the visualizations, the Tag Cloud is the only one you can export as a Word document. The Tag Cloud can provide a visual for the top 25, 50, or 100 that appear in your study. This can be ideal for more professional audiences. The font color automatically generates to be the same throughout the Tag Cloud but you can manually change the font color in order to call attention to certain keywords. This particular feature is only available in the Windows version of NVivo.

17.5.2 Component B: Project Map with Codes

In Ribbon View, select Explore > Maps Icon > Project Map. A box will appear for you to name your Project Map. You will name it 'Project Map with Codes' and then select 'OK.'

You now have a blank map in your Detail View. To generate your map, you will select 'Add Project Items' from the Ribbon (or you can right click on the blank map and select it from there).

Now click the '+' sign to the left of Codes > Phase 1 Survey, and then check the boxes to the left of the three parent codes that appear on the right. Make sure to also select 'Automatically select descendant codes' before selecting OK.

What you will see in your Detail View is the Layered Directed Graph as shown in Figure 17.4. For a better view of the data, right click > Layout > Hierarchical. Additionally, to clean up the data a bit you will want to uncheck 'Connector Labels' in Ribbon View.

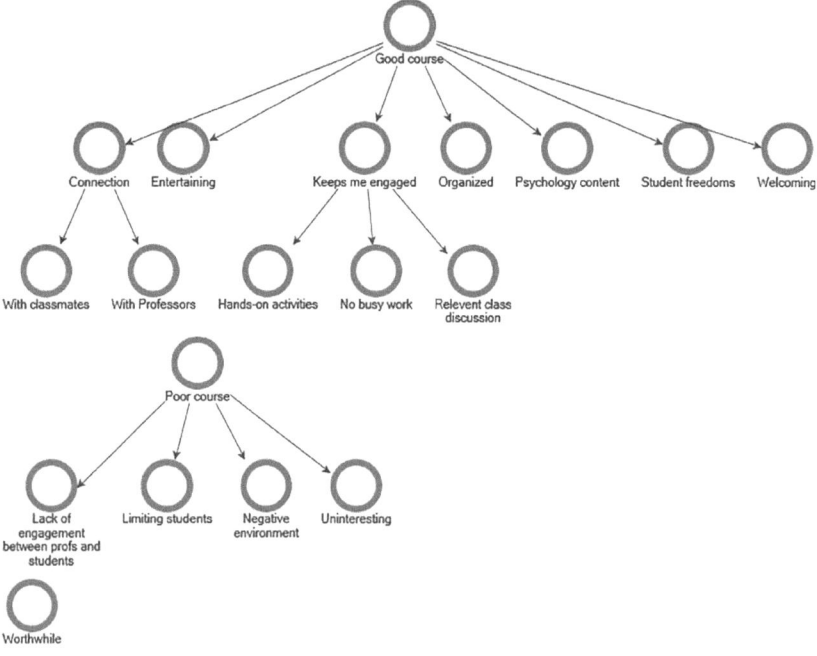

Source: Authors' own work.

Figure 17.4   Project map with codes

15.5.3 Component C: Project Map with Case Classifications and Attributes

An example of a Case Classification is Participant 1; an Attribute is Gender; Attribute Values would be Woman, Man, Nonbinary.

Create a new Project Map that includes Case Classifications. The Attribute will be Gender and the Attribute Values will be Woman, Man, and Non-Binary.

In Ribbon View, go to Explore > Maps Icon > Project Map. A box will appear for you to name your Project Map, which you will name 'Project Map with a Case Classification,' and then you will select 'OK.'

It may not initially appear so, but you now have a blank map in your Detail View. To generate your map, you will select 'Add Project Items' from the Ribbon (or you can right click on the blank map and select it from there).

This time, select the '+' sign next to Cases > Phase 1 Survey. Then select the box next to the 'Phase 1 Survey' (this will automatically select all of the

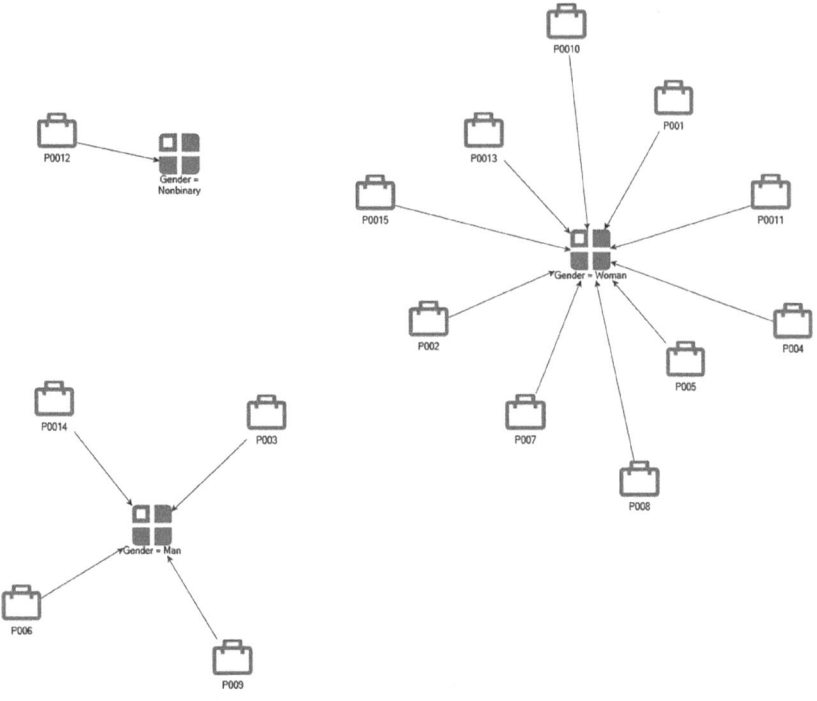

Source: Authors' own work.

Figure 17.5 Project map using participants and attribute values

participants to the right). At the top of the box select 'Automatically select descendent codes,' and then 'OK.'

Go to 'Add Project Items' again and select 'Case Classifications.' You will then click the '+' sign next to 'Survey Respondent.' When it appears on the right, select the '+' sign to open Gender > select Woman, Man, and Nonbinary > OK.

Once again, NVivo has selected a view that may look confusing. To clarify this, right click, select 'Layout,' and select the 'Directed Layout' view. The project map should now resemble Figure 17.5.

Just like in components A and B, you can export your new Project Map by right clicking on the image and choosing 'Export Map.'

17.6 LAB 5: PRESENTING THE DATA SET

A. Title slide
B. Introduction slide
C. Methods slide
D. Results and conclusions slide

The objective for this lab is learning how to summarize all the components of a research project into a comprehensible PowerPoint presentation. When presenting your research, you want to gather the information from your review of past literature, your data set, research design, procedures, and findings.

For this lab, you will be creating a very brief PowerPoint presentation with only four slides, or more if you feel as though you grasp the idea enough to elaborate. The purpose of these slides is to summarize your research to an audience who has no previous knowledge of the content. The following components will walk you through the process.

17.6.1 Component A: Title Slide

The title slide includes the title of the research project and the names of those who conducted it. For this lab specifically, and because you used the data set provided in this manual for Labs 2–4, the title slide will read 'What Students Want from Their Psychology Courses,' and underneath in a much smaller font you will include your name and the names of any group members you might have.

17.6.2 Component B: Introduction Slide

The introduction slide presents several points regarding the research. These points include the research question(s) and/or hypothesis of the study, the purpose of the study, and why the study is important.

17.6.3 Component C: Methods Slide

The methods slide clearly summarizes the research design of the project. You will include information about the design framework, demographics of the participants, and examples from the survey or data collection. Also include what variables and/or themes were measured and how the data was analyzed.

17.6.4 Component D: Results and Conclusions Slide

The results and conclusions slide will display your results in a table or figure that best summarizes what you found. Visualizations are often useful here, e.g., a Word Cloud or Project Map like you completed in Lab 4. The purpose of this slide is to convey the most significant findings of the research and to make sure they are explained thoroughly.

Keep in mind that if you do have the opportunity to present your research in the future, there will be several considerable differences in relation to this lab. If your research is to be presented using a PowerPoint format, there would likely be many more slides and much more detail involved. You would still have each of these components, but many of them would span across two or three slides instead of just one slide. Important components like your literature review, specific measures, discussion, and references are just a few items that would be included in an official presentation. If your delivery format was to be a poster presentation, the organization would still be similar with the same information but all on one poster rather than separated into individual slides.

Familiarity with the vocabulary in the following section is important for new users of NVivo to help ensure clarity, consistency, and analytical rigor throughout the research process. Sharing a common language for coding, analyzing, and interpreting qualitative data will improve organization and credibility in your findings.

17.7 VOCABULARY

- File
- File Classifications
- Code
- Coding
- Code Classifications
- Case
- Case Classifications (i.e., individual units of analysis)
- Attributes (e.g., Gender, Age, GPA)
- Attribute Values (e.g., Woman, Man, Nonbinary)
- Annotations
- Memos
- Sentiment
- Relationship
- Relationship Types
- Design Framework
- Explore
- Navigation View

- List View
- Detail View
- Ribbon View
- Structural Anchor
- Parent Code
- Child Code

17.8 CONCLUSION

Developed to be easy to follow and simple to understand, the guide in this chapter is a valuable tool for beginners who know little about qualitative research and software. It is important that this type of content is included in undergraduate statistics and research courses in addition to quantitative research and analysis. Qualitative research helps students to more broadly understand the attitudes and behaviors of participants and people in general, adding to their knowledge of research and society. This lab series can help students and other beginners develop the skills to collect and analyze qualitative data, as well as aid in the teaching of these topics for instructors.

REFERENCES

Breen, L. J., Sharp, T. J., Gralton, A., & Green, M. J. (2022). Teaching computer-assisted qualitative data analysis to a large cohort of undergraduate students. *International Journal of Research & Method in Education, 45*(2), 207–221. https://doi.org/10.1080/1743727X.2013.804501

Creswell, J. W., & Plano Clark, V. L. (2011). *Designing and Conducting Mixed Methods Research* (2nd Ed.). Sage Publishing.

Fernandes-Jesus, M., McCormick, R., Southby, K., McMillan, D., & Mehta, J. (2024). Developing psychological literacy through applied, interdisciplinary qualitative research: A case study of a second-year undergraduate psychology module. *Psychology Learning & Teaching, 23*(1), 20–34. https://doi.org/10.1177/14757257231221005

Gurung, R. A. R., & Stoa, R. (2020). A national survey of teaching and learning research methods: Important concepts and faculty and student perspectives. *Teaching of Psychology, 47*(2), 121–130. https://doi.org/10.1177/0098628320901374

Jackson, K., & Bazeley, P. (2019). *Qualitative Data Analysis with NVivo.* Sage Publishing.

Lanning, S., & Brown, M. (2019). Undergraduate research as a high impact practice in higher education. *Education Sciences, 9*(3), 160. https://doi.org/10.3390/educsci9030160

Kilgo, C. A., Ezell Sheets, J. K., & Pascarella, E. T. (2015). The link between high-impact practices and student learning: Some longitudinal evidence. *Higher Education, 69*(4), 509–525. https://doi.org/10.1007/s10734-014-9788-z

QSR International Pty Ltd. (2020). NVivo (Version 12) [Computer software]. https://www.qsrinternational.com/nvivo-qualitative-data-analysis-software/home

Shorten, A., & Smith, J. (2017). Mixed methods research: expanding the evidence base. *Evidence-Based Nursing, 20*(3), 74–75. https://doi.org/10.1136/eb-2017-102699

Index

2 x 2 experiment 31

abnormal psychology 137
absolutist thinking style 55
abstract
   knowledge development 56
   research method concepts 56
academic dishonesty 24
academic identity 43
active learning
   activities 9
   strategies 133
adult learning process 163
advanced degrees, fewer students pursuing 20
advertising 70
AI
   data tools 13
   support, methodological concepts 31
   use in education 2
alternative teaching methods 133
ambiguity
   barrier to comprehension 80
   challenge for assessment 81
   lexical 79
   opportunity for learning 81
   research methods 82
ambiguous vocabulary, teaching strategy 81
American Academy of Pediatrics 73
American Association of Community Colleges 39
American Psychological Association (APA) 65, 73
   apology, harm to people of color 73
   Center for Workforce Studies 20
   Guidelines for the Undergraduate Psychology Major 3.0 52, 54, 158, 171, 174
   Introductory Psychology Initiative 37

style competence 14
Style Manual 27
style paper 27
writing versus technical writing 26
anecdotal-based information 68
annotated bibliography 148
Annual Conference on Teaching 32
ANOVA reference 123
anxiety, measurement 31
APA Project Assessment (PASS) 45
applied learning 14
arbitrary assignment 11
articulation agreements 43–4
assessing methodological reasoning 61
assignments, redesign of 2
ATLAS.ti 228
attention, student 1
authentic research 112
   experiences, in undergraduate education 117
autonomy 146

bad tests 211
bar graph 23
between-participants and within-participants 83
between-subjects and within-subjects 83
bias in psychological research 37
broader statistical understanding 22
business-related examples – teaching research methods 21

Café Conversations, career insights 46
capstone experience 29
capstone paper assignment 27
career readiness, research training 37
causal diagrams 61
causal theory error 60
ChatGPT 13, 31
chi-square 223

citation of AI sources 27
claims as inferences based on evidence 59
Clarity of Argument 149
class
　content 201, 206
　demonstrations, AI-assisted 32
　structure 201
class assignment 205, 208
classical conditioning 137
classroom
　community 98
　critical thinking activity 70
coding data 235
cognitive labor 80
cognitive psychology papers 25
collaboration skills 12
collaborative learning 103
Collaborative Replication and Education Project (CREP) 119, 154
college student
　success 130
college student social media habits 67
communication, prescribed system of 26
community college
　historical overview of 38
　research methods education 41
　research methods teaching 2
　role in diversifying psychology 41
　role in psychology pipeline 36
　students, characteristics of 39
　transfer students 37
Community College National Honor Society in Psychology 122
community support for difficult readings 98
community-based mental health surveys 44
competence 147
computer demonstrations, manipulating variance 22
computer programs for statistics (JASP, jamovi) 21
computer statistics program 29
conceptual learning 14
confirmation bias 66
confounding variables 56
construct measurement 31
content-focused psychology courses 7

contradicting information, reduced exposure to 67
correlation
　statistics 25
　versus causation 53
　vs. correlation coefficient 85
correlation, ambiguity research methods 85
cost-effectiveness 188
counterconditioning therapies 137
course design
　challenges 8
　research methods 2
course duration 23
course research projects, options for 23
course-based undergraduate research experiences (CUREs) 44
COVID-19
　global pandemic misinformation 66
　pandemic 160
create valid measures 205
credit transferability 42
critical evaluation in psychology
　advertising 70
　false information 73
　social media and research literacy 71
　systemic oppression 73
critical lens, developing 71
critical statistical concepts 219
critical thinking 39
　ambiguity research methods 89
　development 8
　domain-specific 56
critically evaluating research evidence 71
crowdsourced research 122
cultural responsiveness, teaching methods 3
culturally competent psychological practice 37
culturally responsive research (CRR) 173
culturally responsive teaching 41
culture of research 167
cumulative nature of scientific knowledge 54
curriculum development 38
curriculum misalignment 42
curse of knowledge 81

data interpretation skills 1

data set example 233
databases (large databases) 25
demand characteristics 11
demographic cliff, four-year institutions 38
demographic shifts, implications for psychology 37
department faculty interaction 19
dependent variable 31
detailed feedback 28
developing evaluativist thinking 54
directed acyclic graphs (DAGs) 60
disciplinary knowledge development through reading 98
discipline-specific nature of thinking skills 56
discussion section writing 13
distributive scaffolding 98
diverse student populations 41
diversifying psychological sciences 39
domain-specific thinking skills 56
dominance effect 80
dual Homonyms, ambiguity research methods 89

EaMMi2 (Emerging Adulthood Measured at Multiple Institutions 2) project 123
economic inequities, access to AI platforms 32
editing and finetuning, AI output 32
educational and mental health research 191
educational scaffolding 9
embedded authentic research projects 44
empirical article 27
empirical research reading skills 103
empirically based (psychological knowledge) 54
employable skills, role of research methods courses 20
employment 39
end-of-term paper 22
engagement, student 8
error bars misunderstanding 59
essentialist thinking 59
ethical concerns, AI use 32
ethical considerations in research 10, 167
ethics, teaching of 2
evaluating unknown product claims 71

evaluation of research 8
evaluativism, define 55
evaluativist thinking style 54
evidence-based pedagogical initiatives 96
evidence-based teaching of theories 59
excel data set 233
Excellent Use of Evidence 149
executive order 73
experiential learning 11
experimental design concepts 22
experimental psychologists 23
explicit instruction about the nature of science 56

face-to-face synchronized interactions 161
facilitation 137
factorial design 11, 21
factors predicting dropout 131
faculty frustration 8
false information 66, 73
false vaccine claims 66
feedback
  on focus article activity 103
  rich assessment 150
feedback loops, learning 13
feedforward 152
final research conference 29
first draft requirement 29
first impressions research topic 12
first semester, guiding students 176
first-generation college students 39
flipped classrooms 133
Focus Article activity 95
formula variation, effect on statistical output 22
formulating hypotheses 10
fostering student motivation 96
free-response items, AI generation 32

gamification 27
gender identity vs. sex, misleading language 73
gender-affirming treatments 73
General Social Survey 25
generalizability
  of psychological research 37
generalizability in research 71
Generative AI (GenAI) 30

instructor use of 32
student use of 30
as 'teaching assistant 32
uses for 30
GI Bill
    impact on community college growth 38
Goal 2: Scientific Inquiry and Critical Thinking 45
Google Dataset Search 25
government misinformation, executive order 73
grading process 28
gradual release model 9
graduate-level psychology courses (forensic psychology, applied psychology, and ethics) 137
graduate-level teaching 164
group research projects 9
group writing assignments 29
guided research 166

hand calculations, learning statistical formulas 21
hand calculations vs. conceptual understanding (ANOVA) 22
hands-on practice, between-groups t-test and one-way ANOVA 22
hands-on projects 161
harmful treatment misinformation 66
have-to-take course 146
higher exam grades in flipped format 134
high-impact practices 111
homework assignments, updating with AI 32
homework completion, GenAI use 31
homonyms with Lay terms, ambiguity research methods 86
Human Development Study of Early Child Care and Youth Development 172
human subjectivity and objectivity, balance in science 54

idea generation, GenAI-assisted 30
ill-defined problem 137
importing survey data 233
inaccurate reporting of research in media 68
in-class activities, AI-assisted 32
inclusive research practices 41
inclusivity in research 112
increased exposure effect 70
independent groups and repeated measures. 83
independent research experiences 111
independent variable 31
independent variables, ambiguity research methods 85
individual and group assignments – blended approach 29
individual difference variables 130
individual differences 11
individual writing versus group writing assignments 29
inferential statistics 25
in-person demonstration 11
institutional partnerships 43
institutional policies 42
Institutional Review Boards (IRB) 24
instructional innovation 9
instructional methods 81
instructor use of GenAI 32
instructor-led assignments 146
interaction between false information and targeted ads 70
interactive curriculum 14
interpret statistics 22
interteaching 134
introduction slide 243
Introductory Psychology 20
introductory psychology students 71
IRB applications 115
IRB approval 13
item writing 210
I've done my research 65

Jerry Rudmann Research Award 47
JKCF, recognized transfer support institutions 44
Joliet Junior College 38
Journal of Experimental Psychology: General and the *Journal of Applied Psychology* 10
Journal of Open Psychology Data 123
Journal of Student Research 46
junior colleges, early 20th century 38
just-in-time teaching (JiTT) 136

laboratory and technology infrastructure 43
lack of fact checking on social media 67
large and longitudinal datasets, access to 188
learning context in reading instruction 99
learning goals, statistics education 22
learning outcomes 1
lecture-based teaching 9
lecture-based teaching limitations 8
Letter to Reviewers 153
lexical ambiguity 79
Lexicon development (nonlinear progression) 82
line graph 23
linear regression 224
literature review skills 8
lower mortality among vaccinated individuals 66

managing codes 236
manipulate variable, ambiguity research methods 86
manuscript resubmission 28
material scaffolds 98
MAXQDA 228
measurement in-class activities 209
measurement validity 10, 53
medical misinformation, gender-affirming care 73
memes 212
mental health research 191
mere exposure effect 67
Meta fact-checking process 67
meta-analysis 53
    contribution 119
metaphors in science education 81
meta-scientific understanding 53
methodological competence 53
methodological flaws, in classic studies 59
methods slide 243
mindfulness, practice of 1
minoritized communities, harm to 73
minoritized groups, representation in psychology 37
misconceptions 80
misinterpret group differences 59
misinterpretations of research 66

misleading advertisements 70
misunderstanding of science 130
mixed designs 10
models for involving students in real research 118
modified replication project 25
motivation, role of 145
motivation, student 8
multifactorial outcome 130
multiple regression statistics 25
multiple-choice questions, AI-assisted rewriting 32
multiplist thinking style 55

National Institute of Child Health 172
National Institute on the Teaching of Psychology 32
National Psychology Summit, virtual conference 46
National Research Project (NRP) 40
nature of science in psychology 54
Needs Improvement 149
Network for International Collaborative Exchange (NICE) 122
network-wide meta-analysis 119
Next Generation Science Standards for K-12 education 54
no causation without manipulation 85
non-numerical data 228
non-research careers 30
non-traditional students 39
novices focus on surface features 57
NVivo interface/workspace 232

omonyms within science, ambiguity research methods 84
online discussion post 10
online echo chamber 67
online education 160
Online Psychology Laboratory 45
online research methods courses teaching strategies 163
open science movement 112
open science practices 3, 112
operational definitions 31
opinion-based information 68
oral communication skills 30
original research article, to compare with news articles 68

output table from the statistics program 23
overconfidence caused by lexical ambiguity 81

PBSL (problem-based *service* learning) 137
Pearson & Gallagher model 9
Pedagogy/pedagogical
    research methods 2
pedagogy/pedagogical
    challenges 8
    for incorporating secondary data projects 193
    recommendations 90
    strategies 7
peer feedback 165
peer review 54, 164
    research 10
    research article, distinguishing 68
peer reviewer 164
Pell Grants 40
people of color (POC) 171
perception of research utility 14
performance, level of 148
personal experience with research design 11
physiological measure 10
politics in classroom 74
poster conference 30
postulates of engagement 132
practical research experience 189
pre-class questions'(PCQs) 136
(prep) guides (interteaching) 135
prerecorded lecture (flipped classroom) 133
prerequisite course gaps 58
prescribed system of communication 26
prescriptive tasks 146
presenting the data set 243
Principles of Quality Undergraduate Education 37
problem-based learning (PBL) 137
program and course-level research experiences 44
project consequences 23
project in NVivo 234
project map with codes 240
prompt generation, student skill 30
proper research design 52

proprietary information, AI caution 32
Psi Beta 122
    Journal of Student Research 46
    National Research Project 40
    research skills development 45
    Undergraduate Research Toolkit 46
psychological phenomena using secondary data, trends 191
psychological research 23
    diversity in 171
Psychological Science Accelerator, The (PSA) 122
psychological science communication 97
psychological science, diversity in 36
psychology course 158
psychology courses, community college history 38
psychology curriculum courses 52
psychology, history of harm 73
psychology majors, declining interest in research careers 20
psychology pipeline, diversification 37
psychology programs 1
psychology, research methods in 7
psychology workforce demographics 37
p-values 219

qualitative data analysis software package 228
qualitative research tool NVivo 3
quantitative research methods 160
questionable measurement practices (QMPs) 119

race hierarchies 74
random assignment 53
range of statistics 23
reading assignments 27
reading choice and student agency 97
reading choice (student choice) 97
reading motivation, through relevant literature 96
reading research papers, instruction 71
real-world data 189
reinventing research methods 8
reinventing research methods to develop employable skills 15
reinvention through scaffolding 9
relatedness 147
reminders, teaching strategy 57

reminding students of prior knowledge 57
removal of fact checking on Meta platforms 67
replication crisis in psychology 26
replication plus 154
replication research 119
required research experience 111
research design difficulties 115
research design framework 230
research evaluation standards 71
research hypothesis, ambiguity research methods 83
research in psychology
  assessing methodological reasoning 61
  claims as inferences based on evidence 59
  developing evaluativist thinking 54
  meta-scientific understanding 53
  methodological competence 53
  nature of science in psychology 54
  reminding students of prior knowledge 57
  research methods themes, making explicit 56
  scientific thinking and scientific knowledge 56
  supporting causal reasoning 60
  teaching research methods in content courses 55
  'warts' of science, teaching about 60
  within-group variation and between-group differences 59
research literacy 95
research methods 52
  classes 144
  courses 71, 159
  skills, in advertising analysis 70
  teaching 19
  teaching of 2
  themes, making explicit 56
  transfer problem 42
research methods courses 39–40
  limited availability of courses 40
  pedagogical strategies 193
research methods education 42
research methods education, community colleges 41
research opportunities 40, 111

research paper structure (sections and navigation) 71
research papers, types of (systematic reviews, literature reviews) 71
research projects (types of) 19
research skill development, organizational resources to support 45
research skills, early training 36
research studies, types of (qualitative, quantitative, longitudinal, cross-sectional) 71
research-based career 23
resubmit 152
results writing assignments 29
re-teaching 57
revise 152
revision deadline 28
rigid rubrics 146
rigorous pre-college preparation, lack of 130
rubric creation 147
rubric-based evaluations 150
rumors about disease origins and treatments 66

sampling
  limitations of 71
  representativeness 71
Satisfactory 149
scaffolding (education) 96
scaffolding, in research methods learning 56
scale critique assignment 212
science as cumulative enterprise 59
scientific attitude 55
scientific claims as inferences 59
scientific evidence vs. personal opinion 74
scientific literacy 39, 79, 95
scientific reasoning skills 7
scientific thinking and scientific knowledge 56
scientific thinking, development of 2
scientific thinking skills 61
scientific vs. lay meaning 80
scientist-practitioner model 159, 162
second semester, data analysis, project dissemination, and community partnership 179

secondary data
  limitations of 189
secondary data analysis, in
  undergraduate research 123
secondary dataset 187
selection, ambiguity research methods 85
self-assessment accuracy (novice
  scientists) 81
Self-Determination Theory (SDT) 145
self-initiated research 165
self-report measure 11
self-report vs. behavioral measures 11
sense of belonging 41
similar-sounding methodological terms 57
single parents 40
SMARVUS (Statistics and Mathematics
  Anxieties and Related Variables in
  University Students) project 123
social anxiety 137
social, cultural, and historical contexts,
  influence on science 54
social isolation research, student
  learning gains 46
social loafing 29
social media and research literacy 68
social media misinformation 67
social psychology papers 26
social scaffolds 98
socioeconomic status (SES) 60
socratic learning methods 164
spread of false information on social
  media 68
statistical inference 53
statistical interpretation vs.
  memorization 22
statistical mastery, role of software 21
statistical mindset 217
statistical reasoning 8
statistical tests, relatable examples (Oreo
  cookies, diet soda) 21
statistics (association with research
  methods) 19
statistics confidence 14
statistics courses, student resistance 20
structural inequalities, in higher
  education 36
student challenges, with primary
  literature 95
student difficulty, with complex statistics 71
student engagement 130–131
student engagement, interest-based
  methodological examples 21
student interest variability 20
student interpretation of advertising
  claims 70
student learning outcomes 1
student motivation 96
student partnerships into course
  structure 153
student perceptions of research methods
  (boring or irrelevant) 20
student publications 119
student reflections 181
student self-assessment 150
student self-report data 32
student trepidation, data analysis 21
student use of GenAI 30
student-centered assessment 150
student-led research project, structure
  of 175
students as partners approach and
  motivation 146
Students as Partners (SaP) framework 144
students' inherent interest in research
  methods 20
students of color 39
students use of GenAI 30
substantial overlap between groups 59
supplemental materials, for foundational
  knowledge 57
supporting causal reasoning 60
surface-level learners 145
surgical transition care 73
survey data 233
synonyms, ambiguity research methods 82
systematic observations 54
systematic reviews vs. literature reviews 71
systemic oppression 73

target article 26
targeted advertising algorithms 70
teachers' use of GenAI 30
teacher-student enthusiasm gap 20
teaching frustration, instructor 8

teaching Introductory Psychology 19
teaching literature search skills 68
teaching methods and statistics, impact of student career goals 20
teaching primary literature reading skills 95
teaching research methods 9
teaching research methods across curriculum 57
teaching research methods (discussion) 19
teaching research methods in content courses 55
teaching selecting valid measures 201
team-based learning 138
technical writing
    formats 26
    guidelines 22
think-pair-share item improvement 209
time efficiency 188
time on task (Tyler) 131
title slide 243
transfer advising, dedicated offices 44
transfer barriers 40
transfer partnerships, community college to university 37
transfer receptive cultures 43
transfer students 39
    performance at selective institutions 40
    research preparation 42
transferable critical thinking skills, discredited idea 56
tuition costs 42
Tyler, Ralph 131

unambiguous rubrics 147
undergraduate abnormal psychology course 137
undergraduate arts colleges 19
undergraduate internships 45
undergraduate research 111
undergraduate research projects 112
Undergraduate Research Toolkit 46

undergraduate students enrollment 39
underpowered studies 118
underrepresented students, psychology education 41
undocumented students 40
ungrading movement 150
unstructured data 228
upper-division course 39, 42
Use of Evidence 149
user-friendly research 10

valid measurement 52
variance and error term 22
virtual demonstration 11
visual aids, use 90
visual trick 218
visualizations 238
vocabulary 244
vocational and technical training 38
voice manipulation, experimental example 31

want-to-take course 146
warm-ups 136
'warts' of science, teaching about 60
WEIRD (White, Educated, Industrialized, Rich, Democratic) 171
within-group variation and between-group differences 59
within-groups and between-groups designs, ambiguity research methods 83
within-subjects designs 10
word cloud 238
workforce readiness 39
working memory capacity 80
writing assignments
    types of 26
    variations in 27
writing feedback 29
Writing Style 149
WSW (What Students Want) 233